The Path of Human Progress

Richard O. Zerbe

Contents

Dedication: This book is dedicated to the memory of my father and grandfather Richard and Riley Zerbe respectively.

Acknowledgement: I wish to acknowledge comments by Stan Chramanski and William Talbott.

Introduction[1]

[handwritten margin note: rising inequality and associated loss of status]

Donald Trump has recently been elected president of the United States. His election has been made possible by ~~the~~ relatively ~~disenfranchised~~ and by the rapidity of social change. People ~~will~~ react m~~o~~re strongly when things are taken away from them, things such as manufacturing jobs, than if they never had them. We live in a time of transition and rapid change. We live, as the Chinese curse has it, in interesting times. Rapid change is difficult for us and for our institutions, as the election demonstrated.

It helps in such a time to understand where we are in our human journey, what we are, ~~and where~~ we might be going. Most nonfiction books focus on some particular topic; they focus more narrowly than we do here. Here, we attempt to cover multiple topics related to the broad issue of human progress. These topics range from the rise of women to economic progress and its future to past and possible futures to evolutional and cultural change in humans and the effects of climate change on culture and progress. ~~Forty-six years~~ ago, in *[handwritten: even some]* ~~1970, a popular~~ book on the future, *Future Shock* by Alvin Toffler, was published. That book went through about thirty-five printings. *[handwritten margin: 30 22 / 52]* The major thesis was that those alive in the latter part of the twentieth century were due for a shock; this was a book, as the author said, "about what happens to people when they are overwhelmed by change." He noted that "normal people" would "face an abrupt collision with the future." We are living now in this future. The world of today *[handwritten: appears to]* ~~approaches~~ a difference from the world in which my father was born, and almost from when I was born, as my father's world was different from Julius Caesar's world.

Now Toffler is being resurrected and for good reason. In the *New York Times* on July 7, 2016, Farhad Manjoo notes that the future Toffler saw is already upon us. He notes that Toffler saw future shock as

---

1   This book arises from an article I wrote on human progress in a book that received support from the Robert Glazer Foundation.

a real psychological malady, the "dizzying disorientation brought on by the premature arrival of the future." Manjoo points out that Toffler noted that "unless intelligent steps are taken to combat it, millions of human beings will find themselves increasingly disorientated, progressively incompetent to deal rationally with their environments." Hence Trump. This has happened, Manjoo notes, at a time when futurism has fallen out of favor. The government agency formed to deal with it in the 1970s, the Office of Technology Assessment, has long disappeared. The University of Washington department with which I was once associated, the social management of technology, has also long been disbanded.

Toffler suggests that there have been about 800 lifetimes over the past 50,000 years and that about 650 of them were spent living in caves. When I was born, norms of behavior were different. People tended to work for one employer their whole lives, children called adults Mr. and Mrs. or Miss, a larger proportion of people went to church, there were fewer Hispanics in the United States, divorce was much rarer, international trade was not as important, and people did not have an international perspective, at least until World War II. The greatest generation fought in World War II. In many respects the economy seemed to peak about 1975, but change went on. Such a collision has occurred, and people are stressed out.

with future shock

Given the times in which we live, a book on human progress could not be more timely. It feels to me, here near the end of my life, that we are on a cusp. Wecan learn how to work together to create a path that makes it more likely we as a species will have a good future, or we can watch as political unrest, environmental challenges, and problems of acting collectively make a bleak future more likely. This book little concerns predictions of the future but with ways to cope with it.

This book is not about predicting the future but understanding it. No one can predict the future except by chance unless he or she has a model capable of explaining the future and the past.   No one has such a model. Yet we can envision alternative futures   in a general way. So we consider here an understanding of such questions as the evolution of culture, whether or not economic growth will become slower and even cease, how the role of women is changing, whether or not growth in income inequality will   create social instability, whether or not war retards or promotes progress, and other questions and issues. The book offers hope of positive changes, a greater understanding of ourselves, a picture of economic progress, and the growth of cooperative culture. Beyond any of these, it explains why culture is crucial.

The central concepts binding these disparate topics are culture and cultural change. I contend the basis for progress is culture   and define *culture* as simply the body of learning that is passed   on within a group. Growth in cultural maturity is reflected in measurable results. Cultural maturity is *the* principal determinant of development. So says Lawrence Huntington (1985, 2), and so also say I. Huntington goes on to say,

> *the creative capacity of human beings is at the heart of the de-velopment process. What makes developments happen is our ability to imagine, theorize, conceptualize, experiment invent, articulate, organize, manage, solve problems, and do a hundred other things with our minds and hands that contribute to the progress of the individual and of humankind... The society that is most successful at helping its people—all its people—realize their creative poten-tial is the society that will progress the fastest.*

Culture can evolve much more rapidly than species. And within cultures humans can trigger dormant qualities that culture brings forth. For example, IQ scores are increasing rather rapidly and must be renormalized so the average is still 100. The ability to think abstractly has improved. This does not mean that we are smarter but that we have adapted better ways to think in the abstract, which is what IQ mainly measures.

Many of us feel that violence is increasing. But on a per capita basis, violence has been falling for some time as a result of culture and cultural institutions.

How can we reconcile this positive view of culture with the fact that humans in their relationship to other species are the most destructive species on Earth? Everywhere that humans have arrived, from Madagascar to Australia, from North America to Europe, they have eliminated a majority of the megafauna. Yet they have done this by their ability to cooperate with one another. The power of cooperation can be extended by culture. It can be extended to reduce species extinction, for example. We can develop sympathy and empathy with others in our group; we can extend this to other groups, to the less well off, to strangers, and to other species. The thesis of this book is that the development of cultural maturity, with its associated empathy and the concomitant institutions that support cooperation, trust, survival, and liberty, is necessary for further human progress. To what extent can our ability to cooperate and to empathize be melded with our aggression to enhance social progress and human prospects for survival? This theme is played out in the subsequent chapters that consider material and ethical progress.

Why did cooperation develop? The answer is simply that it allowed a greater efficiency in obtaining resources for survival, whether for war or for trade. Socially interactive hunters and fighters could more efficiently hunt and fight. Why did morality develop? Because it increased the ability to cooperate. Empathy enhances cooperation; empathy is the foundation of the Golden Rule, a rule basic to all major religions. Thus, cooperation and morality evolved over time. Boehm (2012) suggests, "what put…egalitarianism in place was the ability of [politically unified] groups to 'outlaw' and punish resented alpha- male behavior." It is more than this, however, as Boehm recognizes; cooperation had many advantages.

Although this is an optimistic book, the message here recognizes problems. Institutions require cooperation and can mold culture   in many positive ways. However, they can be stupefying and reduce human initiative, though this depends not just on the scale of institutions (e.g., government) but also on their nature. Institutions in Russia are not the same as those in Europe. We have psychopaths at the head of at least two governments with nuclear arms. But at least one of them may be a realist. Will the United States make another such country with a psychopathic leader and nuclear arms? Would World War III be the result? We appear to be in the midst of a great extinction of animal and plant life and of habitat, the infamous sixth extinction. What problems will this create? Will climate change produce a breakdown in society? Do income and wealth inequality increase the possibility of such a breakdown?

Yet the world's economic per capita wealth continues to increase, even as the rate of increase is falling. The position of women continues to improve, science and technology evolve apace, and medical science produces new remedies. Space beckons, and our world view expands. Physics, at least in the speculations of some physicists, sees multiple universes. Some (e.g., Stephen Hawking) claim that we have already achieved a theory of everything (though, if true, clearly greater integration is desirable). Visionary entrepreneurs look to space. Much can yet be done to strive, to seek, to find, and not to yield.

I suggest, perhaps radically, that some cultures are superior to others and explain on what basis. Here, we consider the components of culture that contribute to culture maturity and to the social progress indices used to measure social progress. We consider how and whether we can successfully weld together the cooperative and aggressive instincts.

But is it all so fragile? An asteroid from outer space, the rise of despotic leaders, a plague, and the decline of human character under stresses, the development of ever more destructive technology. Yes! But what can hold it together are institutions and the concomitant culture that brings out the best in us. As you wind your way through

the disparate topics, from economics to sex to evolution to technology, what holds this book together is what can hold us together, a robust and responsive culture. My fervent hope is that the message of this book can contribute to progress and to holding it together.

I write this both to make better sense of my life and to help others see where we have been and make better informed speculations about where we will go. Writing this has opened to me the pleasure and usefulness of dealing with broad issues instead of the narrower ones that I have focused on as an economist and economics professor. After many technical articles and books, it is a great pleasure to consider these challenging and broader issues.

1

Culture asProgress

The art of progress is to preserve order amid change and to preserve change amid order.
—Alfred N. Whitehead

A people without the knowledge of their past history, origin and culture is like a tree without roots.
—Marcus Garvey

In such condition [a state of nature] there is no place for Industry; because the fruit thereof is uncertain: and consequently no Culture of the Earth, no Navigation, nor use of the commodities that may be imported by Sea; no commodious Building; no Instruments of moving and removing such things as require much force; no Knowledge of the fact of the Earth; no account of Time; no Arts; no Letters; no Society; and which is worst of all, continuall feare, and danger of violent death; And the life of man, solitary, poore, nasty, brutish, and short.
—Thomas Hobbes, Leviathan

My Experience

The Journey

My father, one of five children, was born in 1912 on a small farm in Michigan, near Niles. He first attended a one-room school house and later in high school rode to school on a pony. His family had no electricity, no water heater, and no plumbing; instead, they used a well for water, kerosene lamps for light, and large cubes of ice for food preservation. They had no indoor plumbing and, in place of an oven, used a small wood and coal stove. Children bathed once a week in a wash tub. They were a poor family in monetary terms, but they were content, even happy. The parents and all the children found contentment in their relationships and in a home culture that valued learning, empathy, and kindness. My father and all his siblings were valedictorians of their high school classes, except one, Mary Jane, who chose to be salutatorian out of embarrassment at the success of her brothers. Their children and grandchildren have likewise been successful in their careers, a CFO of a fortune 500 company, several engineers, a chaired professor, several lawyers, and one high-level computer programmer who is also an entrepreneur.

Were my grandparents and their children less well off in material goods than I am now? Yes, certainly. The four-year-old sister, Betsy, who died from misdiagnosed appendicitis, would have lived had she been born today, and it is true that the family has never gotten over this loss. I live in a different physical environment and have more material wealth than my father and his siblings, as do my contemporaries, affording us luxuries that our parents and grandparents did not have. My current way of life is not only different from that of my parents, but also quite different from that of my childhood.

In terms of happiness, nonmaterial goods, and the personal interactions that make life worthwhile, I am not sure I am better off than my parents and grandparents. The local travel done with my grandparents proved to be as rewarding and interesting as any international travel I have done later in life. The physical work I did in caring for animals, cultivating the garden, chopping wood, and the like was a good thing, and I learned the satisfaction that can come with work. Company was rather rare on the farm but all the more appreciated. My interaction with farm animals was a treasure. My father, his siblings, and I have all been avid readers, a passion that I still have today. Yet, in a generation or two, the technological world of my parents' and even my world will be unrecognizable to my progeny; still, a good deal of the previous world's art, music, and books will remain. So the question I raise is whether or not our culture has improved. All the children in my father's family did well. They did well because they were part of a culture that prized hard work, kindness, education, honesty. They were part of the great World War II generation.

Progress and Culture

As progress is contained in culture, so is its decline. I define human progress as the maturation of culture in such a way that it makes for more mature individuals. Yet the very notion of progress suggests the notion of cultural maturity, which is a forbidden concept, as we shall discuss. This maturation may not be possible without a certain level of material attainment, yet we may wonder also if too much wealth in a culture might presage its decline. The key component for progress is culture, not wealth. Changes in material growth, health, life extension, happiness, and so forth are all either secondary to or derived from cultural progress. Why is this? An improved culture is associated with improved honesty, hard work, respect, empathy, and a sense of belonging.[2] These qualities increase prosperity and happiness.

I define *cultural progress* as the growth in the ability of a culture to support individuals in developing more empathic, mature, and intimate relationships with other beings, along with virtues such as honesty and integrity. This definition encompasses art and technology but is not confined to them. Art is a result of emotional learning, and technology can make life more enjoyable and create possibilities of cultural and individual maturity. Cultural maturity is that culture that contains mature individuals.

We speak of progress in peace, in spreading wealth, and in technology. Differences in culture can lead to differences in the rate of technological innovation and in how values are defined, meaning that we can speak of cultural progress in the same sense that we speak of progress across other areas, such as technology. These developments that we call progress are themselves part and parcel

---

2   The same is true for businesses. Those that cultivate a good culture have better results in the long run.

of culture, so culture is more than just an instrument of progress; it also must be an object of it. For Tylor, the cultural anthropologist (1871, 1), culture consists of language, customs, institutions, codes, tools, techniques, concepts, beliefs, and so on. The cultural commentator Jacques Barzun notes that anthropologists went about "defining culture among primitive people as everything they did: the way they ate, their canoes, their marriage customs—nothing was left out. When that idea is applied to history, you find that the arts, social customs, government, religion and so forth all became part of cultural history" (Rothstein 2000, 15).

Cultural maturity, as with individual maturity, does not arise in a vacuum. Cultural maturity is by and large a product of its past, institutions, norms, laws, religion, government, and art. Individual maturity is associated with empathy, satisfaction, cooperation, liberty, and wisdom and contributes to and is nourished by cultural maturity.

Culture Matters: Ghana and South Korea

Samuel Huntington (2000) notes that, in the early 1960s, the economic data on Ghana and South Korea were similar. Huntington notes that by 1990, South Korea had grown economically tremendously, while Ghana had remained stagnant. However, GDP growth in North Korea appears nonexistent, not surprisingly, given their repressive culture. The South Korean economic growth was due to the country's ability to give more scope to individual freedom, new markets, and new enterprise, Huntington notes. The following figure shows Ghana's and South Korea's GDP per capita and growth:

Figure 1.1 A Comparison of Ghana and South Korea in USD

Year	Ghana GDP Per Capita	Ghana growth rates per year Percent	South Korea GDP Per Capita	South Korea growth rates per year Percent
1960			155	
1970	413	1.6	279	6.0
1980	482	3.5	1674	19.6
1990	682	-3.5	6,153	13.9
2000	424	-4.6	11,347	6.3
2010	1326	12.1	20,540	6.1
2012	1605	1.9	22,424	0.9
2015	2015	1.9	27,221	1.8

(From world bank data)[3]

Korea starts at a lower base than Ghana's in GDP per capita in the 1960's or 1970's but greatly surpass Ghana during the 1980s What happened? South Korea's success was due to how it created a culture that accepted markets, reduced corruption, and created political stability. Ghana didn't improve much until at least about 1990. As Huntington says, "culture matters."

Yet in more recent years, Ghana's per capita GDP has grown more rapidly than before. When I noticed this change, I predicted that Ghana would begin more substantial growth due to a positive change in its culture. I was right. As *The Economist* notes,

> *from Ghana in the west to Mozambique in the south, Africa's economies are now consistently growing faster than those of almost any other region of the world. Nor is its wealth monopolized by a well-connected clique. Embezzlement is still common but income distribution is improving.*

What happened? Ghana's culture improved. The Heritage Foundation's Index of Freedom notes that Ghana's income

3   http://www.indexmundi.com/facts/ghana/gdp-per-capita.

distribution has improved in the past decade. Its index in 2014 was 64.2, making its economy the sixty-sixth freest in the world. Ghana's. Freedom score less government control of business, all of which are associated with cultural maturity. So we find that over the twenty-year history of the index, Ghana's economic freedom has advanced by nearly nine points. As the Heritage Foundation notes,

> *With improvements in seven of the nine areas measured, Ghana's overall economic freedom has been undermined only by declines in freedom from corruption and monetary freedom. In the area of market openness that measures trade freedom, investment freedom, and financial freedom, Ghana has made particularly progress. Categorized as a "mostly unfree" economy for much of its history in the Index, Ghana has achieved "moderately free" status in four of the past five years.*

Culture matters!

CultureChanges

The basic nature of mankind has not changed much, if at all, since mankind became *Homo sapiens*. But culture has. Culture change can be much more rapid than genetic change. What has changed for us is the surrounding cultural environment. Some cultures are more mature than others by luck and circumstance. All cultures are the expression of human nature, but human nature is malleable even with the same underlying genetic inheritance. Moreover, the nature of man can change as culture changes. As cultures change, they affect changes in genetic stock, as certain attributes are favored and others not (a process called genetic drift). In this book I attempt, however roughly, to view human progress in terms of culture. Just as there are categories of individual maturity, so I shall say there are comparable categories of cultural maturity. Cultural and individual maturities nourish one another.

What Makes a Culture Superior?

Individuals go through a developmental process recognized by psychologists, psychoanalysts, and others. So too do cultures. An individual's mental maturity can be ranked by Masloff 's (2015) hierarchy of individual maturity shown below. (Notice that by this hierarchy, the current US Congress has not achieved self-actualization or even esteem.)

Figure 1.2: Maslow Hierarchy

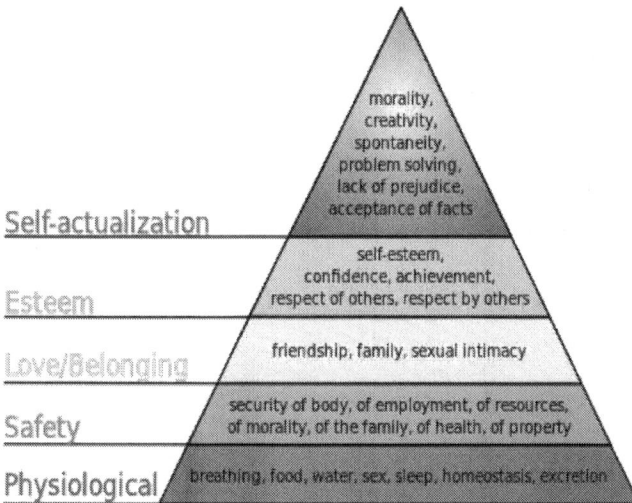

I suggest that cultures may be similarly ranked. A mature society can arise only when basic needs have been satisfied. Such a society is characterized by empathy and sympathy, by justice, by the ability to respond well to pressures that require change. The Maslow ranking, however, is not, and perhaps cannot be, complete. A broader category is well-being, and I would rank cultures on the basis of well-being. Well-being is complex; it is many things. There are many proxies for well-being and for progress. Happiness is not well-being, although it may be part of it. We would not say that a happy drug addict has reached individual maturity, nor that drug addiction is a useful component to well-being. Material gain may not buy happiness yet may be a part of well-being. War may lead to technological development, and technological development may contribute to well-being, but we would not say that technological development at any cost is desirable nor without problem for well-being. A relative of mine lived his life without a cell phone, a computer, or an answering machine; his well-being was high in terms of happiness, material success, the absence of violence, life expectancy, and other measures. There are then many proxies for well-being. There are many pathways to cultural maturity. We will explore these in the remaining chapters.

The first three ranks—physiological, safety, and belonging— have been fundamental to survival of the human race. These levels of attainment, however, support only a crude culture. The top two tiers are fundamental to the long-run cultural survival in a more technology-reliant world. Esteem and self- actualization require cooperation, empathy, and a rule of law. They suggest a lack of political corruption, trade for mutual gain, and an ability to trust when trust is given appropriately.

We may measure the value and maturity of a culture by its liberty and by the way it cares for the old, the young, and the sick, and we may measure a culture by its art and by the happiness of its people. The term I emphasize in characterizing the development of a moral sense is *empathy*. Empathy is not the vague impulse to do good. Empathy is not simply charity or just attempting to do good but something more complex—the empathic understanding of what others need to support their journey to a more mature personality.

The
My focus in the forthcoming chapters will be on the growth in the ability to empathize as a measure of the level of maturation in both individuals and cultures. The stronger the sense of empathy with others, the more likely one is to cooperate. Imagine, for example, that you are working with someone you care about deeply. My assertion is that you would be more likely to cooperate. The ability to care for others grows with maturity, and therefore, so does cooperation.

The measures of progress we will examine include growth in income and happiness, declines in violence, increases in life expectancy, the rise of women, technological change, equity and income distribution, the rise of institutions, and the proper level and type of government spending. We will say that increases   in per capita income, increases in happiness, increases in life expectancy, and increases in income equity all generally increase well-being and are associated with, though not identical to, progress as defined here. Progress in the short run may, however, lead to retrogression in the long run. Income at one time may increase at the expense of the income in the future. The use of certain drugs may increase current euphoria but lead to the ruin of life. An increase in equality of income may itself be desired but may dampen further economic growth. We then will consider and discuss those personal and institutional characteristics that appear to foster progress.

What Causes Societies to Change?

We attempt to measure progress but also need to consider what changes society. Change is caused by both external and internal forces (Chirot 1994). External forces include the threat of war; a society that is not doing well and does not respond to such a threat will disappear. Another external signal that something is wrong is when the performance of other societies is superior. This sort

of comparison has only become possible in the industrial age. Russia seemed to respond, if slowly, to the superior performance of the West, until the rise of Putin. China has responded as well by a move toward coordinated capitalism but struggles with the conflict between sources of wealth being created outside the party, as such wealth can also be a source of power. Internal signals can be economic or political. Bleak periods of economic failure result in mass disruptions, internal war, or suffering.

In the United States, we can think of the effect of the Great Depression in creating new social programs, such as Social Security. And within Germany, the Depression, combined with harsh reparation payments imposed by World War I, created a fascist society that was defeated only through war. Within a society, a clash of cultures such as occurred with the US Civil War resulted in change that we are still trying to sort out. Pressures to change can also be technological. The ascendance of the computer and the Internet have led to new bodies of law, to the rise of different sorts of firms, and to the decline of literature. Ideas, the core of culture, can also cause internal pressures that result in change. Keynes's ideas on business cycles, John Stuart Mill's *On Liberty,* Turing's and von Neumann's ideas on computers, Copernicus on the movement of the Earth around the sun, northern abolitionists on slavery, and the early writers on Christianity and Buddhism are but a few examples of ideas that resulted in major changes. See how ideas of respect and freedom have gradually changed society's culture in the United States. In my own narrow fields of law and economics, the ideas of Nobel Prize winner Ronald H. Coase changed the face of both. The basic point is that without pressure to change, there would be almost no social change. Our job is to make that pressure and to make it toward a good end, as far as we are able.

The figure below ranks countries by a social progress index SPI (2015). Consider possible reasons for the ranking. You will understand them better after reading this book. For now, consider the rankings in the social progress index and the extent to which this cultural hierarchy corresponds to Maslow's hierarchy.

2020

The Social Progress Index 2015

The First 100 Countries

cite

Rank Of First 50	Country	Social Progress Index	Rank Of Second 50	Country	Social Progress Index
1	Norway	88.36	51	ALBANIA	68.19
2	Sweden	88.06	52	MACEDONIA	67.79
3	Switzerland	87.97	53	MEXICO	67.5
4	Iceland	87.62	54	PERU	67.23
5	New Zealand	87.08	55	PARAGUAY	67.1
6	Canada	86.89	56	THAILAND	66.34
7	Finland	86.75	57	TURKEY	66.24
8	Denmark	86.63	58	BOSNIA & HERZEGOVINA	66.15
9	Netherlands	86.5	59	GEORGIA	65.89
10	Australia	86.42	60	ARMENIA	65.7
11	United Kingdom	84.68	61	UKRAINE	65.69
12	Ireland	84.66	62	SOUTH AFRICA	65.64
13	Austria	84.45	63	PHILIPPINES	65.46
14	Germany	84.04	64	BOTSWAND	65.22
15	Japan	83.15	65	BELARUS	64.98
16	United States	82.85	66	TUNSIA	64.92
17	Belgium	82.83	67	EL SALVADOR	64.31
18	Portugal	81.91	68	SAUDIA ARABIA	64.27
19	Slovenia	81.62	69	MOLDOVA	63.68
20	Spain	81.17	70	RUSSIA	64.64
21	France	80.82	71	VENEZUELA	63.45
22	Czech Rep	80.59	72	BOLIVIA	63.36
23	Estonia	80.49	73	JORDAN	63.312
24	Uruguay	79.21	74	NAMBIA	62.71
25	Slovakia	78.45	75	AZERBAUAN	62.62
26	Chile	78.29	76	DOMINICAN REPUBLIC	62.47
27	Poland	77.98	77	NICARAGUA	62.2
28	Costa Rica	77.88	78	GUATEMALA	62.19
29	Cyprus	77.45	79	LEBANON	61.85
30	Italy	77.38	80	MONGOLIA	61.52

- Brld

Rank Of First 50	Country	Social Progress Index	Rank Of Second 50	Country	Social Progress Index
31	Hungary	74.8	81	KAZAKHSTAN	61.38
32	Latvia	74.12	82	CUBA	60.83
33	Greece	74.03	83	ALGERIA	60.66
34	Lithuania	74	84	INDONESIA	60.47
35	Mauritius	73.65	85	GUYANA	60.42
36	Crotia	73.3	86	SRI LANKA	60.1
37	Argentina	73.08	87	EGYPT	59.91
38	Uae	72.79	88	UZBEKISTAN	59.71
39	Israel	72.6	89	MOROCCO	59.56
40	Panama	71.79	90	CHINA	59.07
41	Brazil	70.89	91	KYRGYSTAN	58.58
42	Bulgaria	70.19	92	GHANA	58.29
43	Jamaica	69.83	93	IRAN	56.82
44	Serbia	69.79	94	TAHISISTAN	56.49
45	Malaysia	69.55	95	SENEGAL	56.46
46	Kuwait	69.19	96	NEPAL	55.33
47	Montenegro	69	97	CAMBODIA	53.96
48	Columbia	68.85	98	BANGLADESH	53.39
49	Romania	68.37	99	INDIA	53.06
50	Ecuador	68.25	100	LAOS	52.41

The Second 131 Countries

Rank Of Bottom 31	Country	Social Progress Index
101	LESOTHO	52.27
102	KENYA	51.67
103	ZAMBIA	51.62
104	RWANDA	51.6
105	SWAZILAND	50.94
106	BENIN	50.04
107	REPUBLIC OF CONGO	49.6
108	UGANDA	49.49
109	MALAWI	48.95
110	BURKINA FASO	48.82
111	IRAQ	48.35
112	CAMEROON	47.42
113	DIUJIBOUTI	47.27
114	TANZANIA	47.14
115	TOGO	46.66
116	MALI	46.51
117	MYANMAR	46.12
118	MOZAMBIQUE	46.02
119	MAURTANIA	45.85
120	PAKISTAN	45.66
121	LIBERIA	44.89
122	MADAGASCAR	44.5
123	NIGERIA	43.31
124	ETHOIPIA	41.04
125	NIGER	40.56
126	YEMEN	40.3
127	ANGOLA	40
128	GUINEA	39.6
129	AFGHANISTAN	35.4
130	CHAD	33.17
131	CENTRAL AFRICAN REPUBLIC	31.42
132	OTHERS NOT AVAILABLE	X

Clearly there are patterns here. Find them!

Summary

Progress is determined by culture. Material progress is itself derivative of culture, though not just culture. A superior culture is a necessary but not always sufficient ingredient for human progress. The maturity of a culture may be ranked on a scale of well-being that contains many components, some of which are shown on a psychological scale, such as Maslow's scale for individual maturity.

Questions

1. How would you rank your country's culture on its maturity level?

2. What do you think or feel are your culture's good and bad aspects?

3. How will the growth of technology influence culture?

4. How will the improvement of health affect culture?

5. How will the rise of women affect culture?

6. How will war affect culture?

7. How will it affect progress?

2

The Fundamental Conflict

(1) "If I am not for myself who is for me? And being (only) for my own self, what am I?" And if not now, when and (2) "That which is hateful to you, do not do to your fellow. That is the whole Torah; the rest is the explanation; go and learn."
—Hillel[4]

Current Problems

Consider a potpourri of current problems: nuclear war, terrorism, climate change, species extinction, the warming and acidification of the oceans, and overpopulation, among others. What do these have in common? They share the same solution: cultural maturation.

Forces in Conflict

The basis for progress is culture.

The following paragraph is paraphrased from several pages in the neat, 1988 science fiction novel by Iain Bains, *The Player of Games*. This is the story of a man who went far away for a long time, just to play a game. It ends with a game that is not a game. The story is one of a game (that is not a game) between the two great forces, survival by power (the Empire) on the one hand and survival by cooperation (Culture) on the other. One of the great players of the Culture (Gurgeh) plays the decadent Emperor, the greatest player of the Empire of Azad. Gurgeh survives competing against the greatest players of Azad until he arrives at the final match with the greatest player, the Emperor. The Emperor had

---

4   Hillel is one of the most renowned of Jewish scholars. He lived in Jerusalem in his later life until about 9 CE. There seems to be clear overlap between his ideas and those of Jesus; for example, the Golden Rule is cited.

set out to beat not just Gurgeh, but the whole Culture. Gurgeh had finally realized that the Emperor made the game board his Empire, complete and exact in every structural detail to the limits of definition the game's scale imposed. Gurgeh, up to that point losing, realized his best strategy was to make his play represent the Culture, the Culture militant. The cooperative and empathic Culture against the aggressive Empire. At last hehad found a way to play. The game went on and on. 'It goes on until it ends,' Gurgeh thought to himself one day, and at same time as the banality of the thought struck him, he saw that it was over. He had won. The Culture had won.

We associate the forces of cooperation—cultural and individual maturity, peace, and empathy—with cultural progress and well-being. Yet those forces we associate with survival—war, aggression, selfishness—are also part of our culture, genetic inheritance, and even cultural maturity. The major theme of this book is that both these forces, the cooperative along with the aggressive, contribute to human survival and progress. The challenge of human progress is in arranging these conflicting forces such that they promote advances in human maturity.

Having starkly stated these moieties, they may seem obvious. These two sides of social forces contend for dominance in human history and may be characterized as aggression versus cooperation, war versus peace, anarchy versus law, andcivilizationversus barbarism. Even in our sexual roles, the dichotomy is apparent to the extent to which men tend to be more physically aggressive and women more empathic, although this dimorphism is considerably more complicated than this simple categorization.

In an important sense, cooperation is the child of war. To explain this, Curtis Marean (2015) notes that for tens of thousands of years, anatomically modern humans stayed in Africa. It was only about 70,000 years ago that a small population broke out into Eurasia. Marean asks why.

His answer (Marean 2015, 35) is that the emergence of traits   that made *homo sapiens* peerless collaborators as well as ruthless competitors best explains our sudden rise to world domination over other hominins and other creatures. Groups that are more social than others will tend to dominate, as they will better cooperate. The natural force that gives rise to and promotes such cooperation is the need to band together to fight for static food supplies during periods of intense climate change. Seaside environments provided a static food refuge for bands of humans and a cause of war against other bands. From cooperation came success in war and a growth in technology. The growth of cooperation was greatly boosted by the growth oftrade. Marean
(39) notes that when glacial conditions returned about 70,000 year ago, the modern human population actually expanded with its diversity of hunting tools.

Both of these types of forces, aggressive and cooperative, have contributed to progress and at times have detracted from it.[5] Evolution itself will tend to balance these parts in such a way that promotes survival. Cultures that do not or cannot defend themselves die. Given the greater probability of bad events for early man to deal with, it is no wonder that, as the essayist and novelist Marilynne Robinson notes, "I think a default position of human beings is fear" (*New York Times Magazine*, October 5, 2014, 24). This duality may explain in part how the forces of aggression act as a counter to fear. Cultures that do not promote civilization and internal and external cooperation will be less likely to survive and will tend to die out. Cultures that cut themselves off from others delay their own development, as is evident from the former Chinese and Japanese civilizations. The

---

5   Imagine for a moment that, at some future point, we are able to create super intelligent machines. We would want to program them to take care of themselves, to repair themselves, to adapt to new environments, and to have our values. Could we then pull their plugs (as it were)? If not, would machine (digital) life take over? Or could we program in core values that would govern their decision making and then set them free? Such also is our dilemma for ourselves as we seek cultural maturity; to progress, future humans must move toward a mature culture. See James Hogan's, science fiction novel The Two Faces of Tomorrow for aspects of this dilemma.

trick is to balance these forces in a way that is consistent with mature decision-making.

There has been an increased ability for abstract reasoning of the type used for scientific and moral reasoning. Michael Shermer (2015) notes that this sort of increased ability may be a factor in increasing our moral sensibilities. In the 1980s, James Flynn discovered that IQ scores have been going up by about 3 percent every ten years on average for the past one hundred years. This shows up on IQ scores as an increase in average IQs from 100 to 130, although normalization keeps the putative average at 100. The scores on arithmetic, and vocabulary have increased little; it is rather the increase in abstract reasoning that has increased. Shermer (2012) notes tests that ask questions such as "What do dogs and rabbits have in common?" To answer that both are mammals, says Flynn, means that you are thinking as a scientist, who uses abstract classifications. If you answer instead that "You use dogs to hunt rabbits," you are thinking concretely. According the Shermer, Flynn and his brother tried to reduce their father's prejudice of his generation by a thought experiment: "What if you woke up one morning and discovered your skin had turned black? Would that make you any less of a human being?" The elder Flynn responded, "Now that's the stupidest thing you've ever said. Who ever heard of a man's skin turning black overnight?" The father lived in a much more concrete world, a world focused on natural reality, not on abstractions. The rise in the ability to think abstractly is a rise in scientific thinking. Philosophers such as William Talbott (2005, 2010) have extended scientific thinking into the development of moral theory. At a more concrete level, Shermer notes that the increase in abstract reasoning ability is related to the ability to cooperate. The economist Stephen Burks and colleagues administered a test of abstract thinking ability to a thousand truck drivers and had them participate in games of prisoner's dilemma. Those with higher scores in abstract thinking were more likely to cooperate in this game, achieving what in real life would presumably be a better social outcome.

The Collective Action Problem

Societies are continually faced with problems that require social cooperation to solve, so the failure to cooperate leads to a loss of opportunity. These types of problems are called collective action problems and typically involve situations in which individual gain conflicts with social gain. Economists tend to see these problems through the lens of external effects. Such effects are those that are not taken into account in the decision-making process and thus are not captured through the price system.

A common form of such problems is the prisoner's dilemma (PD). The classic problem supposes that there are two criminals who are caught. Each prisoner must decide, "Should I inform on my partner?" If neither cooperates, and they do not inform on each other, they both would receive a reduced sentence, as the evidence of criminality is weak. But if one informs on the other, the other receives a longer sentence but the informer a lighter sentence. If each informs on the other, they both receive long sentences. Thus, both players may inform, giving a bad result for both. Logically, each player will realize that if his or her partner does not inform, he or she is better off playing the other for a sucker so that he or she informs. He or she also realizes that if the partner cheats, he or she is also better off cheating. So the prisoner cheats.

The results of the PD decisions are as follows:

Figure 2.1: A Prisoner's Dilemma Game

	B (cooperates)	B informs
A (cooperates)	3, 3	9,4
A (informs)	4,9	5,5

If both prisoners cooperate with each other, each receives an sentence of three years as in the box AB above. When one person attempts to cooperate but the other does not, the informant receives a sentence of 4 years but the cooperator receives a sentence of 9 years, as the cooperative person is played for a sucker. If neither prisoner cooperates, each serves five years. The non-cooperative result in which each serves 5 years will be reached when the participants think as follows. If the other person cooperates, I am better off not cooperating. If the other person does not cooperate, I am better off also not cooperating. Yet, if there is non-cooperation, the total years served is 10 rather than the 6 that would have been served if both had cooperation.

The game becomes more complex, however, when it is a repeated game. Cooperation is more likely among more moral or empathetic societies. The joint optimum for the two prisoners is clearly for them to cooperate. How is this result to be obtained?

There are many examples and variations of this type of dilemma, including nations stockpiling nuclear weapons, nations not restricting CO_2 emissions, advertisers determining their advertising budgets, and OPEC controlling oil prices. The following problematic but interesting example is from a blog by Shannon Larson reported in Quora.

> *Women wearing makeup. Society would likely be better off if we all didn't. Each day across America, several million man-hours (woman-hours, actually) are devoted to an activity with questionable benefit for society. Foregoing makeup would free up fifteen to thirty minutes (just an estimate as to average makeup application time) for each woman every morning. However, if no one wore makeup, then there would be great temptation for any one girl to gain an advantage versus everyone else by breaking with the norm, using mascara, blush, and concealer to hide imperfections and enhance her natural beauty.*

Once a critical mass wears makeup, the average facade of female beauty is artificially made greater. Bucking the trend and going au naturel means foregoing the artificial enhancement to beauty. Your beauty relative to what is perceived as average would decrease.

Most women therefore wear makeup. We end up with a situation that is not ideal for the whole or for the individuals but is based on rational choices by each individual.

Note that the above commentary, however, may be too simple. It does not consider the satisfaction women may receive from looking nice, regardless of what other women do. This also brings up the question of why men don't usually wear makeup. Why do they shave?

Consider now a more complex example: Suppose that C1 and C2 are cooperators, and NC1 and NC2 are not. C1 and C2 follow a tit-for-tat strategy in which they first cooperative and then continue to cooperate only if the other person also did in the previous round. Let the gains be 3 for each party in a cooperative trade, the loss be -5 for each party in a non-cooperative trade and -9 for the cooperator when dealing with a cheater and +8 for the non-cooperator when dealing with a cooperation. In this example, however, the non- cooperators are cheating businessmen. The cooperators honor their contracts; the non-cooperators do not. If we consider two-party trades, there are six two-party combinations. In the first round of trades, suppose that C1 and C2 cooperate with each other and with NC1 and NC2, even though N C1 and NC2 don't cooperate with them or with each other. At the end of the first round of six trades, A and B each will lose fifteen, but C and D will have each have gained 11., and total social gains are a negative eight C1   and C2, however, are not suckers but rather mature individuals. They play a game in which they cooperate on the first round and continue to cooperate as long as the other player also cooperates. This strategy is called tit for tat (Axelrod). In the second round of

Figure 2.2. The Extended Prisoners Dilemma Game

ROUND ONE: TWO COOPERATORS					
	C1	C2	NC1	NC2	TOTAL
C1	0	3	-9	-9	-15
C2	3	0	-9	-9	-15
NC1	8	8	0	-5	11
NC2	8	8	-5	0	11
Total					**-8**
ROUND TWO: PUNISHMENT					
	C1	C2	NC1	NC2	
C1	0	3	-5	-5	-7
C2	3	0	-5	-5	-7
NC1	-5	-5	0	-5	-15
NC2	-5	-5	-5	0	-15
TOTAL					**-44**
ROUND THREE: TWO NEW COOPERATORS WITH PUNISHMENT					
	C1	C2	NC2	NC2	TOTAL
C1	0	3	8	8	19
C2	3	0	8	8	19
NC1	-18	-8	0	3	-5
NC2	-9	-9	3	0	-6
TOTAL					**27**
ROUND FOUR: ALL COOPERATORS					
	C1	C2	NC1	NC2	
C1	3	3	3	3	12
C2	3	3	3	3	12
NC1	3	3	3	3	12
NC2	3	3	3	3	12
TOTAL					**48**

trade, C1 and C2 cooperate with each other but not with NC1 and NC2. Should C1 and C2 no longaer trade with NC1 and NC2, C1 and C2 will gain three in each trade round, and NC1 and C2 will each lose -5 from trading with each other. Suppose, however, that C1 and C2 continue to trade with C and D in an attempt to teach them a lesson in the hope that they will become cooperators. In the second round of trading, C1 and C2 each will gain three from trading with each other but will lose ten from trading with C and D, who also will each lose ten from trading with A and B but each will lose an additional five from attempting to cheat each other. The results are shown in figure 2.2., The total loss of C1and C2 after the first two round is -22 each, but now the non-cooperators also have losses. NC1 and NC2 can fold their tents, take their losses of -3 each and leave, or they can change their behavior.   If they leave, C1 and C2 continue to trade with each other, reaping gains of three on each round so that they come out winners.

If NC1 AND NC2 change their behavior in round 3, they will be punished by their round 2 behavior.. Figure 2.2 shows the results. In round four all become cooperators assuming NC1 and NC2 have learned their lessons. Total social gains are -8 in round 1, negative 44 in round 2 , a positive 27 in round three and a positive 48 in round four. Clearly society gains from cooperation.

From a social point of view, the best strategy is to cooperate from the beginning. In this case, each person gains 12 per round or 120 after 100 rounds.

The trick is to get people to cooperate. There are many devices and institutions to enhance the value of cooperation: enforceable contracts, laws against fraud, escrow against non-cooperation, the ability to develop trust, the ability to play the long game, and   so forth.[7] Without such institutions there often is a tendency for cooperation to break down. For example, it pays to cheat on the

---

7   A and B could each insist on contracts with C and D to help ensure cooperation or at least cooperative-like performance.

last round and, this being the case, to cheat on the next to last and so on. Perhaps the best solution is a social culture of cooperation. Zerbe and Anderson (2001) show that among the English-speaking miners, mainly American and British, California gold miners in 1848 together created a sort of spontaneous governmental structure such that predicted violence did not take place among those of the same cultural background. A number of other examples are provided by Elickson (1994) and by Elickson, Rose, and Smith (2014). Clearly there are a number of other complex games and strategies. Yet the fact is that the tit-for-tat strategy works well against almost all strategies and teaches others the benefits of cooperation. The point is that punishment for cooperative behavior encourages cooperation. Thus people react strong to what they see as unfairness.

Consider two different societies, perhaps countries, one in which NC1 and NC2 are in fact cooperators along with C1 and C2, the other in which they are not. Suppose further that, in the first society, the cooperators have a better sense of empathy because their genes produce more oxytocin, a substance that induces warm feelings toward those we know. The first society will do better than the second. Thus there will be both genetic and cultural drift as the first society produces more cooperative individuals.

The Lighthouse

In the figure below, consider a rocky promontory that ships sailing toward a safe harbor are apt to crash into during a storm. A village rests on the mainland near where the ships are swept ashore. When there are ships to be salvaged, the village gains the salvage; in addition, surviving sailors may stay in the village and marry local girls. In fact, salvage is the main business of the village. On stormy nights, one of the village men takes his donkey up on the ridge and walks it along the ridge with the lantern attached. From the sea, this looks like another ship and encourages the ship to sail closer to the coast and crash onto the rocks.

Suppose there are nine shipping companies, each with five ships. On the average, one ship per year is lost, and this loss is randomly distributed among the nine companies. Thus, on average, each company loses one-ninth of a ship per year. Now, for the equivalent cost of one-third of a ship per year, a lighthouse could be built that would prevent the wreckage of ships. No one company would build the lighthouse unless they could charge for it. The owner of the lighthouse would save one-ninth of a ship per year at a cost of one-third of a ship per year, in which case he or she would lose seven-thirtieths of a ship per year. Buy how could the owner of the lighthouse prevent other companies from using it for free? The other companies would all gain one-tenth of a ship per year, and the builders of the lighthouse could not compete. Thisagain is a collective action problem. The setting is shown in the figure below:

Figure 2.4: The Lighthouse Problem

Companies	Cost Savings from Lighthouse on Average in Ships per Year	Cost of Lighthouse If All Share Cost Equally	Cooperative Gain per Company	Total Social Gain
1	0.1	.03	.07	.07
2	0.1	.03	.07	0.14
3	0.1	.03	.07	0.21
4	0.1	.03	.07	0.28
5	0.1	.03	.07	0.35
6	0.1	.03	.07	0.42
7	0.1	.03	.07	0.49
9	0.1	.03	.07	0.56
9	0.1	.03	.07	0.63
9	0.1	.03	.07	0.70
TOTAL	1.0 Ships Per Year	0.3 Ships per year	0.7 Ships per Year	0.70

Even if four companies built the lighthouse, they would be at a competitive disadvantage.

Consider the possible solutions: (1) The shipping companies could cooperate to build the lighthouse, but some may opt out, hoping to get a free ride. In response, the companies could require a contract that stated that no lighthouse would be built unless all contributed. (2) The government could build the lighthouse and charge the shipping companies. This shows the possible advantage of government coercion. (3) The owners of the harbor that the ships are sailing toward could build the lighthouse and charge the ships a harbor fee to cover their costs. The latter was in fact the solution used in the era of sailing ships in England and Ireland (Coase 1974).

These sorts of problems arise whenever there is a divergence between purely private interests and the interests of others. For example, where there is unrestricted access to a valuable asset, say grazing on open range, problems of the commons arise (called the tragedy of the commons). The problem arises from the fact that the asset will not be used in a way that maximizes its total social value. These difficulties arise in commercial fisheries, in air or water pollution, in congestion (e.g., traffic congestion), or with too great a growth in population. Fisheries can become overfished, the polluter does not take into account the harm he or she is causing to others, the highway driver does not consider the increased congestion caused by his or her travel nor do parents consider their contribution to population growth.

The most important collective action problems are those of political agreement, such as developing constitutions and rules of conduct. The US Constitution is a tribute to the wise men who fashioned it. Groups that operate purely for their own political interests can represent a norm that leads to political breakdown and the noncooperative solution. Because the noncooperator does better than the cooperator in important cases, there needs to be some incentive for cooperation.

The most efficient incentive is furnished by culture. There are certain features of culture that are known to promote cooperation. It is well known that people are more likely to cooperate in the PD game if is a repeated game (Axelrod 1984). Successful noncooperation, which occurs when one party cooperates and the other wins by noncooperation, is less likely in repeated games. People are less likely to be a sucker repeatedly than a sucker once. This result also requires some ability to think ahead, a signal of mental maturity. What if you are playing a repeated game with someone whom you are certain will defect? What is a mature strategy? Not always to cooperate. A sucker is not self-actualized. Rather, what if you cooperate on the first round and thereafter   do what the other person did in the previous round? This tit-for-   tat strategy opens the door to cooperation and is remarkably successful against other strategies (Axelrod 1984). It also has the potential to teach cooperation, since the defector will not do as well as a cooperator if many others play tit for tat. But it only works well if there are other potential cooperators. Cooperation is easier under certain conditions. For example, group homogeneity, as evidenced by common culture, promotes cooperation. Zerbe and Anderson (2001) show that while conditions in the California gold fields promoted cooperation among English speakers, intra-ethnic cooperation was much easier to   achieve   than inter-ethnic cooperation. Without some substantial level of maturity, inter-ethnic cooperation may be impossible, as it requires a greater ability to understand or empathize with those who are substantially different. Further examples are discussed by Elickson and by Elickson and Rose . In a sufficiently primitive society where few think ahead, an individual who pursues cooperation may not fare well even if the game is repeated.

Culture and Cooperation

Aspects of culture can affect the likelihood of cooperation. For example, a recent (2014) meta study provides a meta-analytic test of the idea that video games affect social outcomes, depending on their content.[8] Data from ninety-eight independent studies with 36,965 participants reveal that for both violent video games and prosocial video games, there is a significant association with social outcomes. Violent video games increase aggression and aggression-related variables and decrease prosocial outcomes, while prosocial video games have the opposite effects. These results indicate that there are both short-term and long-term effects to these games.

Luhrmann (*New York Times*, December 4, 2014, A 29) points out that the American and European cultures stand out from the rest of the world in the greater sense of ourselves as individuals. He notes, "We like to think of ourselves as unique, autonomous, self-motivated, self-made" and that people in the rest of the world are likely to understand themselves as more interdependent with other people. Nisbett (2005) and others find that these differences affect cognitive processing. Americans, for example, are more likely to ignore context, while some Asian cultures would be more attentive to it. When shown a school of fish in which one fish is significantly larger than the others, Americans notice earlier and pay more attention to the large fish, while Asians notice first the background and remember the seaweed and other background objects better.

Thomas Talhelm et al. (2014) suggest that these differences arise from the different social worlds of rice and wheat. They tested 1,162 Han Chinese participants in six cities and found that the rice-growing Southern China culture is more interdependent and holistic thinking then the wheat-growing North, where efficient farming was not as interdependent. Rice paddies require complex irrigation systems that are interdependent with other systems. In China, the Yangtze River divides Northern wheat farmers from Southern rice growers. Han Chinese from each region were asked questions such as which two of the three items belong together: a bus, a train, train tracks. (What is your own answer?) The more

---

8 Prior to the study mentioned above, there had been a difference of opinion as to whether or not aggression was increased by violent video game play.

individualistic Northerners paired the bus and the train, while the more interdependent Southerners paired the train and train tracks. The bus and the train do similar jobs. The train and the tracks work together. When asked to draw their social networks, the Northern Han drew themselves larger than their neighbors; subjects in the South drew their neighbors larger than themselves. Both groups were also asked how they would respond if a friend caused them to lose money in a business. The Northerners were more punitive.

In economics, it is well accepted that losses mean more than equivalent gains. For example, the amount you would pay to gain a chance of winning a hundred dollars is less than the amount you would pay to avoid the same chance of losing a hundred dollars. My prediction is that losses mean less in the rice-grower cultures than in the wheat-grower cultures.

Cooperation as a Vehicle of Progress

What I call culture and well-being is in considerable part a reflection of cooperation among humans, especially the ability to specialize. An orchestra consists of individuals playing different parts cooperatively to produce a harmonious whole. As this cooperation has become richer, so has culture, and this growth in richness is cultural progress. Cooperation grows not only in complexity, but also in spatiality. The social advantage of cooperation is that it increases the size of the social pie across economic, technological, artistic, and social measurement.[9]

Cooperation can take three forms: one rooted in self-regard, another in empathy or sympathy. First, parties can cooperate for mutual advantage, a scenario that would be more likely if empathy and the third in both. The first form of cooperation involves the ability to solve collective action problems. To solve a normal collective action problem requires a sort of prescient

9   Cooperation is analyzed by the sociologist Marcel Mauss (1922) in terms of gift exchange, which he finds has profound social significance.

self-regard in which individuals care about themselves and about others.[10] Cooperation will then emerge more easily if they also have regard for others, the mixed option.

The second form of cooperation is subtler. It occurs when at least one party is able to empathize with others in quite different positions. Cooperative ability captures the important parts of individual development as growth in empathy. This second form of cooperation, which I shall call empathic cooperation, concerns society's ability to provide individuals with the culture milieu that is most supportive of their individual development, as defined in terms of individual maturity.

Cooperation can extend beyond self-regard. This second form of cooperation requires a willingness to reach out sympathetically and empathetically to the disenfranchised so as to move toward a society in which each person has an equal chance at life's prospects. To move toward an ideal environment for individual development requires something more than prescient self-regard —it requires cooperative empathy, which is part of cultural maturity. Culture maturity imagines not just simple cooperation but a cultural ideal that gives the individual the best chance of realizing his or her maximum potential. As Erikson notes, society should be "so constituted as to meet and invite this succession of potentialities for interaction and the proper sequence of their enfolding" (Erikson 1963, 271). These two ideas of cooperation are my defining measures of cultural progress.[11]

In the development of the Jewish culture, Cahill (1998, 198) sees a tit for-tat mentality operating until the time of David. David's sins are worse than Saul's, but David is better treated by God, for David discovers forgiveness and redemption. This is not surprising, as David's interior discovery of the sense of self

---

10   The ability to plan ahead appears to be a product of culture, including education.

11   With respect to cooperation, the very development of the human brain, the answer to why our brain is relatively large, has been explained in terms of the benefits of social cooperation and the mental complexity needed to handle it Wright 1995.

is apparent, and a sense of self is necessary for a full sense of others and therefore to full cooperation. With the exception of the Psalms, the sense of I is absent from ancient literature and is not discovered again until the humanistic literature of the early modern period (Cahill 1998, 199).

Cooperative empathy requires the ability of one class, group, or country to extend opportunity and justice to another. This ability is akin to the notions advanced by Rawls (1971), who asks us to form basic rules by imagining what our choice would be in an initial or original position. This position is one in which the rule chooser does not know, among other things, what position he or she will occupy in the society until after the rule is chosen. That is, the person could be anyone; this procedure envisions empathy.

E.O. Wilson (2012), the justly famous evolutionary biologist, contends that the pathway to human cooperation (eusociality)[12] was a product of conflict between natural selection based on the relative success of individuals within groups and relative success among groups. The latter required "a mix of closely calibrated altruism, cooperation, competition, domination, reciprocity, defection, and deceit." This required the evolution of a higher degree of intelligence. Sympathy toward other, however, does not require great or even significant intelligence. Recently, voles were shown to offer comfort to those whom they know when they suffered.

This raises the question of the nature of altruism. Or we might ask, "Are genes selfish?" For some time, most evolutionary biologists believed in the selfish gene; altruism was seen as an aberration or as directed only toward kin.[13] Cultures in which cooperation helps increase the society's fitness will tend to survive, where in noncooperative others, survival is less likely. This is likely to

---

12   Wilson defines *eusocial* as "group members containing multiple generations and prone to perform altruistic acts as part of their division of labor" (16).

13   The exception being Ernst Mayr.

be true even when the cooperation considered is at the expense of individual lives. That is, there would be no reason natural selection would not include a genetic predisposition toward cooperation if cooperation increases the likelihood of the survival of this genetic predisposition. Evolution can affect group survival as well as individual survival. Consider two groups, with one group more cooperative than the other, because its individuals are more cooperative both by genetic disposition and by culture. If a cooperative group is more likely to survive than a noncooperative one, then individuals who are more cooperative by reason of both genetics and culture are more likely to survive.

The evolutionary biologist Richard Dawkins invented the term meme to stand for the cultural evolution analog of the gene in biological evolution (Dawkins 1986).[14] A meme or set of memes can be ideas, technologies, religious or political philosophies, or any other components of culture. The critical similarities they share with genes are 1) they are passed on through time and across cultures, 2) they exhibit variation through time and space, and

3) some memes are better than others at propagating themselves. These are unusual concepts to apply to ideas and cultures, but it is clear that if there is any hope of progress or sense in human cultural history, there must be some sort of genealogy of cultures. Cultures and societies do not spring up anew from amorphous bands of people, and some ideas are clearly better at being spread than others. For example, a philosophy that requires its adherents to commit suicide in silence is less likely to grow and gain new believers than one that requires its adherents to teach. The classic example is that of the Shakers who, believing sex to be morally wrong, died out (A. N. Wilson 2001, 375–6). Therefore, ideas can be thought of as competing in a cultural landscape, just as genes compete in a biological landscape. But a cultural version of biological descent with modification is not

---

14   Genes themselves can also cooperate (Ridley 2001).

enough. I suggest that the features of cultural maturity I have identified give cultures a competitive advantage and thus have survivorship value.

Consider the early Christian community The sociologist Rodney Stark (1996) analyzed and modeled the early growth of Christianity in the context of the Roman Empire. He found that, regardless of metaphysics or miracles, many features of the new religion associated with empathy gave it an advantage in the sense of evolutionary fitness, as it was able to propagate itself more effectively than its competitors. These advantages led to an increase in the numbers of Christians in the empire relative to pagans, leading eventually to the domination of Europe by the Catholic Church in the Middle Ages. This type of competitive advantage does not necessarily imply conflict, conquest, or subjugation, but merely a superior ability to attract adherents.

The Rise of Christianity

Early Christianity showed a feature of cultural maturity with the enhanced status and increased respect women and female children were given in the church, relative to pagan attitudes. In Greco-Roman society, females had been treated with little respect for their humanity (Stark 1996). Female children were routinely disposed of, and even large Roman families seldom raised more than one daughter. Women and marriage were held in low regard, and many Roman men remained single, ignored their wives, or avoided having children. Abortion was incredibly common, and due to the crude methods of the time, it frequently killed both fetus and mother. As a result of these attitudes and practices, the core areas of the Roman Empire faced severe population shortages before the Christian era.

By contrast, the earliest Christians found the Roman practices immoral and reprehensible and instead created a significant expansion of empathy and compassion. Wives were treated more fairly, with rights to love, attention, and fidelity from their husbands. Family life and procreation were stressed as godly, in opposition to the casual promiscuity of the Romans. Therefore, not only were more women attracted to the new religion because of their higher status, but their average fertility rate was improved by the practices of Christianity. The new religion was able to grow and eventually dominate Europe by a combination of conversion and reproduction.

Twice in the early years of the Christian era the Roman Empire was swept by epidemics, and the responses of the people demonstrated the improved cultural maturity of the Christian religion. In the late second century, a massive plague killed as much as one-third of the population, including the Emperor Marcus Aurelius, and a similar epidemic caused massive mortality about a hundred years later. The established religion and philosophies of the Roman Empire were unable to provide their followers with solace or guidance against these disasters, resulting in panic, despair, and abandonment of the sick and dying. Stark quotes Dionysius, bishop of Alexandria, writing that "At the first onset of disease they [the pagans] pushed the sufferers away and fled from their dearest, throwing them into the roads before they were dead" (Stark 1996, 83). By contrast, the Christian community found in their religion both metaphysical justification for suffering and the comfort of an afterlife. Even more important from the viewpoint of cultural progress, the Christian ideal of love for their fellow men as an expression of love for God motivated care of the sick and dying of both the Christian and pagan communities. While modern treatments for the diseases were of course unavailable, simple nursing care was effective in reducing death rates. Thus, the compassion and empathy of the Christians led to an increase in the relative proportions of Christians, through improved survival and powerful incentives for potential converts. The Christians were better cooperators.

A similar process may have operated in the cities of the Roman Empire during nonplague times. Stark (1996) demonstrated that Christianity was a largely urban movement in the early empire. The cities of the period were incredibly crowded, filthy, and disease ridden, with death rates so high that they could persist only with constant emigration from the countryside. "Given limited water and means of sanitation, and the incredible density of humans and animals, most people in Greco-Roman cities must have lived in filth beyond imagining" (Stark 1996, 153). In the face of disease, natural disasters, war, and the constant population flux, Christianity provided both mental and physical comfort.

As Stark (1996, 161) wrote,

> *To cities filled with the homeless and impoverished, Christianity offered charity as well as hope. To cities filled with newcomers and strangers, Christianity offered an immediate basis for attachments. To cities filled with orphans and widows, Christianity provided a new and expanded sense of family. To cities torn by violent ethnic strife, Christianity offered a new basis Christianity for social solidarity. To cities faced with epidemics, fires and earthquakes, offered effective nursing services.*

These factors gave Christianity improved survival, fertility, and success in propagation. Cultures such as Christianity evolve and are subject to the rules of natural selection. But they evolve much more rapidly than species do. This suggests that empathetic ethical superiority increases the probably of cultural survival and increases the possibility, according to Ernst Mayr (1997), of the survival of generic impulses toward caring. The increasing progress of democratic rule and of enfranchisement suggests the cultural survivability of cooperation.

Have We Made Progress?

We have. Thomas Hobbes (1651) famously noted that "[In a state of war or nature there are] no arts; no letters; no society; and which is worst of all, continual fear and danger of violent death; and the life of man, solitary, poor, nasty, brutish, and short." Life for many now is not so solitary, poor, nasty, brutish, and short. We have made progress. The more difficult question is whether the progressive trends will continue.

Cultural Relativism Explained

Are the trends I will discuss really improvements in culture? Some people have and some still maintain that cultures cannot be compared and that contentment and well-being or even happiness cannot be measured. To maintain that there is a hierarchy of cultures implies that cultures have different values and that different cultures are not of equal value, contrary to an older and rapidly decreasing view of modern cultural anthropologists, who believed that the concept of cultural progress is anathema.[15]

This cultural relativism in which all cultures have equal value is itself the result of a sort of psychic trauma within the profession. Cultural relativism serves to eliminate assertions of cultural superiority as a justification for unjust impositions of one culture on another. Such impositions have a bad history, so it is easy to understand the appeal of cultural relativism. Concepts of culture superiority have been used to justify the most egregious behavior. The conquistadors used this argument, especially as it pertained to the superiority of the Catholic religion, to enslave native tribes.

15 There are more sophisticated versions of cultural relativism that are not addressed here. If
my picture of it is a caricature, it is nevertheless a useful one. As economists are fond of saying "all models are wrong, but some are useful," by which they mean not "wrong" but "incomplete." The cultural relativist holds that it is inappropriate to judge members of one culture by the norms of another. Rather, they say, members of each culture should be judged by the norms of their own culture (Talbott 2000, 19). For useful references, see Cole and Scribner (1974) and White (1959 and 1998).

For example, in 1519, Hernan Cortes began the conquest of Aztecs on the high central plateau of Mexico. In 1531, Francisco Pissarro set out on a similar conquest of Peru. The conquerors sought wealth, power, the greater glory of the crown, and the spread of Catholicism. The moral justification for the brutal subjugation of   a brutal (Aztec) people was religious; from the start the monarchy believed it had a moral and Christian mission in the New World. The church worked for three centuries to "civilize" the Native Americans. They took Indians from their tribes and villages to teach them Christianity, with poor results for the children.

Figure 2.5[16]

Southern slaveholders used their belief in the superiority of Christianity to justify slavery. The Nazis believed not only in their racial but also in their cultural superiority. The colonization by Western Europeans was rationalized by religious arrogance and was noteworthy for insensitivity to native religious practices and customs. The Marxist values of equality were perverted to eliminate or displace millions of relatively well-to-do Russian farmers

16   See http://www.economist.com/news/world-week/21639585-kals-cartoon?fsrc=scn/tw/te/kal/jan17.

(Kulaks).[17] The current mess in the Middle East is in part, perhaps considerable part, due to the arrogance of England, France, the United States, and Germany in their interventions in the Middle East prior to and after World War I.[18] Cultural or value superiority has in fact been used to justify the most appalling treatment of others. Cultural relativism arose to combat this sort of arrogance. A cultural relativist says you cannot justify treating the natives as if they are inferior; their culture is as good as yours.

In 1918, an essay in *The American Anthropologist* attacked the idea of cultural evolution (by which they meant cultural progress) as "the most inane, sterile, and pernicious theory ever conceived in the history of science" (Wright 2000, 15). By 1939, another anthropologist reported that cultural "evolutionism can muster hardly a single proponent" (Wright 2000, 15). One sort of music is not superior to another; one sort of art is not to be compared unfavorably with another sort.[19] Nor should one set of values be set superior to another set. So the condemnation of brutality and of moral arrogance by anthropologists was welcome. The idea of cultural relativism was created to condemn the infliction of violence by more technologically advanced countries onto less advanced ones.

The anthropological literature offers us, even today, little in the way of a concept of cultural progress. Joseph Campbell (1983) seems to have captured the prevailing anthropologists' view in his contention that all religions are cyclical, mythical, and ahistorical. This cyclical and semi-stagnant view, associated with Eastern philosophy, stands in contrast to the view arising from the Jewish and Greek cultures. The Greeks and Jews appear to see a more linear development. That is, they read human

---

17 Marxism as envisioned by Marx, not as it appears today, appears to be the apotheosis of Nietzsche's warning, "What if morality should turn out to be the danger of dangers?" so that today it has evolved into tyranny.

18 I recommend in this regard the movie Lawrence of Arabia.

19 Economists have also maintained that de gustibus non est disputum (tastes cannot be disputed), and for certain applications, this is a reasonable assumption, but as a general statement, it is wrong, as this chapter suggests.

history from a teleological perspective, so that, in short, they are more likely to see historical progress.

Thus, for some time it has been politically incorrect to speak of the possibility of cultural progress. The notion of progress suggests the notion of cultural maturity, which is a forbidden concept. Our own culture is said to have a self contradictory "dogma of otherness" (Brin 1994, 90), a belief that all cultures are of equal merit—that there should be no cultural dogmas (Brin 1994, 90; Talbott 2000). This attitude is part of a more general postmodernism view in which "there are no clear lines of advance and in which people accept futility and the absurd as normal" (Rothstein 2000, quoting Barzun). The postmodern culture is simply decadent in Barzun's terms (Barzun 2000, 9). Thus the condemnation of brutally and of moral arrogance by anthropologists was welcomed.

The Internal Contradiction of Cultural Relativism

Although cultural relativism arose out of attempts to eliminate unjust judgments of cultural inferiority, it is the wrong tool to condemn unjust treatment; it is logically inconsistent. In its extreme form, it says that all cultures are equally valuable. But the idea of incomparability is wrong and misleading and results in foolish choices. In this form, it has no standing to condemn the acts of a brutal culture, as it cannot say a culture is brutal or unjust, or it can say that it is brutal but cannot say that brutality is bad. Cultural relativism has no answer to the imperialist defense that exploitation of others is just a part of its culture if all cultures are of equal worth. Talbott (2000) asks, suppose you came across a sixteenth-century conquistador threatening to kill any native who did not convert to Catholicism. You attempt to preach tolerance. But the conquistador replies that you are attempting to subvert his culture, which has no such norm of tolerance. A culture that fully acts upon a belief in cultural relativism and as a result did not defend itself would be eliminated by more aggressive cultures. Moreover, cultural relativism carries a cost abdication of cultural responsibility for others and an inability to act to improve culture. Yet just as clearly, cultural absolutism leads to the very sorts of unethical behavior that cultural relativism was created to condemn. However, there are better grounds than cultural relativism or absolutism to condemn colonial exploitation. I will suggest that concepts of individual development and the idea of empathy can be adapted to do this work.

We can accept the view that each culture is often an appropriate adaptation to its circumstances without giving up the notion of cultural maturity. One might reasonably consider cultural relativism as the view that all cultures are simply the most appropriate adaptation to the environment given the circumstances, so that each culture might be seen as appropriate to its past challenges. In this sense, no culture is superior to another, just different. This is similar to the psychoanalytic view that individual development comes from adaptations to external and internal circumstance. This psychoanalytic view, however, says that these short term, perhaps necessary, adaptations may no longer be helpful, and one is better served by changing them. By considering cultural maturity, we can consider ways in which it can be achieved, just as an analyst considers ways in which an individual may better gain greater maturity.

More technologically advanced cultures assume that they are superior in some general sense. Yet technological advancement only captures a part, and a small part at that, of well-being. In the latter part of the nineteenth century, Cynthia Ann Parker, a child of nine, was captured by the Texas Comanche.[20] She

---

20   See S. C. Gwyne (2014).

was raised by them in a hard but rewarding and happy life, producing two sons in a happy marriage one of whom, Quanah, become the most powerful chief of the most powerful American Indian tribe. Cynthia Ann was a physically strong, smart, and competent. After some years, she was recaptured by the Texans, met with relatives, and learned to read. The Texans, relatives and others, attempted to convert her into a proper Christian lady. She attempted many times to return to the Comanche but was kept a prisoner, taught from the Bible but feted at public occasions. After some years, she committed suicide by starvation. The Comanche were a war culture with a strong spiritual base, never properly defeated by the Texans, but cholera, small pox, and new guns of the Texans convinced them to go onto a reservation. One can point to the atrocities of the Comanche, but these were made with the purpose of keeping settlers from their land, and one can point to atrocities of the Texans. One would be hard pressed to say that the Texan culture was superior to the Comanche's, though Texans were technologically superior. The Comanche were superb horsemen and great fighters, apparently happy with the competence to be able to live and survive in difficult territories. This lesson in the failings of arrogance does not mean there are no metrics on which cultures can be ranked.

Certainly in more recent times, we can find reason for hope in cultural progress if we consider past examples that we have been able to ameliorate. We need not go back more than a century and a half in the most economically advanced countries of Western culture to find a good deal of abuse of animals and human beings—the extensive existence of slavery, marked cruelties in the treatment of criminals, the brutal beating of small children, little interest in the poor except on the basis of personal almsgiving, and the incredible horrors in the treatment of the "feebleminded" and insane. In the years since then, the condition of these groups has been transformed: slavery is regarded as immoral though it still exists; animals are better protected; there is a current trend toward treatment rather than punishment for some criminals; the treatment of the sick, the insane, and various physically and mentally defective and sick persons has greatly improved; women have moved closer to an equality with men; and extensive philanthropic movements have been directed toward the relief of distress and the reduction of poverty (Bossard and Boll, 534, citing Maurice Parmelee, *Poverty and Social Progress*, Chapter 17, 1916).

A critic might say that my adoption of empathy as a vehicle of cultural progress is a mere value judgment. Of course, it is a value judgment, but it is a thesis of this essay that value judgments have survival value and are thus not "mere." Empathy and its associated ability to cooperate are themselves products of evolutionary forces with survival value. Nor do I maintain that empathy by itself is the measure of cultural progress; as I said there are many factors, but empathy is one as is self-regard.

Summary

I suggest that we rank cultures on the extent to which they promote individual maturity. Such maturity requires empathy, an ability to cooperate, and a sufficient sense of self to protect oneself and survive. The dilemma that arises is that what is best for an individual may conflict with what is best for society. These sorts of problems are known generally as collective action problems, of which a subcategory is the prisoners' dilemma problems. In economics, these sorts of problems are associated with the concept of externalities or external effects. Examples of collective action problems in which cooperation provided solutions are shown by the rise of Christianity and the behavior of miners in the California gold fields from 1848 to 1850. The concept of cultural relativism in which cultures cannot be compared or judged is not a useful approach.

Questions

1. Can you give examples of the fundamental conflict between cooperation and aggression?

2. How can the conflict be resolved for the good of culture?

3. Is this conflict the one between good and evil?

4. Although we have not discussed law, I ask if the major role of law is to resolve collective action problems. How?

3
The Shape of Progress and Change

In this and subsequent chapters, we will consider topics in which graphical representations are useful and statistical terms are used. These representations and statistics deal with the nature of past trends and future projections. We ask first what has been the nature and shape of these trends, and then we ask to what extent and how past trends of human progress can be extended to predict the future. What would the shapes of such extrapolation look like? The curves shown in this chapter are typical of the shape of human processes and changes. Some important questions include which curves have we inhabited until now, and on which part of a larger curve do we currently lie?

Very few individuals did well more than a hundred years ago in predicting change. The exception is John Watkins, an engineer who in 1900 made the following predictions for the year 2000:

1. Digital color photography.
2. Quick conveyance of photographs from one country to another.
3. Rising height. (The average male was sixty-six to sixty-seven inches tall in 1900; now the average height is close to seventy inches.)
4. Mobile phones.
5. Pre-prepared meals.
6. Slowing population growth figures.
7. Television.
8. Tanks.
9. Bigger fruit.
10. Faster trains.

This is an enormously prescient list. His misses were that the letters C, X, and Q would no longer be used; that everyone would walk nine miles a day; that there would be no more cars in cities but rather subways; and that there would be no more mosquitoes. Still, these all may happen—particularly, I would say no more cars in cities. The attack on Zika may also eliminate mosquitoes. Thus, imaginative extrapolation may not do so badly in some cases.

Another type of prediction is based on an understanding of the underlying mechanism. Einstein predicted gravitational waves more than one hundred years ago, on the basis of his general theory, which itself is a theory of gravity. These waves have been found. One should take this sort of prediction seriously, as it is based on an understanding of underlying mechanisms. In fact, such an understanding can correctly predict better than the creator of the understanding. Einstein's theory implied black holes, but he didn't think they would be found or would exist. Yet there they are.

Correlation and Causation

A most important idea here is that a *relationship between two things does not mean that one causes the other. Correlation does not mean causation.* In addition, if we use simple extensions of existing trends, (a correlation with time), we will make poor predictions and create quite inaccurate positive or negative expectations. Many forecasts are wrong because they are poorly reasoned extrapolations of trends whose natures are not well understood. It can be quite misleading to project trends without knowing something about the underlying mechanism that created the trend. Calkins (2012) notes that it is good fun to read predictions from one hundred years ago, or even twenty years ago, and see how far off they are, but it is also dismaying. Short-term predictions overstate changes, while long-term predictions understate them. It is easy to build narratives but difficult to build good ones, as suggested by the cartoon below.

A WEIGHTED RANDOM NUMBER GENERATOR JUST PRODUCED A NEW BATCH OF NUMBERS.

LET'S USE THEM TO BUILD NARRATIVES!

ALL SPORTS COMMENTARY

All predictions miss the mark, and most predictions miss the mark by wide margins. Predictions always will always be inaccurate. Even predictions of the past are inaccurate; the past is never fully certain. People speak of Bannister's 4-minute mile, but his time was not 4 minutes; it was 3.94. Yet surely it was not exactly 3.94, maybe something like 3.943. People who actually witnessed long past events are no longer alive and their written accounts probably differ.

The issue is whether or not the predictions are accurate enough to be useful. Therefore, choosing the appropriate curve or trend can be one of the greatest challenges, as incorrectly doing so may cause misinterpretation leading to faulty conclusions.

A simple example of mistaken extrapolation is height predictions. One might say, "John was growing at a rate of 2 inches a year from age five until age nine, by which time he was 5 feet 4 inches tall. (This characterization of the past will itself not be entirely precise; John may have grown by 2.01 inches per year.) On this basis of the 2 inches per year trend, one might suggest, foolishly to be sure, that by the time John reaches seventeen, he will be 14 inches taller (2 inches for seven years) or about 6 feet 6 inches tall. Probably not! His growth rate will likely change. Perhaps a more reasonable estimate could be made from his growth rate at age nine or from the height of his parents. The growth rate from ages five to nine might be useful data along with other data in predicting height, but taken alone, a linear extrapolation is clearly a poor bet. A graph using a linear extrapolation of John's height in inches would be as follows:

Figure 3.1: John's Height vs. Age

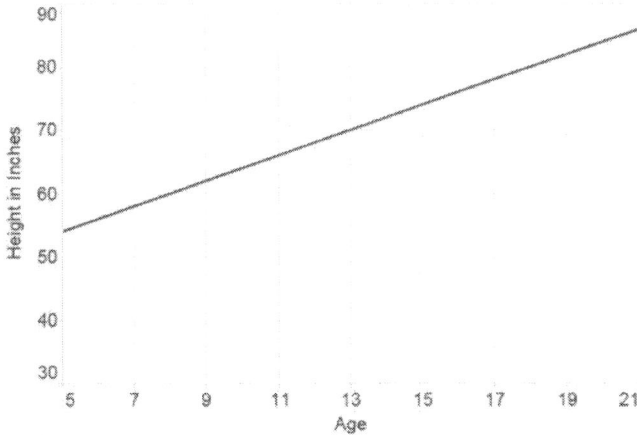

Notice that the linear extrapolation has John at 84 inches, or 7 feet, by the time he is twenty! We see then that linear extrapolation is an inappropriate mechanism by which to predict growth. Similarly, neither economic growth nor the decline in per capita violence nor changes in life expectancy, for example, have shown linear relationships.

One of most troubling causes of ill health is obesity. Predicting the prevalence of obesity in America is another example in which determining the correct growth trend, or "shape of the curve," is important. The National Health and Nutrition Examination Study (NHANES) is a program of the Centers for Disease Control and Prevention that collects health study data about the proportion of the population that is overweight, defined as having a body mass index (BMI) of 25 or higher. The BMI is defined as the body mass divided by the square of the body height and is universally expressed in units of kg/m^2, resulting from mass in kilograms and height in meters. (What is your BMI? Mine is 25.2, so I am overweight by this measure.) To be considered not just overweight but obese according to NHANES, one would have a BMI over 30.

Jordan Ellenberg, a mathematician at the University of Wisconsin, looking at work by Youfa Wang, reported that in the early 1970s, less than 50 percent of the American population had a body mass of 30 or higher (Ellenberg 2014).

By the 1990s, that proportion had risen to 60 percent, and by 2008, it had risen to almost 75 percent. Per Ellenberg, Youfa Wang goes on to note that at this rate, by 2048 everyone in the United States would be obese.[21] This is by definition true. But it would be a poor prediction, and for that matter using obesity would be a poorer choice for prediction than body fat. BMI is a poor measure of obesity, as it does not distinguish body fat from muscle.[22] A really ripped guy or gal, for example, is considered obese by BMI standards, as muscle is almost twice as heavy as fat. Also the measure of obesity should be adjusted for age and sex, as muscle mass declines naturally with age. A much better measure of obesity is percentage of body fat, as given below, adjusted for age. The following figures of body fat are typical:[23]

Figure 3.2: Body Fat Percentage: Women

Age	Lean	Slim (healthy)	Fit (fair)	Average (high)	Obese (very high)
19-24	< 19%	19 - 22%	22 - 25%	25 - 29%	> 29&
25-29	< 19%	19 - 22%	22 - 25%	25 - 29%	> 29%
30-34	< 20%	20 - 23%	23 - 26%	26 - 30%	> 30%
35-39	< 21%	21 - 24%	24 - 28%	28 - 31%	> 31%
40-44	< 23&	23 - 26%	26 - 29%	29 - 33%	> 33%
45-49	< 24%	24 - 27%	2 - 31%	31 - 34%	> 34%
50-54	< 27%	27 - 30%	30 - 33%	33 - 36%	> 36%
55-59	< 27%	27 - 31%	31 - 34%	34 - 27%	> 37%
60+	< 28%	28 - 31%	31 - 34%	34 - 38%	> 38%

---

21 I am using Ellenberg's account of Wang. I have not read Wang; thus, my remarks should not be taken as a criticism of him.

22 I would like to thank Jared Erickson, fitness trainer, for pointing this out.

23 Adapted from http://www.brainyweightloss.com/body-fat-percentage-chart.html.

50

Figure 3.3: Body Fat Percentage: Men

Age	Lean	Slim (healthy)	Fit (fair)	Average (high)	Obese (very high)
19-24	< 11%	11 - 15%	15 - 19%	19 - 23%	> 23%
25-29	< 13%	13 - 16%	16 - 20%	20 - 24%	> 24%
30-34	< 14%	14 - 18%	18 - 21%	21 - 25%	> 25%
35-39	< 16%	16 - 19%	19 - 23%	23 - 26%	> 26%
40-44	< 17%	17 - 20%	20 - 24%	24 - 27%	> 27%
45-49	< 19%	19 - 21%	21 - 24%	24 - 28%	> 28%
50-54	< 20%	20 - 23%	23 - 26%	26 - 29%	> 29%
55-59	< 20%	20 - 23%	23 - 26%	26 - 29%	> 29%
60+	< 20%	20 - 23%	23 - 26%	27 - 30%	> 30%

In addition, we can be confident that the current trend in BMI increases will not continue. Ellenberg (2014) notes that, as the proportion of the population that is obese grows, the number of average or healthy weight people who become obese will become smaller, and the growth rate will slow down. Furthermore, those remaining at "normal" weights may be the most resistant to becoming obese, which would also slow down the growth of obesity. This phenomenon would indicate a declining growth rate of obesity, rather than positive linear growth rate.

The data used by Wang for obesity growth rates do indeed show an exponential relationship. From 1950 to 1990, obesity grew by about 0.56 percent per year. From 1990 to 2008, obesity grew at about 1.2 percent per year. This is an exponential increase; an exponential increase means that there is an exponent involve. Notice that exponential increases will at some point exceed linear increase, meaning that it has a greater slope and rises at a faster rate. For example, a simple exponential function is given by $Y = X^2$.

A graph of this function would look like this:

Figure 3.4: An Exponential Function

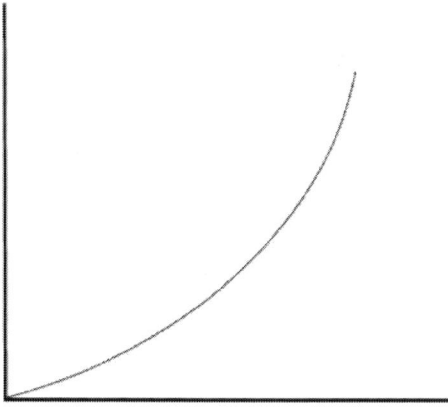

If an exponential curve did explain the rise in obesity, we would soon arrive at 100 percent obesity, and further growth in the obesity proportion would be impossible. This, to say the least, is unlikely. It appears that an exponential curve will not adequately explain future obesity. As the proportion of obese people grows, the proportion would grow more slowly. Thus, the trend shown by the data cited by Ellenberg is unlikely to continue.

The correct graph might look more like the one shown below, with the curve asymptotic to 100 percent at infinity, meaning that it approaches 100 percent quite closely. This is an example of a logistic graph, which is often used to show probabilities (as is done in the next figure). When used with probabilities, it shows the probability line approach certainty, or a probability of one, at infinity or some other ceiling less than one.[24]

---

24   The equation for this graph is taken from https://onlinecourses.science.psu.edu/stat507/ sites/ onlinecourses.science.psu.edu.stat507/files/lesson09/graph_function.gif.

Figure 3.5: A Logistical Graph

Probability of disease

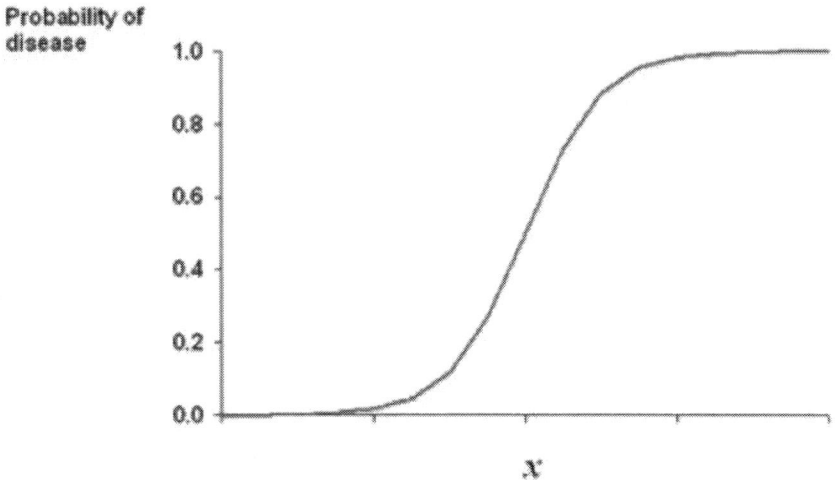

The above graph starts as an exponential curve, then increases more and more slowly until it is almost flat, reaching a probability of one at infinity. The logistic equation is shown in the footnote below and should be read as the probability of obesity at a given time, where e is the natural log, α and β are numbers (parameters) and t is time. Recently, I noticed in a new Center for Disease Control Study also published in JAMA (*Seattle Times*, September 17, 2015, A5) that there were no significant changes in obesity as measured by the BMI from 2003 to 2004 and from 2011 to 2012, as our above graph suggested would happen. However, the report does point out that waist size is up by 3 percent since 2000, suggesting that true obesity (measured by the percentage of body fat) actually is continuing to rise. The report notes that "while the prevalence of obesity [as measured by BMI] may have reached a plateau, the waistlines of US adults continue to expand." Again, if you want a good health measure, use percentage of fat rather than BMI.

Exponential growth cannot continue forever and usually not even for very long. The figure below shows the numbers that a 2 percent annual growth rate would produce, starting with the number one over different time periods from one thousand years to nine thousand years. These periods seem long to us, but in terms of human development, they are small, and in terms of geological time, they are miniscule.

Figure 3.6: Exponential Growth Starting with the Year On

Exponential growth starting with one	Years	Growth rate per year
398,264,651.66	1000	0.02
158,614,732,760,369,000.00	2000	0.02
63,170,641,290,655,500,000,000,000.00	3000	0.02
25,158,633,448,643,400,000,000,000,000,000,000.00	4000	0.02
10,019,794,386,618,500,000,000,000,000,000,000,000,000,000.00	5000	0.02
3,990,529,921,072,670,000,000,000,000,000,000,000,000,000,000,000,000.00	6000	0.02
1,589,287,008,947,340,000,000,000,000,000,000,000,000,000,000,000,000,000,000,000.00	7000	0.02
632,956,837,003,199,000,000,000,000,000,000,000,000,000,000,000,000,000,000,000,000,000,000.00	8000	0.02
252,084,334,203,709,000,000,000,000,000,000,000,000,000,000,000,000,000,000,000,000,000,000,000,000.00	9000	0.02
100,396,279,550,111,000,000,000,000,000,000,000,000,000,000,000,000,000,000,000,000,000,000,000,000,000,000.00	10000	0.02

Consider another example in which population doubles every twenty years. Starting with 2 people, the number of people in one hundred years would be 2^5, only 16 people. In two thousand years, it would be 2^{100} or $1.26765E + 30$. That is, there are thirty-one numbers before the decimal point. The current world population is about 7.3 billion. At a doubling every twenty years, in one hundred years it would be about 58 billion. In one thousand years, it would be—well, you get the idea—very large!

The following graphs show three possible explanations for the growth trend of obesity in the United States. The obesity trend could describe a parabola an inverted U or more complicated shapes. The parabola shape as shown by line A would suggest upward portion of the obesity trend, as its prevalence has risen over time, and then a downturn as we reach an apex. That is, obesity may begin to decrease in the future due to higher prices for food, government regulation of food quality, or an increase in concerns over health. Line B shows an upward trend followed by a downward trend.

Figure 3.7: Obesity Up and Down

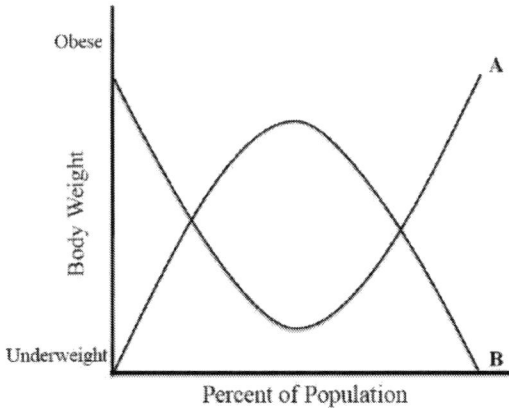

Or these parabola-like trends may follow a continuous cycle of increases and decreases as shown below in the form of a sine curve.

Figure 3.8: Possible Continuous Obesity Trend in the United State

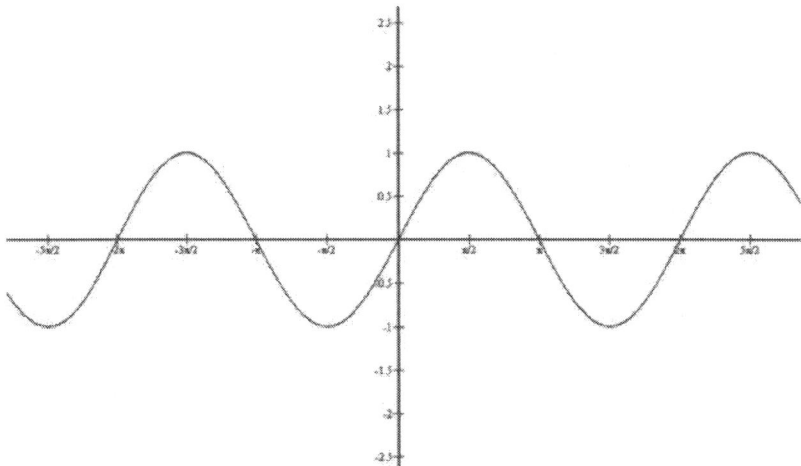

The concept that history creates repeated expansions and contractions has long been a popular view. During famines, obesity would fall, but it would increase depending on the availability of food and on cultural attitudes. The view of the cyclical nature of life was particularly popular among Renaissance thinkers (Dobel and Anderson 2002) who saw patterns of birth, growth, and decay. After all, we are born, we grow, and we die. By some accounts, this same pattern applies to the universe itself. A more pleasant version of this cycle would be a rebirth of the universe with an improved version each cycle, such a pattern as in the sine curve above but with an upward tilt.[25]

One must think hard about the forms the processes one is examining could take. Curves shaped by an inverted *U* or a regular *U* are common in nature. Consider the life cycle of bacteria in a nutrient-rich but closed environment. In this case, we know something of the physical processes that occur, so the form in figure 3.9 is not unexpected. This is shown in the figure below.

Figure 3.9: The Life Cycle of Bacteria

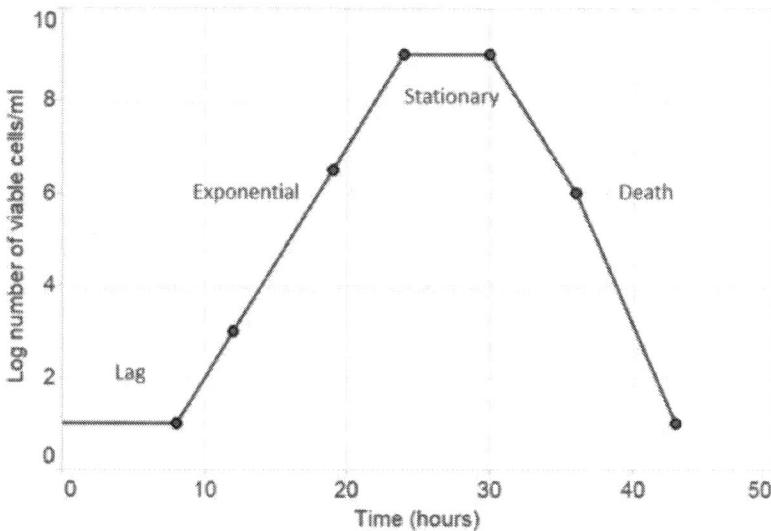

Are we like bacteria in a closed environment? See chapter 8.

---

25   Some physicists have speculated that the universe itself follows a repeating life-and-death pattern.

Statistical Analysis for Prediction

If we be, therefore engaged by arguments to put trust in past experience, and make it the standard of our future judgement, these arguments must be probable only.
—David Hume[26]

How likely is it that it will snow tomorrow, given that it has snowed the past two days? A simple method of prediction for weather is that the weather tomorrow will be the same as it is today. This turns out to be better than a completely uniformed guess. The slightly informed guess is better than the uninformed guess, as it makes use of prior information. What about a guess based on the fact that it snowed the last two days? One approach is to use the Copernican principle that suggests the snow will continue as long as it has existed until now—that is, for two more days. This suggests that we assume the phenomenon, snow falling, will continue as long as it has already. If we know only that snow fell today, per the Copernican principle, the best guess is that it will continue one more day. Christian and Griffiths give examples of its application: the United States will last until the year 2255, Google until about 2032, and so on. Obviously, this method must be modified where other information exists. Yet one might want to sensibly stay away from a website whose signage indicates it has been six days since the last accident but not expect a 90- year-old person to live to be 180. Here we have lots of data that suggests that no one has ever lived to be 180 years old. The lesson here is that the use of prior assumptions and data is crucial to good predictions. (The Copernican principle is simply Bayes' theorem with an uninformative prior.) Christian and Griffiths note the following example in which the Copernican principle was useful. During World War II, the Allies wished to estimate the number of tanks being produced by Germany. Estimates based on the serial numbers of captured tanks suggested 246 tanks per month. The estimate was made by doubling the highest serial number found

---

26 My favorite classical philosopher. Taken from Christian and Griffiths 2016.

for those tanks produced in the month. Estimates based on aerial reconnaissance suggested a figure of 1,400 per month. Records after the war revealed the actual figure as 245 per month.

Prediction involves some ability to determine the shape of the relevant curves we have discussed. Natural phenomena tend to fall into two categories of curves: those that cluster around some central value and those that do not. A normal or bell-shaped curve is an example of the former. Many phenomena fall into the bell-shaped distribution: life expectancy, human height, human weight, measured intelligence, and so on. Normal distributions are symmetrical around the average. The average value is the same as the median value, the value in which half the values lie below and half lie above.

A better estimate would be if we knew that for the particular area, most snowfalls lasted, say, two days. In this case, we would predict that the snow will end tomorrow. If we know the average for a particular phenomenon, the prediction is the average. For example, if we are predicting the longevity of a seven-year-old boy, it is simply the average for a seven-year-old boy. If the boy comes from an educated family, it would be the average for seven- year-old boys in educated families, and so on. If we know only the average longevity for people, the predicted estimate would be the population average longevity plus a bit more, as he has already lived seven years.

Other distributions are very different from the normal—for example, the distribution of income or wealth or the likelihood of solar flares. The number of people with wealth below the average is much greater than the number of people with wealth above the average. For the United States, the ratio of average wealth   to median wealth is about 6.9. It is highest for the Russian Federation with 12.6 and lowest for Slovakia at 1.31.[27] In the United States, for example, the top four hundred wealth holders

---

27   Based on Credit Suisse Report—Wealth Distribution and Gini (2013).

58

have more wealth than 50 percent of the population. That is, the predicted net wealth of a newborn child would not be the average wealth of, say, $350,000, since there is a much smaller chance of achieving that than the median net wealth of about $45,000. That is, there are many fewer people in the United States with wealth at or above $350,000 than there are people with wealth at or below $45,000.

These sorts of distributions are power law distributions: that is, the distribution is a function of X raised to some power. A general form would be that $Y = \delta x^N$, where X is the variable, δ is some constant, and N is the power. Climate change damages are power law distributions in the sense that extreme damage has some significant probability.

Some of the graphs we will encounter show a statistical relationship, a correlation or association between one variable (the dependent variable) and one or many other variables (the independent variables).[28]

Correlation

Correlation shows the extent of joint positive or negative variability. The correlation coefficient varies from -1 for a perfect negative correlation to +1 for a perfect positive correlation. An example of perfect correlation would be one in which variable X goes up by 9 percent and variable B also goes up by 9 percent and so on for any percentage increase. A perfect linear correlation would occur if variable X went up by, say, five, and so did variable Y and so on. If you actually get a perfect correlation, then you are almost certainly just comparing a variable with itself.

---

28   See http://xkcd.com/552. I am indebted to my colleague, Mark Long, for this figure.

It should not be thought that correlation means causality, as the cartoon below suggests.

Figure 3.10: Causality

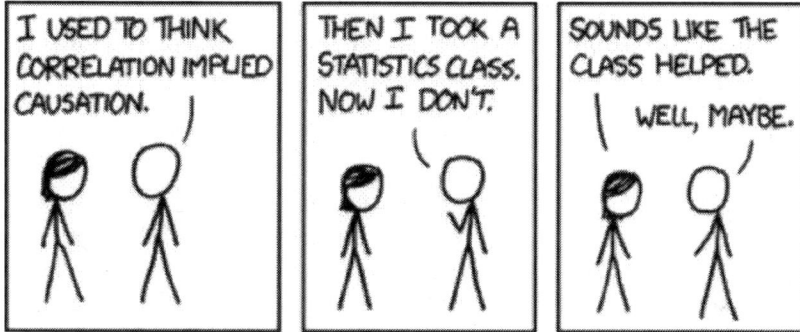

Both John's growth in height and the growth of a tree in his yard may be correlated, but we would not think that one caused the other. Why not? Because we have no knowledge or understanding of any underlying mechanism that could provide such causation.

We could suggest that food and water affected the growth of both. We do understand what causes growth in John and in the tree, but there no linkage of causation between the tree's growth and John's; if the tree is chopped down, John will continue to grow.

To access correlation, one typically uses regression analysis. This sort of analysis creates a line, the regression line that shows the most efficient path or "best fit" between the dependent variable and the independent variable. This line measures whether or not the relationship is significant and at what level. For example, the graph below might show the correlation between the growth of the tree and the growth of John. The horizontal axis shows the growth of the tree on the assumption (hypothesis) that the growth of the tree causes John's growth, as shown on the vertical axis. Clearly there is a relationship, but it is not causal; fertilizing the tree may increase its growth but will do nothing for John's growth. It is hardly possible to overemphasize that there must be reasons (theory) to believe variables may be causally related and not to just assume it because of their correlation. Correlation does not mean causation. The tree has grown taller as John has grown taller, so their growth is correlated, but one has not caused the other. In contrast a correlation between the amount of rainfall and the growth of the tree could potentially lead us to discover a causal relationship that we could further investigate.

Figure 3.11: John's Growth vs. Tree Growth

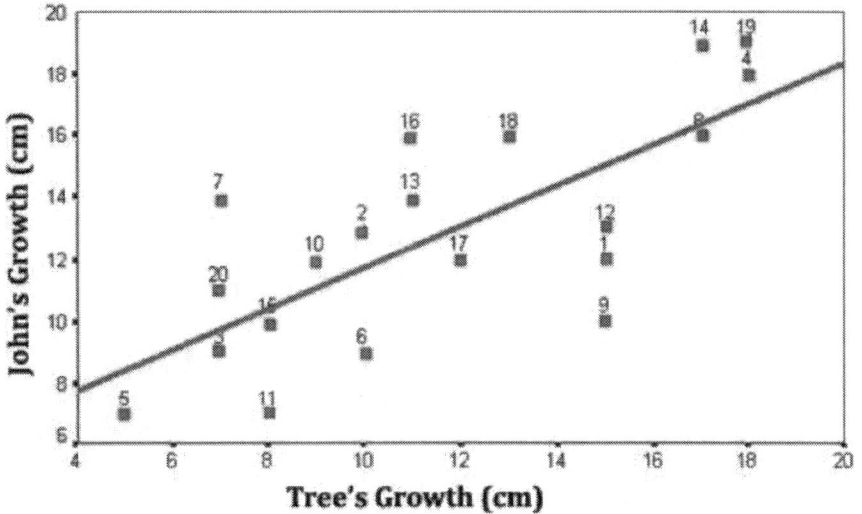

The red squares are the data points relating the growth of the tree and the growth of John. The red line shows the best fit relationship between the growth of the tree and the growth of John. The best   fit line minimizes the sum of the squares of the distance between the data point and the red line. The closer the dots are to the line (regression line), the more confidence we may have that we have captured an association. However, we know of no underlying mechanism by which tree growth will affect John's height, except for time. Nor can we rule it out, but we can argue that such a relationship is very unlikely. Thus, we cannot assume there is a causal mechanism connecting John's growth to trees. We could, however, show a possible causal relation between John's height and time, on the basis that known physiology suggests it. We could then explore what causes John's growth over time and why this growth stops at some point in time.

A plausible hypothesis is that John's weight is related to his height.

The following graph shows a correlation (regression) line between John's height and weight. Notice that these black data points lie closer to the regression line than in the relation between John's height and the tree's height. We might have greater confidence in the height-weight relationship if we could describe just how this relationship works.

Figure 3.12: John's Weight vs. Height

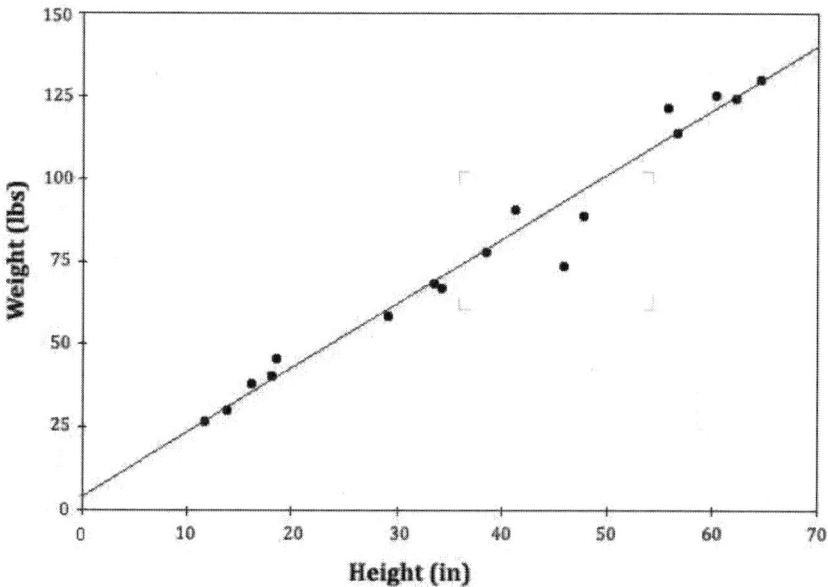

Christian and Griffiths present a nice framework for prediction developed from Simon LaPlace (see Bell's *Men of Mathematics*) and generally referred to under the rubric of Bayes' theorem or rule.

Economics of Finance and the Discount Rate

Costs and benefits of climate change action

Take a simple example based on calculating present values. Present value is the sum today that we could invest that would yield a future stream at a given interest rate. One hundred dollars invested today at 9 percent forever would yield nine dollars ($100 x .01) every year forever. A stream of nine dollars per year forever, then, has a present value of one hundred dollars ($100/.09) at a 9 percent discount rate. When the interest rate is used to find the present value, it is called the discount rate, so that the discount rate is 9 percent. The present value of a stream of values, benefits, or costs that goes on forever (or in practice for a considerable time) is found by S/R where S the yearly amount and r is the interest rate.[29]Thus, the present value of one hundred dollars forever at 9 percent is just one thousand dollars. That is, if the interest or discount rate remains constant, one thousand dollars invested today will yield one hundred dollars per year forever. The present value of an infinite stream is not much different from the present value of a finite stream, depending on the discount rate and the time length. The figure below shows the relationship for the PV of one dollar.

Figure 3.12: Present Value of $1.00

Discount Rate	5%	9%
PV of $1 per Year Forever: Perpetuity	20	9
PV 30 years	$15.37	$9.43
PV 50 years	$18.26	$9.91
PV 100 years	$19.85	$9.00

---

29   The calculation is 20 trillion/(.07-.02) or 20 trillion/.05 = 400 trillion. To fully understand this, see chapter 3 in Zerbe and Dively (2004). There is much controversy about what dis- count rate to use. The 7 percent figure would be regarded as high by many but not by me and many others. It is true that the rate of time preference for many may be lower, but one must also take into account the displacement of private capital.

Summary

Fundamental to questions of change is an understanding of the forces of change. Graphs of change can show patterns that are useful for depicting change, but correlations between variables in themselves don't mean much without an understanding the underlying forces that produce the correlations. If we use simple extensions of existing trends, we often, but not always, will make poor predictions and create unreasonable expectations. Examples of unwarranted extensions are legion and include extensions and predictions of height and the BMI measure of obesity. We don't yet have flying taxis, a well-known prediction for the year 2000, made about 1900.

The shapes of common phenomena include linear, exponential, logistic, sinusoidal repeated wave, and elliptical. Relationships that appear to be one sort of curve—for example, linear or exponential—often turn out to be more complex. For example, recent growth in obesity, as measured by BMI, has appeared exponential but cannot continue to be so. Graphs can show statistical relationships, but they do not prove causation. The relationships between variables need to be explored carefully and thoughtfully, both in terms of causation and predictability.

Questions

1. Do you prefer histograms (bar graphs) or line graphs? (Most people like histograms better.) I don't know why. Do you?

2. Why does association not imply causality?

3. Give examples of an association in which causality is unlikely.

4. Easy-to-use statistical packages make analyses easier but might degrade quality. Why do you think this could be the case?

5. Is the following a power law distribution? What is the equation for it? What is the average of the outcomes Y, and what is the median?

X	Y
1	1
2	4
3	9
4	16
5	25
6	36
7	49
8	64
9	81

6. Make predictions for what the world will be like in nine years, in thirty, in fifty, in one hundred. If I am alive in nine years, send these to my publisher.

7. My esteemed colleague Milton Friedman told of an experience he had working for the government as a statistician during the war. The military approached his group and asked them how to make a trigger that would fire with 100 percent accuracy. The statisticians told them this was impossible. What further advice did they give do you think? What might you suspect the device was?

4

Economic Progress

It can't continue forever. The nature of exponentials is that
you push them out and eventually disaster happens.

—Gordon Moore (creator of Moore's law)

Growth in per Capita GDP

Many associate progress with material progress, and it does seem
that the growth of cultural maturity for a society seems unlikely
without some level of economic attainment. Otherwise, people's
energy is devoted to basic survival, as Maslow's chart suggests.

Now it happens that growth in per capita GDP shows no
advancement during the first thousand years of the Common Era
(CE), as shown below. This does not mean there was no progress,
but it does suggest a lack of material progress that inhibited other
forms of well-being. This is shown in figure 4.1.

Figure 4.1: Growth and Growth Rate in GDP per Capita Is Increasing

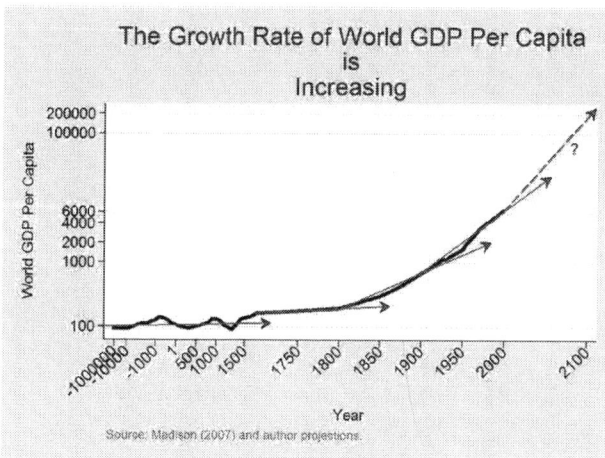

Source: Madison (2007) and author projections.

Impressive economic growth has occurred over the past millennium, but most significantly after the Napoleonic Wars. The causes are disputed, but it seems clear that a number of factors contributed, including population growth, greater capital investment, and the innovative effect of war.

In the one hundred or so years since 1815, there has been a fourteen-fold increase in per capita income, and a GDP[30] increase of more than three hundred, along with a twenty-three-fold population increase. It is not surprising to find that per capita wealth and income have been increasing for some time. However, it may be somewhat surprising to find out that the growth rate itself of income per capita has been increasing for more than a thousand years. What does the growth rate in per capita GDP look like; what shape has the curve followed over time? To determine this, we examine the figure below. This shows that since the year 1000 CE, there has been a systemic increase in the growth rate of the world's per capita income.[31]

---

30   It is useful to think of GDP as just an approximation for national income. GDP is the sum of gross value added by all resident producers in the economy, plus any product taxes and minus any subsidies not included in the value of the products. It is calculated without making deductions for depreciation of fabricated assets or for depletion and degradation of natural resources. GDP per capita is gross domestic product divided by midyear population.

31   The above figure was developed from data collected by Angus Maddison. From Wikipedia, the free encyclopedia: "Angus Maddison (6 December 1926–24 April 2010) was a British economist specializing in quantitative macroeconomic history, including the measurement and analysis of economic growth and development. He was Emeritus Professor at the Faculty of Economics at the University of Groningen (RUG). In 1978, Maddison was appointed historical Professor at the University of Groningen. Maddison was a pioneer in the field of the construction of national accounts, where a country's accounts are calculated back in periods of several decades all the way to the year 1. To this end he combined modern research techniques with his own extensive knowledge of economic history and in particular countries' performances in the field of GDP per capita. His work resulted in a deep new understanding of the reasons why some countries have become rich whereas others have remained poor (or have succumbed to poverty)." I think it safe to say that Maddison is regarded as one of the world's most prominent scholars in the field of data creation.

Figure: 4.2: Economic Growth over the Centuries

Years	12 Western European Countries	20 Western European Countries	World Average
1-1000	0.03%	0.03%	0%
1000-1500	0.13%	0.12%	4%
1500-1600	0.13%	0.14%	0.05%
1600-1700	0.13%	0.14%	3%
1700-1820	0.15%	0.15%	0.07%
1820-1900	1.86%	1.86%	0.08%
1900-2000	1.84%	1.94%	1.90%

What Figure 4.2 shows is that from the year 1 CE to the year 1000 CE, there was no growth in world or European per capita GDP. But at the end of the first millennium, per capita income rose. Thus, the annual rate of per capita growth of GDP in Europe from about 1000 CE has been exponential. In addition, the growth rate itself shows almost continual increases since the end of the first millennium (except between 1600 and 1700), when considering the data century wide. This is shown in Figure 4.2. As we can see from the above figure, the Growth rate has been, and still is, increasing. Between 1900 and 2000, the growth rate begins at 1.9 percent and increases by about 0.184 percent per year. I present some extrapolations here, not as predictions but to provide some possibilities for the future. Starting in 2015, suppose the growth rate continues to increase at the rate of 0.184 percent per year for fifty years. This would give us a growth rate of 9 percent per year after fifty years. The rate will not be this high, so let us be more conservative; suppose the growth rate stays constant at 1.9 percent. Current world GDP per capita is about $12,000, using purchasing power parity or PPP. With this growth rate, fifty years hence, the world GDP per capita at our current population would be about $31,000 in 2015 dollars. This is possible and maybe even likely.

68

Figure 4.3: Yearly Increase (or Decrease) in World Growth Rate in per Capita GDP

	Annual Growth Rate in GDP Per Capita in West + Japan	Annual Growth Rate in GDP Per Capita in the World
Years		
0-1000	0	0.13
1000-1820	0.13	0.05
1820-1998	1.67	1.21

Years	Yearly Increase in World Growth Rate
1000 to 1500	0.00%
1500 to 1600	0.04%
1600 to 1700	-0.26%
1700 to 1820	0.39%
1820 to 1900	2.03%
1900 to 1975	0.44%
1975 to 2008	0.17%

At the approximate 2 percent annual growth rate, the growth in per capital GDP remains impressive. World per capita income in 2015 was about twelve thousand US dollars. (One can approximate the doubling time for growth by dividing seventy by the growth rate, here 2 percent.) This means that per capita income will double in about thirty-five years.[32] Thus, in a hundred years, per capita income will increase by almost nine times. This is possible, if perhaps optimistic, as the increases in the growth rate are slowing down. Figure 5 shows the current situation.

The growth rate continues to increase but at a decreasing rate. In the future, this increase in the growth rate could fall to zero, in which case we still might have constant growth at a fixed rate. Figure 4.4 shows not that we have a collapsing growth rate, but

32   The doubling rule is derived for exponential growth as follows: Let $P(e^{gt}) = 2P$, where P is the starting value, e is the natural log, g is the growth rate and t is time. Solving for t, the doubling time gives $t = \ln 2$, which is about 70 percent. At 1 percent, the growth doubling time would be 70/1 = 70 years, so that the world would be twice as rich as now in per capital income in seventy years. At a rate of 3 percent per year, the doubling time would be about twenty-three years.

that we have a collapsing rate of increases; the growth rates are slowing, beginning about now. If the increases in the growth rate become zero, we will have a constant growth rate with a steady doubling period.

Figure 4.4: Increases in the World's Growth Rate

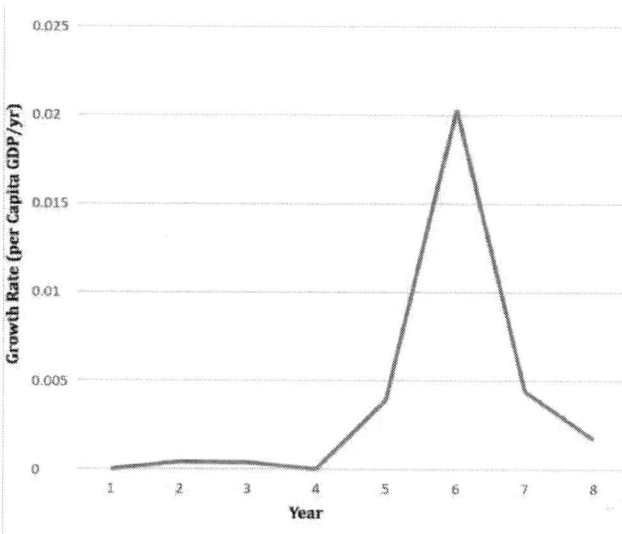

Doomsday Predictors and Predictions

Imagine, however, that the increases in the growth rate fall below zero so that the growth rate is falling. As noted earlier, when you put bacteria into a closed environment rich in nutrients, they experience exponential growth until the number remains constant for a bit but eventually collapses, as they run out of nutrients and die from their own waste. If we are like bacteria, growth will cease and death will ensue. As Kenneth Todar explains it,[33]

> *In the laboratory, under favorable conditions, a growing bacterial population doubles at regular intervals. Growth is by geometric progression: 1, 2, 4, 9, etc. or 20, 21, 22, 23...2n (where n = the number of generations). This is exponential*

---

33   http://steadystate.org/paul-krugman-on-limits-to-growth-beware-the-bathwater/

growth...When a fresh medium is inoculated with a given number of cells, and the population growth is monitored over a period of time, plotting the data will yield a typical bacterial growth curve which ends with the expiration of the population.

Todar notes that when bacteria are grown in a closed system (also called a batch culture), like a test tube, the population of cells almost always exhibits these growth dynamics: cells initially adjust to the new medium (lag phase) until they can start dividing regularly   by the process of binary fission (exponential phase). When their growth becomes limited, the cells stop dividing (stationary phase), until eventually they show loss of viability (death phase). Growth   is expressed as change in the number of viable cells versus time. Generation times are calculated during the exponential phase of growth. Time measurements are in hours for bacteria with short generation times.

Note that the bacterial growth curves bear a resemblance to the increase in the per capita human growth rate in GDP; both are upside-down letter Us (or Vs). The logs (LN) on the vertical axis have the effect of making a straight line from an exponential function. The bacteria grow first at an exponential rate. In reality, even in batch culture, the exponential phase growth for bacteria   is not ever a constant rate, but instead a slowly decaying rate, a constant stochastic response to pressures both to reproduce and   to go dormant in the face of declining nutrient concentrations and increasing waste concentrations.

On this sort of basis, there are of course doomsday predictors. I am not one of them for the remotely foreseeable future. Certainly there will be major setbacks but probably not for the reasons the doomsayers believe. Brian Czech is such a doomsayer. He attacks Paul Krugman for believing growth will continue as follows:[34]

---

34   The Daly News, Ceter for the Advancement of the Steady State Economcy, http://steadys- tate.org/paul-krugman-on-limits-to-growth-beware-the-bathwater/)

Having delivered the keynote address—on limits to growth no less—at the Australian Academy of Science's annual conference on environmental science, it struck me that decades of careful research could be undermined by the presumptuous pen of a well-placed economist. Something is wrong with that picture.

However, it is Czech who is being presumptuous; the picture he paints is incorrect, and he is not alone. He is inappropriate in attacking Krugman, who is dealing with shorter time periods, whereas the case for doomsdays require longer time periods. Czech does not account for innovation. There are perhaps many who see the future as a steady state or a no-growth economy. But before we get to a no-growth economy, we would have to first get to a constant growth economy, which would not happen soon. As we have seen, a modest growth rate for only a few hundred years can accomplish a lot.

We are not just like bacteria, or at least we have a larger playing field than bacteria in a bottle. We have people in a world or maybe, maybe, people in a universe. Bacteria are more adept than we are in changing their phenotype, but we are adept in creating new resources. Fusion will probably make an entrance at some point; innovation continues apace; the ability grows to create vaccines more quickly. Beyond this, outer space and its resources beckon. Collapse does not appear to loom in any foreseeable time range. Climate change will cause problems, but this may hopefully be surmounted.

Economic Well-Being

For some time, it has been suggested that progress indicators other than GDP per capita should be used. Per capita GDP measures total spending, not well-being. A measure that has been suggested is the genuine progress indicator (or index). This index starts with personal consumption and adds in the value of housework, volunteer work, and government services. It subtracts the cost of crime, family breakdown, and underemployment; the cost of commuting; the cost of pollution abatement and auto accidents; and a number of environmental impacts. For the United States, the index is available for the period 1950 through 1994. The values for the GPI and the GDP for selected years is shown below.

Figure 4.5: Comparison of per Capita GPI and GDP in 2000 US Dollars

Year	Per Capita Genuine Progress Index (GPI)	Per Capita GDP	Per Capita GPI Divided by Per Capita GDP
1950	8612	11672	0.738
1955	9785	13336	0.734
1960	10136	13847	0.732
1965	11592	16423	0.706
1970	13034	18395	0.709
1975	14471	19961	0.725
1980	14730	22666	0.650
1985	15124	25386	0.596
1990	14892	28435	0.524
1995	14409	30131	0.478
2000	15145	34764	0.436
2004	15035	36596	0.411

extend Between 1950 & 1975

Since 1950, the GPI has risen by a factor of 1.74 or 1.27 percent per year. It has been slowly going down since 1985. Between 1950 and 1975, the index was growing by 2.1 percent per year. Between 1975 and 2004, it grew by 0.1 percent per year. Do you think the expectations of those living in 1975 about the near future might

turn into graph

have led to unrest and unhappiness? The GPI has even fallen for some Scandinavian countries. See the graph below for Finland.

Figure 4.6: Development of GDP, ISEW, and GPI Indicators in Finland in 1945–2010 (per Capita in Real Prices)

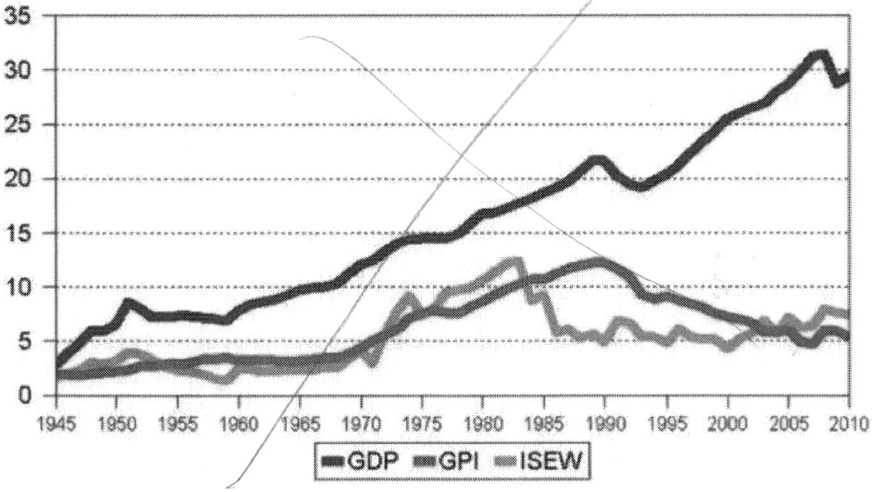

Economic growth in absolute but also in per capita terms has since, say, 1815 been spectacular, after the Napoleonic Wars. Yet it is possible to imagine an array of negative possibilities: the stress of change might lead to war with disastrous results. Our technology may surpass our ability and wisdom and lead to unhappy world. Economic growth may stagnate and fall into decay. On the positive side, economic growth may stagnate but happiness increase. The rate of change may slow or people may adapt to it. The positive trends we will examine may continue, and the world would become a better place. All this depends on nature's laws and our own abilities to grow morally and in wisdom.

Summary

The world has shown exponential growth in GDP per capita since about the year 1000 and seen not just growth, but also an increasing growth rate, especially since about 1815 so that the world and Europe's growth rates are highest at this time. However, the rate of increase in the growth rate has been falling. Even with a lower growth rate, cultural maturity can increase and thus, so can well-being.

Questions

1. When will economic growth end? Will It?
2. Will greater national wealth solve all problems?
3. Will it solve any problems?
4. If so, which ones?
5. Which problems will remain?

5

Financial Stability

Has Financial Stability Increased?

The financial stability of nations is of constant concern. Economic growth shows a positive relationship with the stability of an economy. Moreover, stability itself is desirable at any level of income, because psychology dictates that losses are weighted more heavily than equivalent gains. Thus, stocks that have less variability (lower betas) are more highly valued. This chapter mainly concerns the United States. The figure below shows the pattern of economic expansion and retreat for the United States since 1923 with its increasing financial stability, and the pattern suggests the possibility that such stability can be achieved elsewhere in the world.[35]

Figure 5.1: Annual US GDP Growth From 1923–2009 [36]

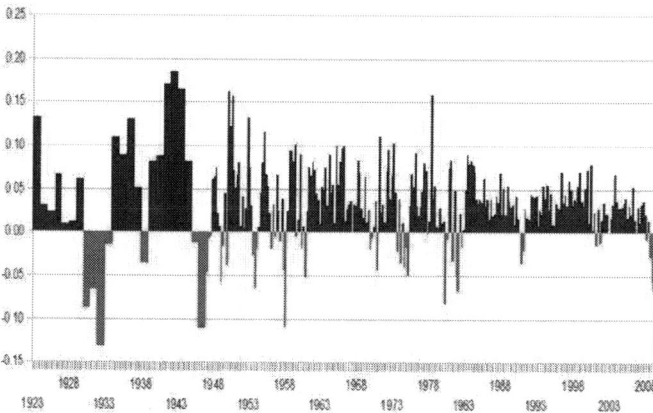

From the above graph, it is apparent that business cycles have become less severe since 1928.

---

35   The Great Depression occurred mainly because the Fed failed to deliver funds to support banks whose customers panicked about their money, even though the banks were otherwise solid. As a result, the amount of money in the economy fell by about one-third.

36   Jay Henry. Created October 17, 2009. After 1948, quarterly data are used.

Consider a more detailed measure of variability. I calculate the number of years of recession or depression from 1785 until 2007 by period. (As is common practice, I will use the word recession for both a recession and a depression.) The official definition of a recession is "a period of general economic decline, typically in GDP, for two or more consecutive quarters."[37] (There is no definition for a depression.)

In the twenty-nine-year period from 1785 to the end of the Napoleonic Wars in 1815, 78 percent of the years were recession years in the United States. This was a period of unusual volatility. For comparison, from 1816 through 1857, 34 percent of the years were in recession. And for the fifty-three years from 1860 through 1913, 46 percent were in recession.

Congress created the Federal Reserve System in 1913 to provide greater business cycle stability by controlling the money supply. For the fifteen years from 1913 to 1928, 32 percent were recession years. The Great Depression was a massive failure on the part of the Fed and was the consequence of bank failures, as Milton Friedman and Anna Schwartz (1963) have showed. Friedman notes that these bank failures could have been prevented if the Fed had stood ready to supply liquidity to the system. That is, the banks were mainly sound, but panics resulted in people taking their money out of banks, thereby causing banks to fail. The Fed could have supplied cash as loans on a temporary basis but didn't.[38] Has the Fed learned anything from this?

---

37 http://www.investorwords.com/.

38 Almost the whole period from 1929 through 1940 was a period of lower GDP.

Figure 5.2: Years of Recession

Period	Total Years	Percentage of Years in Recession
1785–1821	36	65%
1821–1860	39	36%
1861–1914	53	49%
1914–1928	14	32%
1914–1933	19	48%
1933–2007	74	17%

Note that the last period shows a smaller percentage of years in recession. Has the Fed created more stability in the economy? Apparently yes. Although correlation is not causation, it would appear that it has, as it is difficult to find any other explanation for the economic stability. The period of 128 years between 1785 and 1913 shows that 50 percent were years of recession. The 107-year period from 1914 through 2007 shows only 24 percent of the years were of recession. This difference between the pre-1914 period and the post-1914 period is huge: stability is twice as great in the more recent period. It seems that the Fed learn from the Great Depression. The record after the Great Depression, since 1940, is better than its overall record, with only 18 percent of the years in recession. We could reasonably hope that central banks everywhere can make the same progress shown by the Fed.

$$65$$
$$36$$
$$49$$
$$150$$

Summary

The Fed has appeared to increase economic stability and to some degree learned from past mistakes. This bodes well for what central banks worldwide might be able to achieve.

How Did the Fed Increase Stability?

All this suggests that the Fed has materially decreased economic instability. How did it do this? We can gain insight into this by looking at the relationship between money, its rate of being spent, and GDP in the context of the Great Depression.

The relationship between money and GDP is captured by Irving Fisher's famous equation of exchange:

$$MV = PQ = GDP$$

M is money stock. V is velocity of money—that is, how quickly the money stock is spent. For example, if M is one hundred and   if each dollar is spent four times each year, V, the GDP would   be four hundred dollars. P is the price level, so an increase in P indicates inflation. Q is output. GDP is the gross domestic product, a measure of national income. If M increases and V stays the same, what must happen? Either price increases or output increases or both. When the economy is at full employment, which in practice means something like between 4 and 5 percent unemployment due to people changing jobs and the like, and there is an increase in M, then either P or Q must increase. However, Q cannot increase in the short run, as the economy is at full employment, so inflation occurs instead; P increases. If there is significant unemployment, new spending will increase mainly Q and also reduce unemployment. Who controls M? The Federal Reserve. During a period of significant unemployment, the Fed should increase M.

What if M increases, but V falls? If V decreases proportionally with the increase in M, nothing happens, except that there is now a greater amount of money sitting in checking and savings accounts not being spent. In this case, the policy instrument available during a recession is to increase government spending temporarily. But will the increase turn out to be temporary?

To see this more clearly, let us examine the causes of the Great Depression. The Great Depression was caused essentially caused by a decrease in M. The decrease in M in turn was caused mainly caused by bank failures (runs on banks), which wiped out checking and savings accounts, the major part of the money supply. There has never been a time in which M fell in any significant degree and was not associated with a depression or a recession; in the early 1930s, the fall in M was particularly large. The Fed could have prevented this by acting as a supplier of ready funds to banks. They had the authority (Friedman and Schwartz 1963). The conclusion remains. Bottom line: the Great Depression was caused by bank runs and collapses that depleted checking and savings accounts, which the Fed could have prevented. The increase in stability after this time as well as Fed documents suggest, however, that the Fed has learned to increase the stabilization of economic activity.

On the other hand, in our recent Great Recession of 2008, there was a collapse in V. The traditional remedy was to increase government spending—that is, to promote an increase of V. The Obama stimulus was the government response, but it was too little and a bit late.

Because M2 growth tracks all previous inflation-disinflation cycles, it goes a long way to avert the suspicion that the relationship between monetary growth and inflation is spurious. Monetary historians, such as Milton Friedman and Anna Schwartz, confirm that inflation is everywhere and is at all times a matter of the monetary supply. They cite evidence that the long-term relationship between monetary growth and inflation has remained much the same throughout history. For example, when monetary growth accelerated in the 1890s due to engineering advances increasing gold output, there was an associated inflation. Gold was then a standard into which currencies could be converted. When monetary growth collapsed in the early 1930s because of bank failures, there was an associated deflation. Similarly, recessions are associated with a slowing down or fall in changes in the money supply.

Summary

The US economy has been more stable since the Fed was created in 1913—even when counting the Great Depression. The Fed appeared to have learned from the Great Depression, as the stability after 1939 has been the greatest of any period in US history. The improvement in stability appears to be a result of the Fed's actions. Greater stability probably promotes economic growth and, as we shall see, happiness.

Questions

1. Currently, there are attempts to reduce the power of the Fed. Is this a good thing? Why or why not?

2. Is it likely that the Fed's record of relative stability will be duplicated by Europe or elsewhere? Explain.

3. What is the parallel between what happened to bank deposits in the Great Depression and what is happening in 2015 in Greece?

4. Has there ever been a material reduction in the money supply unaccompanied by a recession? Check this out and report what you find.

Add in Status Paper

6 7

Happiness, Status, and Well-Being

The world is so full of a number of things, I'm sure we should all be as happy as kings.

—Robert Louis Stevenson, A Child's Garden of Verses

It was the symbolism as much as the actual dollar signs that mattered. It meant a lot just to be recognized, appreciated. As a human being, all of us want to feel loved and appreciatedand valued. Andthen when you put a number to it—honestly, it's not really about the money.

—Seattle Seahawk football player Doug Baldwin [39]

The Two Forms of Happiness

We are becoming richer. But are we happier? If we are happier, have well-being and cultural maturity increased? The field of subjective well-being (SWB), or happiness, has recently become a thriving area of science, with more than nine thousand publications on the topic in the last year alone.[40]

Recent research by Deaton and Kahneman (2014) suggest that happiness has two somewhat different psychological states, life satisfaction and emotional well-being.[41] They suggest that these involve two different but interconnected feelings. Emotional well-being contributes to life satisfaction and vice versa, but it is

---

39   Upon receiving a four-year, $46 million contract in 2016, as reported in the Seattle Times, August 1, 2016.

40   Perhaps this is explained as the search for happiness through a race for tenure and status, as happened in the legal literature on "the race to the bottom."

41   Angus Deaton and Daniel Kahneman analyze more than 450,000 responses from Gallup-Healthways Well-Being Index. Daniel Kahneman and Angus Deaton find "High income improves evaluation of life satisfaction but not emotional well-being. Crossmark, 2010, vol. 107, no 38

possible to be emotionally happy but have low life satisfaction or vice versa?

Life satisfaction stems from a retrospective evaluation of achievements in relation to goals. Life satisfaction is likely to be higher if (a) one has accomplished or surpassed one's goals, (b) one has status, and/or (c) one is financially secure. Income and education are related to life satisfaction, and generally the closer one is to achieving one's goals, the greater one's happiness.

Lesson One: Thus, a source of unhappiness is to set one's goals too high.

For example, China's rapid economic growth has been accompanied by increased unhappiness by promoting an unrealistic increase in people's expectations and goals. Hilke Brockmann et al. (2009) found that between 1990 and 2000, happiness in China plummeted despite massive improvement in material living standards. This finding contradicts the notion that income growth at low living standards leads to gains. Brockman et al. explain this puzzle by drawing on the concept of "frustrated achievers," who are achievers who nevertheless did not meet their own expectations. They find that income inequality in China became increasingly skewed toward the upper income strata so that the average income and financial position of most Chinese in fact worsened. Moreover, the Chinese growth raised expectations faster than gains were realized. Consequently, financial dissatisfaction rose and became an important factor in the decreasing levels of happiness among the Chinese population.

The second component of happiness—emotional well-being—refers to the emotional quality of everyday experiences, measuring the frequency and intensity of experiences of joy, stress, sadness, anger, and affection that make one's life pleasant or unpleasant. Health, caregiving, loneliness, and shared experiences are relatively stronger predictors of daily emotion. The strongest is shared relationships.

Lesson Two: People attain greater emotional well-being primarily through social contact.

People are happiest when they spend time with people they like, and loneliness leads to emotional unhappiness no matter how rich you may be. For emotional well-being, money helps only up to a point. According to Diener et al. (2012), subjective well-being contributes to good health, more effective functioning, and a longer lifespan.

Lesson Three: Money doesn't buy as much emotional happiness as we might expect.

STATUS   2 type

Happiness and Income

An income of about $75,000 in 2014–2015 for a family of four is enough to achieve emotional happiness, even in the most expensive cities; it is enough to have rewarding and rich social experience and to feel financially secure. This amount can be even lower in less expensive locations. In developed countries income is far from being among the most important components of happiness. For example, in developed countries the increase in income needed to affect the adverse effect of unemployment for individuals is huge, aside from the income loss due to unemployment. Unemployment apparently reduces the sense of self-worth with attendant significant negative social effects, such as spousal abuse and crime (Winkelmann, Liliana, and Rainer Winkelmann 1998). The relation between income and happiness is considerably stronger in developing (or more politically correct, transitional) countries than for developed countries. Although higher income is related to better psychological adjustment and life satisfaction, Gebauer et al. (2013) propose that religiosity attenuates this relation when it de-emphasizes wealth, as I have noted earlier. Their study involving 187,957 respondents from eleven religiously diverse cultures showed that individual- level as well as culture-level religiosity weakens the relation between personal income and psychological adjustment. This weakening is stronger as religion promotes anti-wealth norms. Religiosity's moderating effects were so pervasive that religious individuals in religious cultures reported better psychological adjustment when their income was low than high.

In terms of life satisfaction, however, greater personal income is associated with greater satisfaction. When plotted against (log) income, life evaluation rises steadily. Additional income increases life satisfaction but at a diminishing rate. Low income apparently exacerbates the emotional pain associated with such misfortunes as divorce, ill health, and being alone. Deaton and Kahneman conclude that high income buys life satisfaction but not emotional happiness and that low income is associated both with low life evaluation and low emotional well-being.

National income, as opposed to individual income, has effects on SWB over and above those of personal income. To assess the incremental effects of national income on SWB, a recent study conducted cross sectional, multilevel analysis on data from 838,151 individuals in 158 nations. Higher national income at a given level of personal income turned out to lower daily feelings of well-being, showing that individuals in richer nations experienced more worry and anger on average. Now ask yourself if you would be happier in a richer country if your situation was the same as it is now. Would you prefer to be relatively rich in a poor nation or relatively poor in a rich nation, even if your absolute level of income were higher in the rich nation? Would you prefer to have high emotional happiness but low status or to have high relative income and little emotional happiness?

The income-SWB relationship was stronger across countries at higher levels of national income, a result that might be explained by cultural norms, as money is paradoxically valued more in richer nations. (The SWB of more residentially mobile individuals was less affected by national income.) Overall, results suggest that the wealth of the nation one resides in has, in itself, consequences for one's happiness.

The happiness of American blacks has in recent years risen more than that of whites. White women in the United States have been the biggest losers since the 1970s; their happiness has fallen, particularly those who did not graduate high school. The group who did not finish high school has shown also recent decreases in life expectancy.

Certainly the United States has been losing rank among other countries in terms of life expectancy, even though ours has been increasing. Is the same true of happiness? I think so, as human relationships seem to be subverted by the digital age.

Is Emotional Happiness More Important Than Status?

I would like to think that emotional happiness trumps status happiness, and although the evidence is insufficient, I believe it to be true. In an important sociological study of a working-class neighborhood (Bethnal Green) in the East End of London, it was found that although housing was quite crowded, with different generations living together, there was extensive interaction among the community. These interactions were often centered around local pubs. Status was based on personal characteristics, including how people treated others (including spouses) and whether they were honest and paid their debts. The level of income or job was unimportant in the ranking. A new public housing development resulted in the neighborhood being transferred to high-rise public housing in a different neighborhood. This changed the status scale, reducing personal interaction. This study suggests that physical arrangements affect happiness and social interaction.

These sorts of determinants of well-being are similar among cultures. Well-being is U-shaped in age, with people being happier earlier and later. The social loss of events like unemployment and divorce are large. A lasting marriage (compared to widowhood), for example, is estimated to be worth $100,000 a year.

Figure 6.1: The Inverse Correlation Between Hypertension and Life Satisfaction for Some Developed Countries

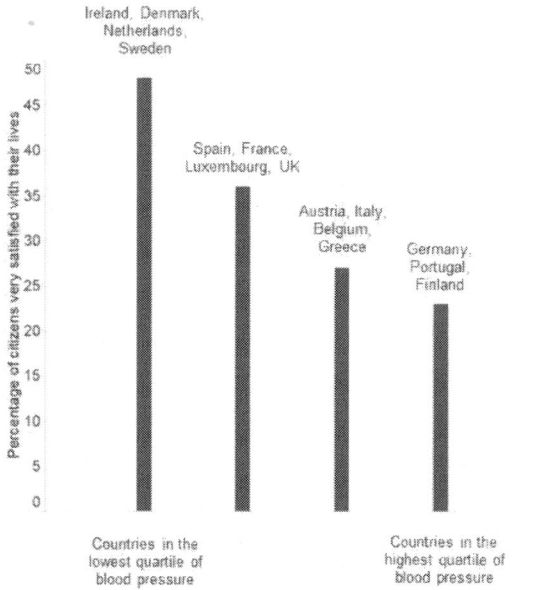

Is Happiness Growing?

Happiness is good, but can you get it? Would an increase in income alone bring you happiness? While increases in income can improve happiness, it is dependent on how much income one already earns. For example, if you earn more than $75,000 a year, an increase in income would likely not result in a substantial improvement in happiness. The figure top right shows the level of happiness over time for five European countries. (A similar relationship has been found for the United States.)

Figure 6.2: Life Satisfaction for Selected Developed Countries

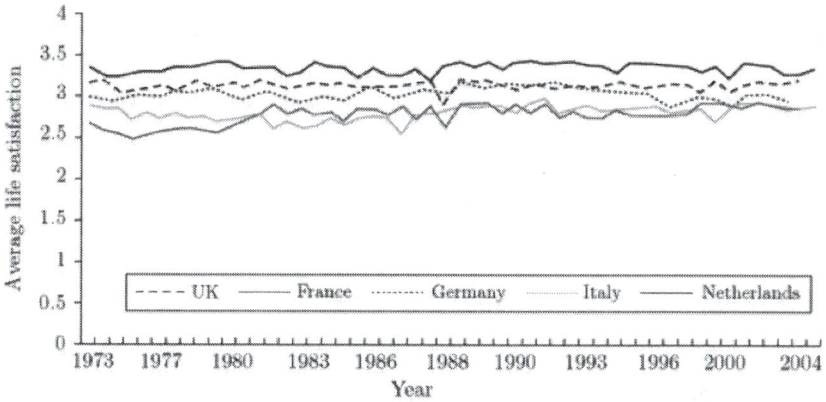

The relationship over time and between less developed and more developed countries is also shown by Clark et al. (2008).[42] There is a stronger correlation between income and happiness for developing countries. For such countries, there is a positive association between income and happiness, whether or not fixed effects (e.g., personality traits, age, unemployment) are accounted for.

---

42   Economists talk about utility. But utility is self-defined as whatever is maximized by people's decisions. Very often, the only arguments in the utility function are income or goods that can only be bought with income, but what people maximize is considerably more complex. The focus should be on those components of decision-making that are measurable (i.e., the arguments in the function). One difficult to measure argument is status.

The figure below shows the relationship between happiness at the individual level (the dots) and at the aggregate level (the line) over time.

Figure 6.3 The Relationship between Income and Happiness at the Individual and Aggregate Levels

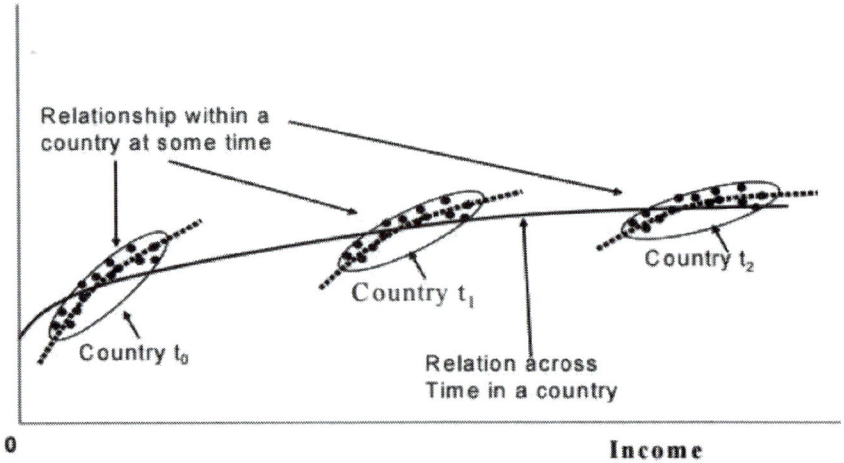

The dotted lines within the ellipses show the relationship between income and happiness for an individual at a given point in time. The solid line shows the level of aggregate happiness as income increases. Both at the individual and aggregate levels, the increase in happiness from an increase in income is greater among poorer countries. That is, an increase in income means more if you are poor relative to your reference group, and, as a country becomes richer, the increase means less in aggregate and at the individual level happiness. An increase in income will increase both of these in the poorer countries but only life satisfaction in the richer countries so that the flatter slope of the aggregate happiness curve at higher incomes is to be expected. For emotional happiness, each additional increase in income beyond some point, let's say $75,000 following Kahneman, is worth less.

Economists call this a decreasing marginal utility of income; that is, each additional dollar one gains is worth less to the individual than the previous one.

Is Status a Zero-Sum Game?

Status contributes to life satisfaction if not to emotional happiness. A zero-sum game is one in which the gains of some exactly equal to losses of others. Several economists argue (Clark et al.[43] and Coelho [1985], for example) argue, along with, that status is a zero- sum game and therefore cannot contribute to aggregate happiness. This seems incorrect. Consider status as simply that characteristic of rank that contributes to biological success, reproduction. Under this definition, status ceases to be a zero-sum game from a species point of view if total biological success can be extended and an expansion of success appears possible. Biological success is not a zero-sum game. Humans have taken over almost everywhere.

Next, consider status as occurring both within and between groups. Groups can be expanded or contracted. Suppose that status can   be expanded by the creation of new groups and that the ordinal amount of status is found by multiplying within group status by the status of the group and summing across groups. The total status is given by

(1) $S=V1 \ N/N + V2 \ (N-1)/N + ... Vm \ 1/N$

where the Vs represent vector of ranking of within group status, which is purely a function of the number within the group, N is the number of original groups, and N/N is the status of the top group. Consider the simplest example of two groups with two members each:

Figure 6.4: Status in a Four-Person Society

	Individuals	Individual Status Within Group	Group Status Rank	Total Status
Group One	A B	1 0.5	1 1	1 0.5
Group Two	C D	1 0.5	0.5 0.5	0.5 0.25
			Total Status	2.25

I assume that a new group will be formed whenever there are potential members, each of whom can gain status from group formation. Total status can increase even if the new group enters at the bottom of the status grouping. A new group could be formed by members of an existing group or groups or by others. Consider the addition of a second group consisting of individuals E and F, though it could also be made up of existing members of groups (i.e., A, B, C, D). As shown below, the addition of the new group will increase total status from 2.25 to 3.0. New groups will be formed whenever there is a net gain in status for the new members, although groups will not form without limit, as the formation of a new group has costs. Consequently, new groups will form when the gain in status to their members is greater than the costs. In general, the change in total status from the formation of a new group is found by differentiating equation (1) with respect to N, subject to a cost constraint representing the cost of group formation.

Figure 6.5: The Change in Total Status from a New Group

	Individuals	Within Group Status	Group Status	Total Status
Group One	A B	1 0.5	1 1	1 0.5
Group Two	C D	1 0.5	0.67 0.67	0.67 0.33
Group Three	E F	1 0.5	0.33 0.33	0.33 0.17
			Total Status	3.00

The formulation here also shows that as N increases, the gain from a new group falls. For example, in moving from two to three groups, the increase in total status is 0.75. In moving from three to four groups, the gain would be 0.525, and so on. The process of group formation described here would not yield the optimum number of groups. If groups enter at the lowest status, there will be too few groups, as new group formation raises the status of all other groups except the first. If a group enters at the top, there will be too few groups. An external effect exists because the change in total status from a new group will not (in general) be the same as the change in status to the members forming the group. In the example just discussed, the new group has the lowest status, and total status increases by 0.75 units. Individuals C and D gain a total of 0.25 status units. In general, if the new group is the bottom status group, total status must increase by more than the gain to the new group members, because the addition of the new group will increase the status of all other groups. If the new group becomes the top status group, the change in total status would be less than that gained by the new group members, because the introduction of the new group lowers the status of groups below it. This sort of treatment of status as an economic good and groups as producers of status implies that reductions in costs of group formation will increase the number of groups.

The process of group formation described here would not yield the optimum number of groups. An external effect exists because the change in total status from a new group will not (in ·general) be the same as the change in status to the members forming the group. In the example just discussed, the new group has the lowest status, and total status increases by 0.75 units. Individuals B and D gain a total of 0.75 status units. In general, if the new group is the bottom status group, total status must increase by more than the gain to the new group members because the addition of the new group will increase the status of all other groups. If the new group becomes the top status group, the change in total status would be less than that gained by the new group members, because the introduction of the new group lowers the status of groups below it. This sort of treatment of status as an economic good and groups as producers of status implies that reductions in costs of group formation will increase the number of groups.

Summary

There are two interrelated sources of happiness, emotional happiness and life satisfaction. Emotional happiness is day to day and is particularly related to human interaction. Life satisfaction is mainly related to life achievements relative to one's expectations. Income increases for individuals do not add to emotional happiness beyond an income level of about $75,000 in the most expensive cities and less elsewhere. Income increases do add to status and life satisfaction. Increases in income increase happiness faster in poorer countries. Increases in national income without an increase in one's own income tend to make people less happy, because they lower the status of some. In developed countries income is not the most important determinant of happiness, even of life satisfaction. Status seeking need not be a zero-sum game

Questions

1. Are you happy? Why or why not?

2. Have you thought of lowering your expectations?

3. Have you thought of moving to a location in which your status would be greater? The big fish in a smaller pond effect.

4. How much is your happiness tied up with the happiness of those you care about?

5. Are some people happy with less status?

7 Status, War and the Rise of Institutions

*Let's kill something. Land a man in a landscape and he'll
try to conquer it. Make him handsome and you're a fascist,
make him ugly and you're saying nothing new. The conqueror
suits up and takes the field, his horse already painted in
beneath him. What do you do with a man like that? While
you are deciding, more men ride in. The hand sings weapon.
The mind says tool. The body swerves in the service of the
mind, which is evidence of the mind but not actual proof.
More conquerors. They swarm the field and their painted
flags unfurl. Crown yourself with leaves and stake your claim
before something smears up the paint. I turned away from
darkness to see daylight, to see what would happen. What
happened? What does a man want?*

Power.
I prefer to blame others, it's easier. King me.
—Richard Siken Landscape with a Blur of Conquerors, *excerpt*

*Mr. Siken shows us how institutions are created. Consider
the role of war. Sun Tzu notes that "war is a matter of vital
importance to the State, the provider of life or death, the road
to survival or ruin."*
—Sun Tzu, The Art of War

Introduction

This is a thesis of war as an originator of civilization. Once war became sufficiently important and large scale, survival meant recognizing the relationships among wealth, technological change, and the ability to wage war. To be successful at war, whether offensive or defensive, requires material resources. Indeed, history shows that those with greater resources tend to win.

What Are Institutions?

Institutions are private organizations, laws, customs, agencies, and governments. For example, the Chicago Board of Trade is a private organization with its own building and its own set of more or less complicated self-regulations. You can lose your membership for violating its regulations. 2) Law is the bedrock of at least more advanced civilizations. Law, along with government, has the power to coerce, for example by requiring that taxes be paid. At least as important, government and law use this power to lower transaction costs of private agreements, thus increasing economic efficiency.

3) Customs represent norms of behavior and can substitute for law in many cases. For example, in Shasta County, California, custom says that a rancher whose cows damage a neighboring farmer's crop owes the farmer damages, and although the law suggests otherwise, custom prevailed (Elickson 1986).

Governments are institutions that at their best attempt to monopolize the means of violence and thereby reduce it. 5) Agencies are instruments of government.

Why Did Institutions Not Arise Earlier?

Thomas Hobbes's (1651) great insight was the realization that civilization relies on restraints that government and other institutions provide. The genetic basis for human nature has not changed much in a long time. What has changed are culture and institutions as the essence of culture.[44] But why were such institutions so long in arising?

The outstanding feature for most of humanity's economic history has been the absence of material progress, in contrast to more recent history. Homo sapiens appeared about 200,000 years ago, while fully modern, speaking humans appeared about 100,000 years ago. There was no material progress through the first millennium CE.[45] Thus, most of our history has been without much material progress. Why is this?

What makes individuals form families, families form tribes, tribes form villages, villages form towns, and towns form nations? Survival! These formations increase survivability. It is often suggested that the gains to be had from trade led to the creation of institutions, or that it was the desire of leaders to gain status, and perhaps this could be true. But the first mover that created institutions was violence.

Violence was at first more effective under a war leader, and this led to a conflict between social and individual gains. Phil Coelho (1985) suggests that the role of social hierarchies makes individual gains more important than social gain: the old collective action problem. Coelho claims that historically, the status seeking of leaders prevented gains for societies, hence slowing the creation of institutions. We can then rephrase our question about human progress to be "Why did social institutions take so long to evolve?" The answer lies in conflicting genetic traits necessary for survival, aggression, and cooperation. The aggressive trait stresses individual achievement relative to others, which focuses on increasing survival and reproductive success. But cooperative behavior increases the ability to wage war and is necessary for

---

44   Wade (2015) has suggested the slowness to create good government in Africa is due to a genetic basis that makes trust and thus cooperation more difficult. His evidence is weak. Kenneally (2014), a linguist, offers a better explanation with better evidence, showing that cultural trauma can persist for very long times.

45   See Zerbe (2015).

social living. It is only after institutions made the effort necessary for survival less that cooperation became stronger (Pinker 2012).

Both competition and cooperation are crucial ingredients of human evolution. All species that are social animals, in that they reproduce sexually, have social hierarchies, rankings, and dominance and must balance cooperation and competition. In many cases, it is efficient for the competitive instinct to be channeled into a social order, in which the status of each individual is relatively fixed and aggression is channeled toward other tribes or species. This was especially true of early societies.

Primitive societies are not acquisitive, but redistributive for the sake of survival (Lumsden and Wilson 1981, 150–1; Marvin Harris 1991.[46] As Coelho notes, in a primitive world subject to large stochastic variations in morbidity, mortality, and resources, an emphasis on redistribution is adaptive, a sort of social insurance arrangement. In early societies, status was often gained by giving away material goods.

In larger tyrannical societies, the despot finds it easier to maintain or increase his or her status through extractions from other members—the more he or she is deified, the more the population is debased, which has thus been the history of empires. In such societies, there is little rule of law, dispossession of one's goods is always a possibility, and the most rewarding form of competition for many is political, not economic.

For these reasons, trade is a poor candidate as the first mover in the creation of institutions but a very strong second mover. Leaders in a primitive state generally recognize that trade will create wealth in centers of power other than themselves, unless they can expropriate it. But if they expropriate it, there is little incentive to trade. Thus, at times in their history, Japanese and Chinese societies closed themselves off from trade.

---

46 See Zerbe and Anderson 2001 for evidence of sharing behavior among California gold miners.

The Origin of the State

What does it mean to establish a state (government)? First and foremost, it means, as Max Weber (1946) noted, the creation of an institution that must, to a considerable extent, monopolize violence and the means to violence and thus reduce it. Otherwise, the state fails. Second, the state must muster its own defense. This task requires economic growth. Economic growth in turn requires some level of rights for citizens. For example, a capitalist ideology with its concomitant protection of property rights was a further crucial concept in promoting economic growth, and this ideology succeeded because it furnished wealth as a means of war or protection from war. In terms of protection from war, we noted Freud's statement that "Civilization began the first time an angry person cast a word instead of a rock." Thus was the Magna Carta of 1215 turned by the great soldier William Marshall[47] and later by Stephen Lang into a voice against tyranny.[48]

As noted in the Times Literary Supplement, Gaventa reminds us that the exercise of power has as much to do with preventing decisions as with bringing them about. Force, the threat of sanction, the invocation of precedents, norms and rules to squash incipient revolt, the introduction of new rules or barriers—these prevent demands from becoming issues.

Voluntaristic Theories

Theories regarding the origin of the state can be divided into two categories: voluntaristic and coercive theories (Caneiro). Proponents of voluntaristic theories believe that at some point, individuals voluntarily gave up their freedoms and autonomy to be part of a larger community in exchange for protection of their

---

47   William Marshall (first Earl of Pembroke) was known as the greatest fighting man of the thirteenth century, besting more than five hundred knights in tournaments, and was never defeated. He led royal troops in battle when he was nearly seventy.

48   The Economist, December 20, 2014–January 2, 2015, p. 35.

individual rights. A leading historical theory in the voluntaristic camp is the *social contract theory*, developed and promulgated by Hobbes. Another popular voluntaristic theory is the *hydraulic hypothesis*, developed by Karl Wittfogel. This stated that in arid and semi-arid agricultural regions, farmers realized that it would be advantageous to merge into one cohesive unit capable of building and maintaining large-scale irrigation projects. Another voluntaristic theory, the *automatic hypothesis*, states that with increased surplus, food stocks created by agricultural development caused a division of labor and a working class, conditions that then allowed for political integration and state unification. Yet other theories emphasize trade as the organizing force.

Currently, a leading voluntaristic economic theory of the origin of the state is provided by Douglas North (1991), an economist and winner of the Nobel Prize. In his seminal work entitled *Institutions*, North contends that state institutions arose in order to decrease transaction costs for economic growth and development. Human cooperation, a product of institutions, he explained, would facilitate division of labor and specialization, thereby reducing production costs and raising gains to trade. The state was also a necessary body to create rules and standards to regulate trade. This theory, then, rests on economic gain, rather than violence and warfare, as the initial impetus for state development. I contend that this theory helps explain the growth of government, but not, as is claimed, its origins.

I do not find North's trade explanations persuasive as an explanation of the origin of the state. They are useful in explaining the growth of wealth and with the growth of wealth, greater demands for the services of the state. Yet these views assume that collective actions problems are purely economic problems with economic solutions, rather than complex interactions of cooperative and aggressive forces.

Coercive Theories

Individuals will group around a strong man or woman to protect themselves during or in anticipation of war. (Great examples of this are to be found in various American Indian tribes. One of the best examples of a war culture is the renowned Comanches. Superb soldiers, they suffered from the disadvantage of many such cultures led by a strong man: the followers fled when the strong man was killed.[49]) The strong leader can then organize a state, and sometimes this can lead to civilization, which was in fact the usual pattern (Carneiro 1977). In his seminal work entitled *A Theory on the Origin of the State*, Robert Carneiro, a renowned American anthropologist, explains how the voluntarist theories fail to hold up in practical examination. He states (Carneiro 1977) that numerous historic examples "demonstrated inability of autonomous political units to relinquish their sovereignty in the absence of overriding external constraints." Carneiro has it right. This leaves the coercive theories to explain the rise of state institutions.

Conquest theory lies at the heart of the coercive theories, holding that the state was created as a mechanism by which to control other tribes/villages that it had conquered.[50] Franz Oppenheimer (1914, 15), an early twentieth-century sociologist and political economist, explained that states existed

withthesolepurposeofregulatingthedominionof the victorious group over the vanquished, and securing itself againstrevoltfromwithinandattacksfromabroad. Teleologically, this dominionhad no other purpose than the economic exploitation ofthe vanquished by the victors.

War is also my explanation. I contend that war better explains the origin of the state, although not in all cases; not all states rose from warfare. Why did some (most) states arise from war but some not?

---

49   See the superb book by Gwynne (2010).

50   I had written this chapter before I found the nice book by Nicholas Wade (2014), whose views of war as the creation of the state appear to agree with mine.

Carneiro's *Conscription Theory* addresses this question, as it details necessary conditions under which warfare gave rise to state institutions, making it one of the most developed and respected coercive theories. Under this theory, in areas of circumscribed agricultural land, there was sufficient pressure on population and resources to incite warfare. Once warfare ensued and there was a loser, the loser was forced to remain in the community, thus giving rise to villages and kingdoms, as well as to social structures and hierarchies.

Wealth of the State as a Predictor of Victory

A predictor of military victory in great power warfare is gross domestic product (GDP). As we will see, this theory played out   in the Second World War when comparing the GDP of the Allied countries to that of the Axis countries. The numbers below confirm the belief that the Axis did not stand a chance of winning the Second World War.[51] Consider the ratio of Allied to Axis GDP presented in the following figure:

Figure 7.1: Wartime GDP of the Great Powers

Country	1938	1939	1940	1941	1942	1943	1944	1945
USA	800	869	943	1094	1235	1399	1499	1474
UK	284	287	316	344	353	361	346	331
France	186	199	164	130	116	110	93	101
Italy	141	151	147	144	145	137	117	92
USSR	359	366	417	359	274	305	362	343
Germany	351	384	387	412	417	426	437	310
Austria	24	27	27	29	27	28	29	12
Japan	169	184	192	196	197	194	189	144
Allied/ Axis GDP	2.4	2.3	2.1	2	2.1	2.3	3.1	5

Note first that Germany and Italy together had a greater GDP than the United Kingdom and France in 1940, 534 billion to 480 billion. So an

---

51   *Allied and Axis* GDP by Ralph Zuljan (2003)

economic theory of war would predict that German and Italy would win the war if it was confined to these great powers. Thus one might say, economically speaking, Germany's attacks were not irrational. Once Germany attacked Russia, however, the balance shifted so that the Allies had a total of 897 billion to the German-Italian combination of 534 billion. The addition of Japan gives a more even match, with 897 for the Allies and 726 for the Axis. The entry of the United States, however, tilts the balance decidedly in favor of the Allies, with a combined GDP of 1,840 billion for the Allies to 726 billion for the Axis. With this in mind, was defeat of the Axis inevitable? Perhaps not. A winning strategy for Germany could have been to avoid attacking Russia and to have tried harder to keep Japan from attacking the United States and otherwise working to keep the United States out of the war.[52] The longer the war went on, the more the advantages went to the Allies, such as larger, deeper, more versatile economies and better access to global supplies.

The same analysis applies to World War I. As Broadberry and Harrison conclude (2005), once stalemate set in late 1914, "The greater Allied capacity for taking risks, absorbing the cost of mistakes, replacing losses, and accumulating overwhelming quantitative superiority should eventually have turned the balance against Germany. The Allies had much more potential wealth they could have spent on the war. One estimate (using 1913 US dollars) is that the Allies spent $147 billion on the war, and the Central Powers spent only $61 billion. Among the Allies, Britain and its empire spent $47 billion, and the United States spent $27 billion; among the Central Powers, Germany spent $45 billion. Similarly, the North won the Civil War in the United States mainly because it had greater resources.

Status and Why War Continues

Once a state is created, why does war continue? The answer is status. Consider the American Civil War. Why did the Civil War

---

52 For a more detailed discussion, see http://www.onwar.com/articles/0302.htm.

occur at all? Status! Far fewer resources would have been used if the North had been able to simply buy the Southern slaves and free them. The South, however, wouldn't have sold even if the North had offered. As I have pointed out elsewhere, (Zerbe 2001), the value of slaves to the Southern white society (and to some of the Northern society) was greater than just their economic value. The willingness of the South to accept payment would have yielded   an almost incalculable number. The existence of slaves promoted not only the status of slave holders, but of the whole Southern society. The majority of Southerners were not slave holders, but they gained status by having a social class below them.

World War I also corroborates this theory. World War I was a search for greater status, as with the American Civil War. Its roots were primarily a battle between the German and English aristocracy and was particularly a reach for greater status by Kaiser Wilhelm I that arose out of his jealousy of his English relatives and possibly also out of mortification over his withered arm. (My god, the British yachts were faster than his. See the terrific book *Dreadnaught* by Robert Massey.)

Summary

Civilization relies on restraints that government and other institutions provide. Human nature has not changed in a very long time. What has changed is culture and institutions that are the product of culture. Institutions generally consist of laws, customs, private organizations, agencies, and governments. The outstanding feature for most of humanity's economic history has been the absence of material progress—in contrast to more recent history. The fight for gains in individual status may have slowed social gains and the development of social institutions.

Both competition and cooperation are crucial ingredients of human evolution. All species of social animals that reproduce sexually have social hierarchies, rankings and dominance. It is efficient for the competitive instinct to be channeled into a social order. War and defense, and to a lesser extent trade, explain the origin of the State. Those countries with greater resources usually win wars.

Questions

1. Will warfare be both the beginning and end of civilization?

2. Are the resources of the United States, Britain, France, Germany and Japan greater than those of Russia, China, and Iran?

3. Will Putin go to war against the West? Why or why not?

4. If war is the vehicle for the creation of civilization, what is the engine for the growth of civilizations?

8

Progress, Freedom, and the Growth of Government

No man's life, liberty or property are safe while the Legislature is in session.

—Judge Tucker [53]

Introduction

I consider differences across countries with respect to social progress and economic freedom. The scope here is large and uses macro data sets such as overall government spending as a percentage of GDP or GDP per capita. Hall and Sostice (2001) divide capitalist countries into two types, liberal market economies, (e.g., the United States, Great Britain, Canada, Australia, New Zealand, Ireland) and coordinated market economies (CME) (e.g., Germany, Japan, Sweden, Austria). Those two types can be distinguished by the primary way in which firms coordinate with one another and other actors, such as trade unions. In LMEs, firms primarily coordinate their endeavors by way of hierarchies and market mechanisms. Coordinated market economies rely more heavily on nonmarket forms of interaction in the coordination of their relationships with other actors. I find that there are no aggregate differences between them. I find further that governments with levels of spending in the range of 40 to 55 percent of GDP tend to rank the highest in their level of progress and in economic freedom. Moreover, the growth of government to this range is associated with public demand for government services, not with innate or tipping point growth. Finally, I find that the claim that high economic growth rates

---

53   Gideon John Tucker (February 9, 1826–July 1899) was an American lawyer, newspaper editor, politician. and judge In 1866, as surrogate of New York, he wrote in a decision, "No man's life, liberty, or property safe while the Legislature is in session"(http://en.wikipedia.org/wiki/Gideon_J._ Tucker).

indicate a more desirable level of government is unsupported and in fact contradicted.

Cultures may be placed into multifarious categories. Some of these are more attractive than others. As there is a substantial correspondence between cultural categories and political ones, this raises the issue of whether there are political categories that are associated with more attractive cultures. I address this question by examining the relationship between various categories of social and political culture and a measure of social progress. A related question is whether or not there is a level of government in the culture and the society that corresponds to more and less attractive cultures. In considering this I relate the level of government spending to an important measure of progress. Of course it makes a difference what form government spending takes and how it relates to the capacity of what governments can do and can do best. Additional insight could be gained by finer- grained approaches. The question I seek to address is "What is the appropriate level of government capacity that is associated with progressive countries?"

It is now well established that different types of institutions affect the culture and the society and are in turn part of the culture. For example, Persson and Tabellini (2003) point out that those governments elected by proportional representation will redistribute more that those dependent on majoritarian electoral rules. Iverson and Soskice (2006, 2012) maintain that this is because proportional representation allows the formation of distinctive groups and allows lower income families to form a coalition to redistribute from the rich. Hall and Lamont (2012), Ellickson (1991) and Zerbe and Anderson (2001) have shown the importance of social relations and custom in forming decision- making processes and the type of government.

The scope used here is larger and uses more macro data sets, such as overall government spending as a percentage of GDP or GDP per capita. I consider differences across countries with respect to social progress and economic freedom.

The Size and Growth of Government

War led to the state, and the state led to greater trade and, ironically, to warfare on a larger scale (Caneiro 1970). The rise   of government and associated institutions have reduced violence and brought other benefits, so that if we are doing a simple extrapolation, the implication is the more government, the better. This cannot, however, be correct. Imagine for a minute a one-world government; regardless of how prosperous this might or might not be, it would be too dangerous to liberty and happiness. Perhaps there would be greater peace and less violence, but such a state of the world would be too risky, a sort of potential Orwellian "1984." Nor within nation states will the benefits of growth in government always exceed its costs.

Is there then an appropriate range of government spending beyond which or below which its costs exceed its benefits?

If so, what is this range? I introduce two indices. The first is the Social Progress Index, SPI. Later, I will introduce the Economic Freedom Index, EFI. The SPI ranks countries on the basis of the well-being of their citizens. The components of the SPI are shown below.

Figure 8.1: Components of Social Progress Index 2015

Basic Human Needs	Foundations of Wellbeing	Opportunity
Nutrition and Basic Health Care	Access to Basic Knowledge	Personal Rights
Water and Sanitation	Access to Information and Communications	Personal Freedom and Choice
Shelter	Health and Wellness	Toleration and Inclusion
Personal Safety	Ecosystem Sustainability	Access to Advanced Education

These components of this index might be regarded similarly to Maslow's (1943, 1954) stages of individual maturity, with basic human needs representing the more primitive components, the foundation of well-being the more advanced components, and opportunity the most mature level. (This is not to say that Maslow's criteria are sufficiently inclusive.) The interrelation of the three categories in the SPI is shown below.

Figure 8.2

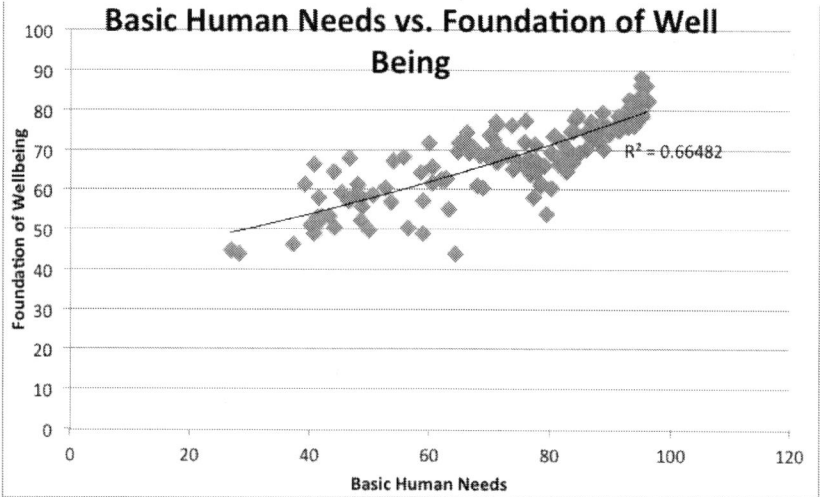

Further, how well a country does on the "foundations of well- being" explains much of how it does on "opportunity," as the following shows.

Figure 8.3: Relation of Opportunity to Foundation of Well-Being

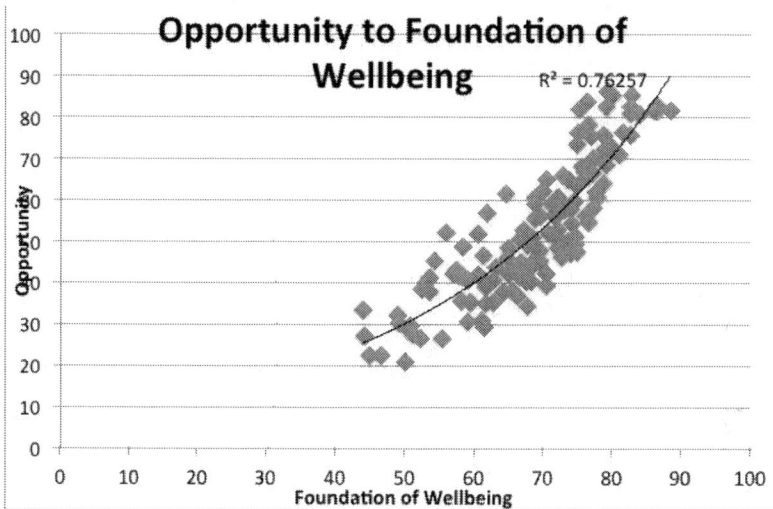

The top fifteen countries on the SPI are shown below.

Figure 8.4: Top Fifteen Countries on the Social Progress Index[54]

Country	Social Progress Index	Basic Human Needs	Foundations of Well-being	Opportunity
Norway	88.36	94.80	88.46	81.82
Sweden	88.06	94.83	86.43	82.93
Switzerland	87.97	95.66	86.50	81.75
Iceland	87.62	95.00	86.11	81.73
New Zealand	87.08	92.87	82.77	85.61
Canada	86.89	94.89	79.22	86.58
Finland	86.75	95.05	82.58	82.63
Denmark	86.63	96.03	82.63	81.23
Netherlands	86.50	94.80	83.81	80.88
Australia	86.42	93.73	79.98	85.55
United Kingdom	84.68	92.22	79.04	82.78
Ireland	84.66	93.68	76.34	83.97
Austria	84.45	95.04	82.53	75.77
Germany	84.04	94.12	81.50	76.49
Japan	83.15	95.01	78.78	75.66

54   The United States is number sixteen.

Capitalistic Countries

Not only are these countries democracies, but they are also capitalistic countries. Peter Hall and David Soskice have developed a classification of two distinct types of capitalist economies: liberal market economies (LME) and coordinated market economies (CME). Those two types are distinguished by the way in which firms coordinate with each other and other actors, such as trade unions. In LMEs firms coordinate their endeavors by way of market mechanisms. CMEs rely more on nonmarket forms of interaction in the coordination of their relationships with others types of actors. In addition to these classifications for more capitalistic counties, there are classifications for countries that are not capitalist. For example, there are planned economies such as Russia and statist countries such as China. The traits associated with CME and LME countries are shown in the figure below:

Figure 8.5: Characteristics of CME and LME Countries

Criteria	LME	CME
Mechanism	Competitive market arrangements	Nonmarket relations
Equilibrium	Demand/supply and hierarchy	Strategic interaction among firms and other actors
Interfirm Relations	Competitive	Collaborative
Mode of Production	Direct product competition	Differentiated, niche production
Legal System	Complete and formal contracting	Incomplete and informal contracting
Institutions' Function	Competitiveness Freer movement of inputs	Monitoring Sanctioning of defectors
Employment	Full-time, general skill Short term, fluid	Shorter hours, specific skill long term, immobile
Wage Bargain	Firm level	Industry level
Training and Education	Formal education from high schools and colleges	Apprenticeship imparting industry-specific skills
Unionization Rate	Low	High
Income Distribution	Unequal (high Gini)	Equal (low Gini)
Innovation	Radical	Incremental
Comparative Advantage	High-tech and service	Manufacturing
Policies	Deregulation, antitrust, tax- break	Encourages information sharing and collaboration of firms

I address whether or not these two sets of capitalistic countries differ in their progress scores. The following figure shows that they do not. Thus, being a liberal market economy offers no advantages on the progress index to being a coordinated market economy and vice versa.

Figure 8.6: Progress Scores for LME and CME Countries

LME Countries	Progress Index	CME Countries	Progress Index
Australia	86.42	Austria	84.45
Canada	86.89	Belgium	82.83
Ireland	84.66	Denmark	86.63
New Zealand	87.08	Finland	86.75
United Kingdom	84.68	France	80.82
United States	82.85	Germany	84.04
Average	85.43	Italy	77.38
		Japan	83.15
		Netherlands	86.5
		Norway	88.36
		Switzerland	87.97
		Sweden	88.06
		Average	84.745

Countries at the Bottom of the SPI

What about the bottom fifteen countries on the SPI? These are shown in figure 8.7 below. Eleven out of fifteen, or two-thirds of these countries, are in Africa. The rest are in Asia, except Yemen, which is in the Middle East but with no material oil. These countries are not democracies and have low incomes per capita, significant corruption, and low levels of individual freedom.

Figure 8.7: The Bottom Countries on the SPI

Country	Social Progress Index	Basic Human Needs	Foundations of Well-being	Opportunity
Myanmar	46.12	58.87	49.19	30.28
Mozambique	46.02	43.13	53.49	41.43
Mauritania	45.85	47.73	59.08	30.73
Pakistan	45.66	56.37	50.71	29.90
Liberia	44.89	41.15	53.23	40.30
Madagascar	44.50	41.93	53.53	38.04
Nigeria	43.31	39.04	61.51	29.37
Ethiopia	41.04	44.04	50.49	28.59
Niger	40.56	40.55	48.99	32.15
Yemen	40.30	49.72	50.07	21.12
Angola	40.00	41.27	52.20	26.51
Guinea	39.60	40.00	51.20	27.59
Afghanistan	35.40	37.17	46.50	22.51
Chad	33.17	28.09	44.12	27.30
Central African Republic	31.42	26.81	44.84	22.62

Note that the bottom fifteen rank particularly low on the opportunity index, the most mature measureorlevel ofculture.

The Size of Government and Social Progress

There is a strong correlation between government spending as a percentage of GDP and the SPI for advanced countries, as the following graph shows.

Figure 8.8: SPI vs Government Spending as Percentage of GDP for the Twenty Top Countries on the SPI

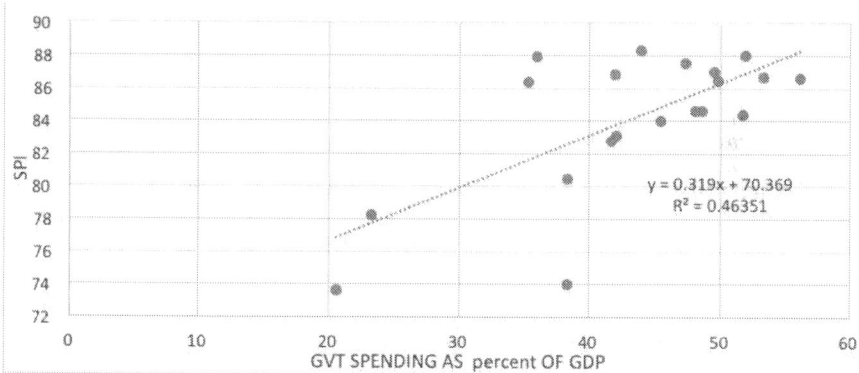

$y = 0.319x + 70.369$
$R^2 = 0.46351$

GVT SPENDING AS percent OF GDP

Why Government Grows

Why do governments grow relative to the economy? I consider three possible explanations, a demand for services explanation, a diseconomies of scale explanation and a tipping point explanation. The tipping point explanation is that there is some level of government spending after which there is necessarily a continual increase of government's size. This does not hold across governments, as the relative amount of government spending tends to flatten out and grow less quickly after it reaches levels   in the 40 to 50 percent range. In the United States, the level of federal spending after World War II was at about 9 percent of GDP after the initial fall in postwar spending. After the war government spending as a percentage of GDP rapidly rose. Would the increase in federal employment result in a tipping point as employees voted to expand the size of their roles? Probably not. Again, for the United States, such a tipping point is unlikely to be a result of the size of federal government employment. Between 1962 and 2012, the lowest figure for federal personnel was 4.127 million in 2007 and the highest was 6.639 million in 1968. The actual number in 2012 was 4,312. This is about 2.9 percent of the total labor force. Federal government workers voting for government growth are too small a percentage of the work force to explain this growth.

The second explanation is on the production side and invokes diseconomies of scale. The diseconomies argument is that for countries with larger GDPs, government's job becomes more complicated as the economy grows so that government needs to grow relative to the economy to perform basic government tasks. That is, does government become less efficient as it grows. If this is the case, we would expect a correlation between countries' GDPs and the relative size of their governments. This relationship does not, however, exist, as shown below in figure 8.9.

Figure 8.9: GDP and Relative Government Spending

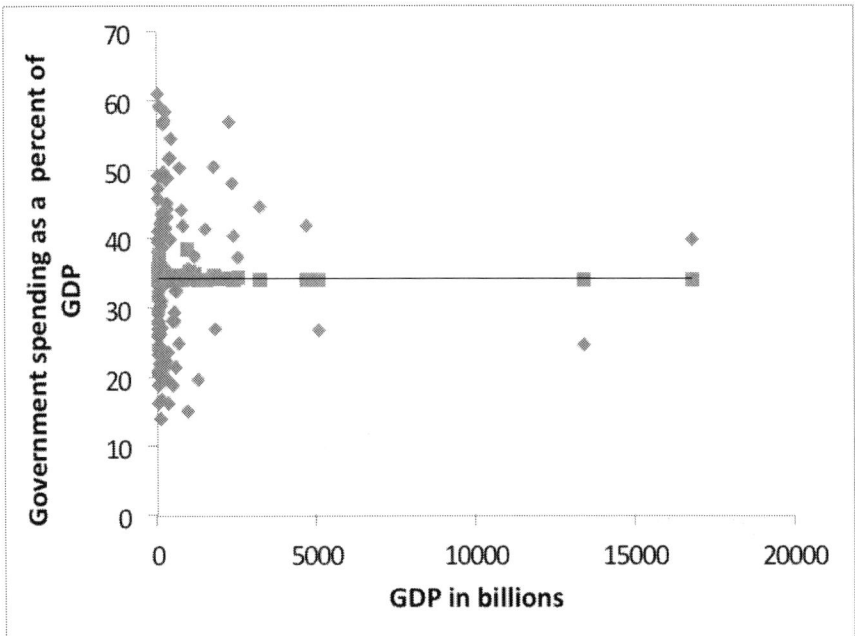

The third explanation is that as per capita income rises, citizens demand more of their government. Here the relation is strong. Per capita income "explains" about 42 percent of government expenditure as a percentage of GDP.[55] My interpretation is that people demand more government services as per capita income grows. The "demand for government services" explanation implies that per capita GDP should be positively correlated with the SPI rankings; higher per capita GDP buys more social progress. This is the case, as shown in the figure below.

Figure 8.10: The SPI and per Capita GDP for All Countries on the SPI

SPI vs Per Capita GDP

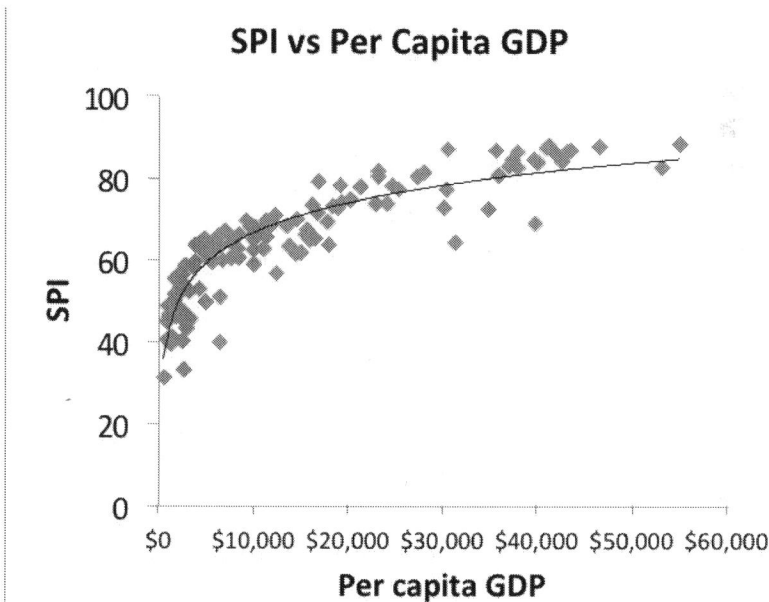

What is striking about the SPI is that the countries all tend to   have fairly high government spending in relation to their GDPs, suggesting that government tends to grow as the economy grows or perhaps vice versa. Denmark has the largest relative government for the top SPI group at about 56 percent, with the other Scandinavian countries close to this. The smallest government spending relative to GDP for fairly well-off countries is shown by Chile. Chile is a bit of an outlier in this regard and does not make the top twenty in the SPI. The figure below shows that the top countries on the SPI have high per capita incomes.

---

55   The F statistic is very highly significant with 158 observations.

Figure 8.11: Top Countries by SPI and per Capita Income

Rank	Country	SPI Score	Per Capita Income
1	Norway	88.36	100,898.40
2	Switzerland	87.97	84,748.40
3	Australia	86.42	67,463.00
4	Sweden	88.06	60,380.90
5	Denmark	86.63	59,818.60
6	United States	82.85	53,042.00
7	Kuwait	69.19	52,197.30
8	Netherlands	86.50	50,792.50
9	Austria	84.45	50,510.70
10	Finland	86.75	49,150.60
11	Iceland	87.62	47,349.50
12	Belgium	82.83	46,929.60
13	Germany	84.04	46,251.40
14	United Arab Emirates	72.79	43,048.90
15	France	80.82	42,560.40
16	New Zealand	87.08	41,824.30
17	Canada	86.89	41,824.30
18	United Kingdom	84.68	41,781.10
19	Japan	83.15	38,633.70
20	Israel	72.60	36,050.70

Note that these countries appear in the top SPI group, with the exception of the UAE and Kuwait; such oil-rich countries are treated as special cases

The Size of Government: Too Much, Too Little, and Just Right

I suggest the Goldilocks rule for government: there can be too much, too little, and just right amounts.

Too much

There can be too much government. Consider the following countries at the bottom of the SPI:

Figure 8.12: Bottom Countries on SPI and Government Spending Relative to GDP

Country	Government Spending as a Percentage of GDP
Kiribati	109.2
North Korea	100
Timor Leste	86.4
Micronesia	65.2
Lesotho	61.1
Cuba	60.2

These are not candidates for countries that are either progressive with respect to the SPI or economically free as measured by the EFI, although Cuba has possibilities. It appears then not unlikely that you can have too much government.

Too little

The thesis of the Rahn Curve below is that, especially in advanced countries, there is too much government and that most countries would be better off without so much. The suggestion is promoted by noting that the economic growth rate is greater in countries with smaller relative governments. This hypothetical curve is shown below.

Figure 8.13: Growth Rates and the Size of Government

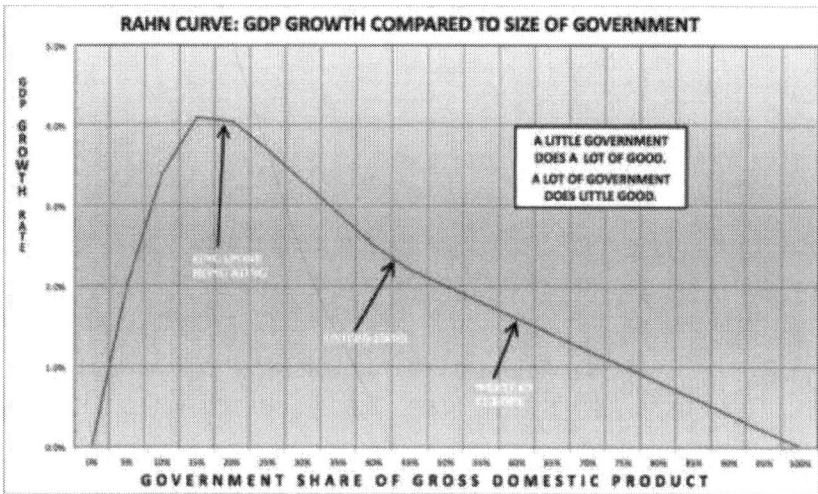

The relationship between the government share of the economy and the economic growth rate is cherry picked and includes cities that act as countries, such as Hong Kong and Singapore. This relationship is then used to suggest the possibility that governments' optimal share of the economy is about 9 percent.

This is a case of confusing cause and effect. More advanced countries have slower growth rates as a natural consequence of the growth process. As economies grow, governments grow disproportionately. Russia, with an inefficiently structured economy, had a large GDP growth rate after the 1917 revolution, so many social scientists were predicting it would sooner rather than later surpass the United States. Warren Nutter at the University of

Virginia correctly predicted this would not happen without a change in the Russian economic system. Similarly, China has had a large growth rate in recent years in its earlier stages of development,   but we do not know that this will continue. Another example of   a country with an immature economy but a high growth rate is Mauritius.

The growth of relative size of government appears to be due to a greater demand for more government with the greater wealth of countries; in economic terms, greater government is a luxury good up to some point. The fact that more mature countries have lower growth rates and less mature ones can have larger growth rates is shown below. Figure 14 shows the negative correlation between per capita GDP and a five-year growth rate.

Figure 8.14: Per Capita GDP vs Five-Year Growth Rates

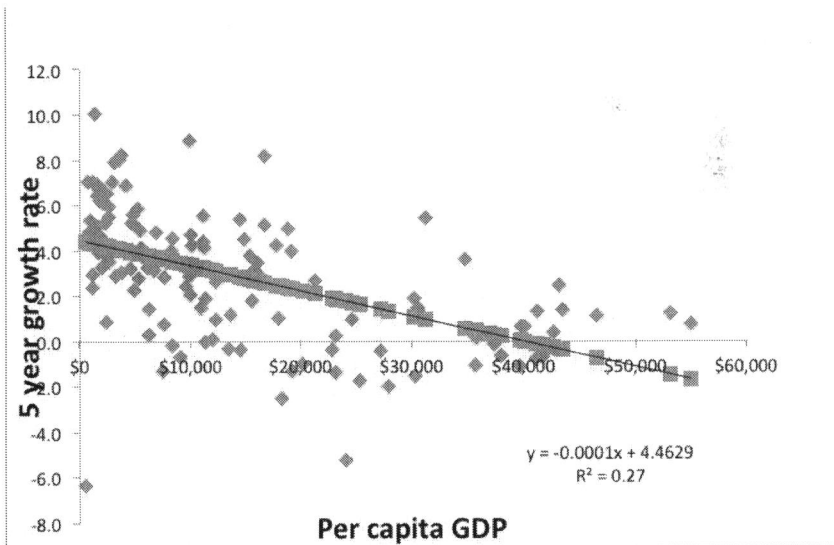

Figure 8.15: Economic Growth Rates for Less Developed Countries

Growth Rates for Some Less Developed Countries	Country
19.7	Sri Lanka
19.6	Peru
19.2	Nepal
19.1	Uganda
19.0	Mali
18.9	Philippines
18.3	Costa Rica
16.9	Ethiopia
16.5	Macau
16.3	Bangladesh
16.3	Central African Republic
15.3	Iran
14.7	Turkmenistan
14.1	Guatemala
13.6	Sudan
13.3	Madagascar

This figure suggests that growth rates are not the appropriate measure of the most attractive range of relative government size as for more advanced countries; nor are the countries listed above high on the SPI.

Just right

Once you get into the 50 percent and 40 percent ranges for relative government spending, however, you get more progressive and freer countries. We showed in that the six countries with the very largest governments relative to the rest of the country are poor ones. However, the next ten countries ranked by government spending relative to GDP and shown below are among the more advanced in terms of the SPI and the economic freedom index, which we discuss next.

Figure 8.16: Economic Freedom and Ten Top Countries with Large Relative Government Spending

Ten Countries with Largest Relative Government Spending	EFI
Slovenia	59.4
Greece	58.5
Denmark	57.2
France	57
Finland	56.7
Belgium	54.7
Sweden	51.9
Austria	51.7
Italy	50.6
Netherlands	50.4

On this basis, I advance the suggestion that government spending can account for a range of about 40 to 50-some percentage of GDP and we still could call it a mature, free and progressive society.   In the United States, government spending is about 42 percent of GDP.

This may be lower less than the desired range, given that a larger portion of US spending is on military programs than it is for other developed countries.

The Economic Freedom Index (EFI) and the SPI

The conservative Heritage Foundation provides an index of economic freedom. They describe it this way:

Economicfreedomisthefundamentalrightofevery humanto control his or her own labor and property. In an economically free society, individuals are free to work, produce, consume, andinvest inanywaythey please. In economically free societies, governments

allow labor, capital, and goods to move freely, and refrain from coercion or constraint of liberty beyond the extent necessary to protect and maintain liberty itself.[56]

There is a strong correlation between the SPI and the EFI for the full joint list of countries as shown below. Those countries that score highly in one index also score highly in the other.

Figure 8.17: Correlation of the SPI and the EFI

SPI vs EFI

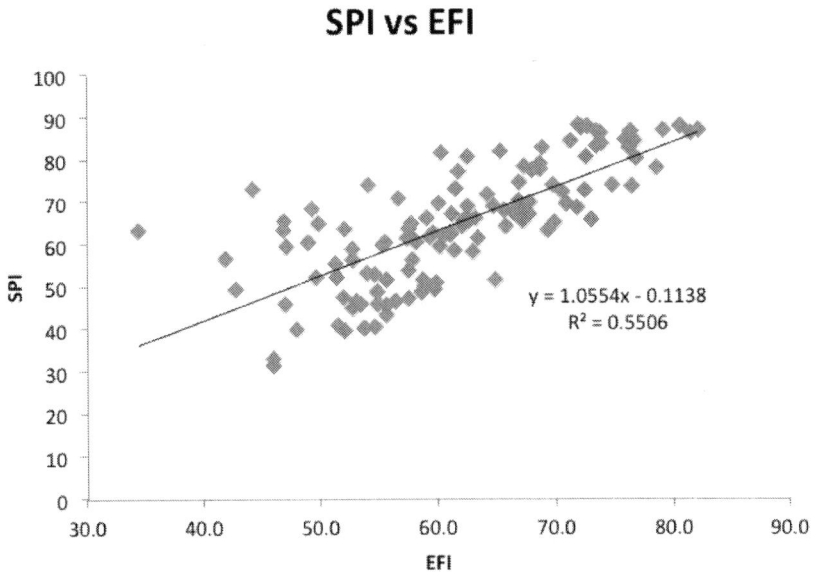

$y = 1.0554x - 0.1138$
$R^2 = 0.5506$

Figure 8.18 shows the twenty countries that lie within the top fifteen in either the SPI or the EFI. The top sixteen countries of the group of twenty as measured by the SPI are all fairly rich, developed countries. The remaining four (Chile, Estonia, Mauritius, Lithuania) are less developed. These four have among the highest EFI scores. These are less developed countries with high rates of economic growth. There is a lot of overlap, and all countries rank highly on both indices.

56   http://www.heritage.org/index/about.

Figure 8.18: Twenty Countries in the Top Fifteen in Either the SPI or the EFI

Country	SPI Score	SPI Rank	Economic Freedom Score	Economic Freedom Rank	Gvt. Spending as % of GDP (ppp)
Norway	88.36	1	71.8	24	43.9
Sweden	88.06	2	72.7	21	51.9
Switzerland	87.97	3	80.5	3	36
Iceland	87.62	4	72	7	47.3
New Zealand	87.08	5	82.1	1	49.5
Canada	86.89	6	79.1	4	41.9
Finland	86.75	7	73.4	18	53.3
Denmark	86.63	8	76.3	9	56.1
Netherlands	86.50	9	73.7	15	49.8
Australia	86.42	10	81.4	2	35.3
United Kingdom	84.68	11		11	48.5
Ireland	84.66	12	76.6	7	48.1
Austria	84.45	13	71.2	27	
Germany	84.04	14		14	45.4
Japan	83.15	15	73.3	17	42
United States	82.83	16	76.2	10	41.6
Chile	78.29	26	78.5	5	23.2
Estonia	80.49	23	76.8	6	38.3
Mauritius	73.65	35	76.4	8	20.5
Lithuania	74	34	74.7	13	38.3

It is interesting, however, that while there is a strong correlation between the SPI and EFI for all countries, there is no correlation between the EFI and the SPI for these advanced countries; the R^2 is only 0.0019 and not significant. What this implies is that across the broad sample of countries, many of the same components contribute to the SPI and the EFI. Yet for the top-rated countries, the SPI and EFI share dissimilar components. That is, all advanced countries rank highly on both indices, but within the top group, there is no apparent relationship between the SPI and the EFI.

Figure 8.19: Lack of Relationship between EFI and SPI for Top-Ranked Countries

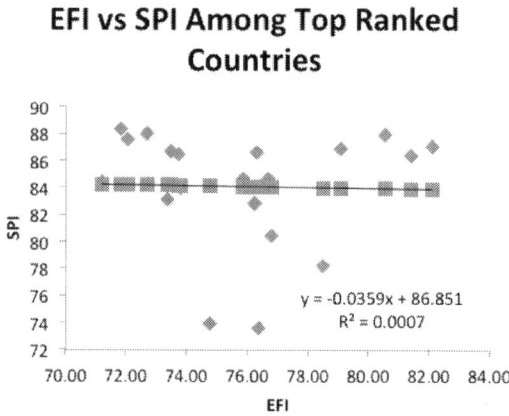

EFI vs SPI Among Top Ranked Countries

$y = -0.0359x + 86.851$
$R^2 = 0.0007$

For the list of top countries in the two indices, there is a small though insignificant positive correlation between governments' spending and economic freedom, as shown below.

There seems to be little reason to suppose less government spending leads to less freedom. For the full list, there is again a small and insignificant positive correlation between relative government spending and the EFI.

Figure 8.20: Government Spending vs GDP and the EFI for all Countries on the EFI Index

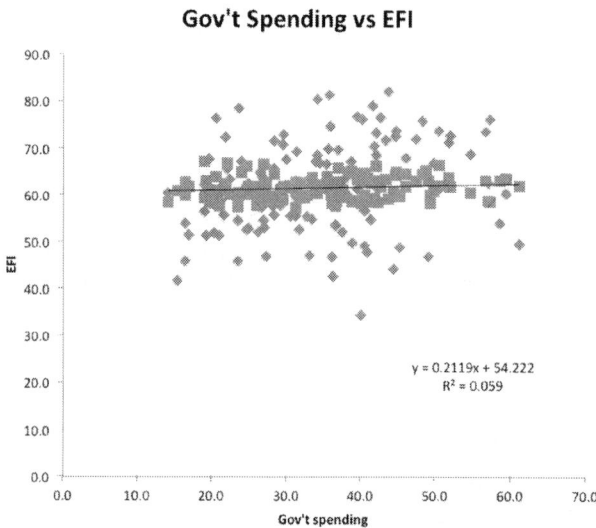

Gov't Spending vs EFI

$y = 0.2119x + 54.222$
$R^2 = 0.059$

There is, however, a negative correlation for the top countries between relative government spending and the EFI. That is, within top countries, it appears there can be too much government in the sense that freedom is less.

Figure 8.21: Government Spending as a Percent of GDP
and the EFI for Twenty Top Counties on the EFI

Gvt Spending as a Percentage of GDP and the EFI

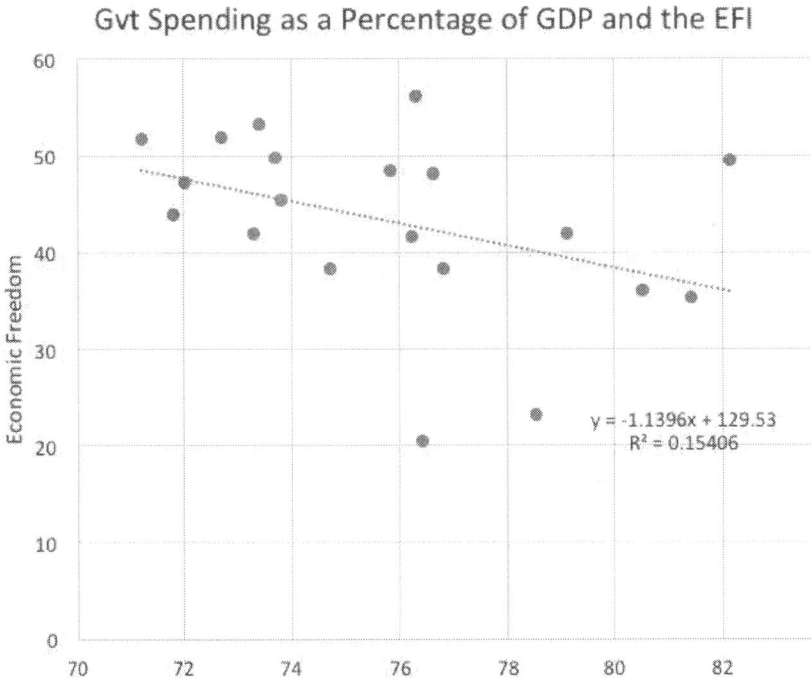

$$y = -1.1396x + 129.53$$
$$R^2 = 0.15406$$

The difference between the effects of government spending as a percentage of GDP between the SPI and economic freedom should not be surprising. Once countries have reached a significant level of per capita GDP, additional government spending relative to GDP appears within limits to improve social programs. But it is mainly unrelated to economic freedoms. Those whose governments spend more will tend to have more economic regulation and hence, a lower economic freedom score.

There is a strong correlation, however, between GDP per capita and the EFI. The relationship tends to flatten out, as there is necessarily a limit to economic freedom, regardless of income. You have to ask whether the high per capita GDP causes more freedom, or more freedom causes the higher incomes. I suggest that they interact with each other. Low relative government spending is not associated with greater economic freedom.

Consider those countries near the bottom of the EFI shown in the figure below.

Figure 8.22: EFI and Government Spending

Country	EFI Score	Government Spending as a Percent of GDP
Madagascar	61.7	13.3
Sudan	N/A	13.6
Guatemala	60.4	14.1
Singapore	89.4	14.4
Turkmenistan	41.4	14.7
Iran	41.8	15.3
Central African Republic	45.9	16.3
Bangladesh	53.9	16.3
Macau	70.3	16.5
Ethiopia	51.5	16.9
Costa Rica	67.2	18.3
Hong King SAR	89.6	18.5
Philippines	62.2	18.9
Mali	56.4	19
Uganda	59.7	19.1
Nepal	51.3	19.2
Peru	67.7	19.6
Sri Lanka	58.6	19.7
Indonesia	58.1	19.7
Guinea-Bissau	52	20

These countries have both low levels of freedom and low government spending as a percentage of GDP. This figure suggests again that a country can have both too little government and also too little freedom.

There is, however, a significant and positive correlations between per capita GDP and EFI as shown below.

Figure 8.23: Per Capita GDP and Economic Freedom

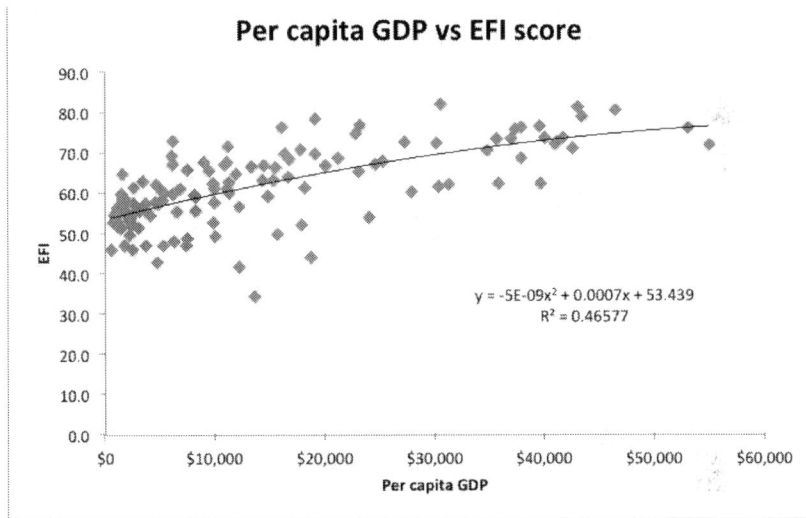

Per capita GDP vs EFI score

$y = -5E-09x^2 + 0.0007x + 53.439$
$R^2 = 0.46577$

A challenge for progress in government for nation states is the maintenance of diversity within unity. The number of states with UN membership has increased from 51 countries in 1945 to 193 today.[57] The current vogue for carving out new nation states is unlikely to be any more successful than the carving out of new states from the Ottoman Empire after 1914. The trick instead to maintaining unity is to devolve and decentralize, as Canada has done with respect to Quebec, while still maintaining a strong central government.

---

57   *The Economist*, "The World in 2015: Splitting Images," p. 31.

Summary

I find that there are no aggregate differences between LME and CME countries in terms of the social progress index. Countries can have too much, too little, or just right levels of government. We find that governments with levels of spending in the range of 40 to 55 percent of GDP tend to rank the highest in their level   of progress and in economic freedom; these are the "just right" countries. Moreover, the growth of government to this range is associated with public demand for government services, not with innate or tipping-point growth. That is, this level of government is driven by the demands of their populations. Moreover, republics with significant democracy rank highest both economically and   in terms of social progress. Finally, I find that the claim that high economic growth rates requires small governments is unsupported and in fact contradicted.

Questions

1. Do you find that I write from a more liberal or conservative perspective, or neither?

2. Do you think the relative size of government will continue to grow or to fall for developed countries? For less developed countries?

9 Chap 6

Inequality

I hadn't the heart to touch my breakfast. I told Jeeves to drink it himself.
—P. G. Wodehouse

Lady Constance Keeble: "Does this pig mean more to you than your nephew's future?"
Clarence, Earl of Emsworth: "Of course it does!"
—P. G. Wodehouse Heavy Weather

Status and the Decline of the British Aristocracy

One of the great drivers of human behavior, status and the search for it, can be gained from titles, money beyond the dream of avarice, a fashionable address, a grand car, servants or slaves and so forth. These are status goods. People strive for status, but a culture can provide different ways of achieving it, some more compatible with social well-being than others. Slaves, for example in much of the world are no longer status goods. There are three ways of gaining status: through one's own achievements, through achievements of one's ancestors (i.e., inheritance), or through preventing others from achieving it. This latter is nicely shown by legislation during the middle and late middle ages, and even into the more modern period, of sumptuary laws forbidding certain types of clothes being worn by various underprivileged social classes constituting the hoi polloi (Costain 1958). Veblen (1934) famously saw that much of human activity was designed to elevate one's social rank. The very wealthy like J. P. Morgan hated Teddy and Franklin Roosevelt because they lowered the power of money and monopoly. Similarly, we now see enmity directed at the Affordable Care Act, known popularly as Obamacare, probably because its expected redistributive effect lowers the status of those who already had health care, although the rhetoric against the act is only about growth of government.

With respect to the British, David Cannadine (1999) notes on his book cover:

> *At the outset of the 1870s, the British aristocracy could rightly consider themselves the most fortunate people on earth: they held the lion's share of land, wealth, and power in the world's greatest empire. By the end of the 1930s, they had lost not only a generation of sons in the First World War, but also much of their prosperity, prestige and political significance.*

He goes on to note (9):

> *In Great Britain for many centuries there were titles of class distinction signifying gradations of wealth, and also status designations signifying precise degrees of lordly rank. These were closely correlated. The status distinctions were in the main the five ranks in order of distinction of the peerage aristocracy— duke, marques, earl, viscount, or baron (the peerage)—to which we should add in most respects the titles of baronet and knight, both of which are "sirs." The landholdings and associated titles were created by British monarchs, to help ensure that the ennobled would come to the aid of the King in time of war by furnishing warriors and financial support. Around 1880 in England about 56% of all land was in estates greater than 1000 acres owned by nobility about 61% in Wales, 78% in Ireland and about 93% in Scotland.[58] That is, over 66% of Great Britain's land was owned by about 9,000 people belonging to the aristocracy. Titles of wealth were simply those held by such as small landowner, more than middling proprietors and territorial*

58   A. Cannadine, p. 9.

*magnates.⁵⁹ Land ownership, wealth and status distinction
governed. Land ownership was especially highly associated
with status designations; yet the aristocracy reached
their apexofpowerinthe 1870s, and then begin a decline.
Within the space of 100 years, that is by the 1970s, the elites
were dethroned, figuratively speaking. It no coincidence that
historians see the 1870 as the start of a new period of prosperity
for Britain.*

The great comic novelist, P. G. Wodehouse (pronounced *Woodhouse*), chronicled this decline with great humor and insight. In one novel (*Ring for Jeeves*), Bertie Wooster's butler, Jeeves, has been sent out to help Lord Rowcester, the owner of a great but decaying manor house. The roof leaks, the farms have been sold, and the park has been leased out to the local golf club. As Jeeves explains to an American visitor amazed at the decay,

> *A house such as Rowcester Abbey in these days is not an
> asset, sir, it is a liability...Socialistic legislation has sadly
> depleted the resources of England's hereditary aristocracy.
> We are living now in what is known as the Welfare State,
> which means—broadly speaking— that everybody is
> completely destitute.⁶⁰*

How did this happen? The short answer is war and taxation. World War I depleted the ranks of the aristocracy; after all, this was in large part a war among aristocrats. The war also depleted their wealth. This fall took place over a one-hundred-year period from about the 1870s through the 1970s. The fundamental reason was a shift in culture that led to a change in British attitudes toward the landed aristocracy. The changing attitudes resulted in demand for franchise extension

59   See Cannadine (1994, 12)

60   See Cannadine, 639, and Wodehouse (1953). I confess to Wodehouse being my favorite comic author.

and in turn the decline in power of the House of Lords and a change in the composition of the House of Commons.

This extension of the franchise was seen all over Europe. In Britain, the growing political strength of the common man resulted in several reform acts, the most notable being the Third Reform Act of 1884–5, which shifted the balance of power away from money toward numbers of people who had the vote. This was helped along by the influx of foreign goods, particularly agricultural goods—globalization, if you will—that led to a fall in land prices and thus, the income of the landed aristocracy. In addition, industrialization shifted relative wealth from landlords to industrialists.

All this is in the context of the decline in power of the king in Britain. This power had arguably declined since Magna Carta and certainly declined precipitously after the time of Charles II in 1630. The kings were the leaders and in the main the protectors of the aristocracy of the realm, and with the decline of the king, the decline of the powers of the aristocracy must and did fall, although both falls were interconnected. The First World War was driven by cross-Europe aristocracy rivalry and especially by the envy of the German Kaiser of the British aristocracy's successes. The First World War led to increased taxation and led in considerable part to the Second World War, which further depleted the wealth of the upper classes.

A pertinent question now is whether a similar decline could occur in the United States in the future. The elite in the United States is primarily a money elite, not a titled one. The money elite in the United States is primarily based on earned income not, as in Britain, on unearned income from land. Nevertheless, taxation and war could create a leveling of income in the United States as well, as we discuss in more detail later in this chapter.

Inequality in Developed Countries

Developed countries fall into two classes of income or wealth inequality: those that are relatively equal (e.g., the Scandinavian countries and Japan) and those with greater inequality: for example, the United States, Great Britain, Italy, and France. For the United States and most OECD countries, inequality of income and wealth has indeed been increasing. Figure 9.1 shows the situation for the United States. How equal do we want the world to be? You would be surprised.

Figure 9.1 Summary of Inequality[61]

Has the dispersion of earnings been increasing in recent decades?	Yes, the top decile of earnings has risin from 150 per cent of median income in 1950 to 244 per cent in 2012.
Has overall inequality increased in recent years?	Yes, especially since the 1980s.
Have there been periods when overall inequality fell for a sustained period?	Yes, from 1929 to 1945.
Has poverty been falling or rising in recent decades?	Official poverty measure fell from 1948 to 1970s, since then there has been cyclical variation around a constant level.
Has there been a U-pattern for top income shares over time?	Yes, top gross income shares fell from 1928 to the 1970s; since mid-1970s have more than doubled.
Has the distribution of wealth followed the same pattern as income?	Top wealth shares generally decreased till 1982 but have not followed as strong an upward trend as for top incomes.
Will the inequality of wealth increase in the future?	Probably

Inequality is best measured by income shares, and researchers tend to prefer as a means of measurement the share of income and wealth in the top 1 percent or 9 percent. Afvaredo et al. (2011) show that the magnitude of changes toward less equality in the United States are substantial. The share of total annual income received by the US top 1 percent has more than doubled from 9 percent in 1976 to 20 percent in 2011 (Picketty and Saez 2003). There have been rises

---

61   Source: http://www.ted.com/talks/dan_ariely.

for other top sharers, but these have been much smaller: During the same period, the share of the group from ninety-fifth to ninety- ninth percentile only rose by three percentage points. The rise in the share of the top 1 percent has had a noticeable effect on overall income inequality in the United States (Alvaredo et al. 2011). The growth in inequality in the United States since the 1980s has been from labor income.[62] The working rich have replaced the rentiers at the top of the income distribution.

Piketty

Recently, Thomas Piketty caused a minor firestorm with his book *Capital in the Twenty-First Century* when he discussed the level of inequality and suggested that it would grow worse in much of the developed world and that it would probably lead to substantial problems.[63] His book, set a record for the least read best seller.[64] Piketty (2013) famously asserts that income equality

---

62 The share going to the top 9 percent or even 1 percent is now regarded as a better measure than the Gini coefficient. The Gini coefficient measures total inequality as a percent of total income as shown below. In this graph the Gini coefficient for the United States is about the same as for China, with Brazil the highest. The Gini coefficient is the ratio of area A to areas A+B.If income were perfectly equal, the relevant curve would be the line of equality, the straight forty-five degree line, there would be no area A, and the Gini coefficient would be zero (0). If one person or family held all income (or wealth), the relevant curve would be the x and y axis so that areas A and B were the same so that the Gini is one (1). Derived from File:Gini since WWII.gif by Citynoise (en.wp), released under PD-self. Colored using Inkscape. This vector image was created with Inkscape. Gini indices of selected countries are from publicly available data from the World Bank, Nationmaster, and the US Census Bureau. The Gini index is the Gini coefficient expressed as a percentage and is equal to the Gini coefficient multiplied by one hundred. The Gini coefficient requires that no one have a negative net income or wealth. Worldwide, Gini coefficients range from approximately 0.249 in Japan to 0.707 in Namibia.

63 Inequalityissaidtobeaproblem, butfromtheworld'sperspective, inequalityismainlydecreasing. Theworld'smostextensivedatabaseon thissubjectof inequalityistheWorldTopIncomes Database (WTID), availableat (http://topincomes.parisschoolofeconomics.eu/).Alonger time series for the eightlargestdevelopedcountries is available fromT.Piketty, andC Zucman,*QuarterlyJournal of Economics*, forthcoming available at http://piketty.pse.ens.fr/file/PicettyZucman2013WP.pdf. (http://en.wikipedia.org/wiki/Economic_mobility).

64 Piketty's *Capital in the Twenty-FirstCentury* was honored as the least read best seller. Jordan Ellenburg, UniversityofWisconsinmathematician,hasdevelopedawhimsicalindexbasedonKindle records thathecallsthe Hawking Index (HI): "Takethepagenumbersofabook'sfive tophighlights, average them, and divide by the number of pages in the whole book. The higher the number, the more of the book we're guessing most people are likely to have read." Previous record holder, Stephen Hawking, *A BriefHistory ofTime* HI=.066. Piketty's *Capital in the Twenty-FirstCentury* HI=.024 (The Pikettypassages were all before page 26.) (*WallStreetJournal*, July 3, 2014).

is a bad thing that is increasing in developed countries and that it will continue to increase if nothing is done, leading to dire consequences. He advocates much higher taxes on the wealthy as one remedy. He and his colleagues track the distributions of income and wealth and their evolution over time for the United States, Japan, and major European economies, some of it covering more than two centuries. He develops a relatively simple model to help understand the workings of capitalist economies and the consequences of wealth and income distributions.[65] His work has been attacked by some the political right, but the statistical work has emerged unscathed to an appreciable degree. His policy conclusions of course may be questioned.

He makes the following key conclusions regarding inequality in the United States and most of Europe:

1. From 1980 to the present, there has been an unprecedented increase in income inequality in the United States, with concentrations in the top 9 percent and particularly in the top 1 percent, exceeding those for the United States in the 1920s and those for France in the periods before and after World War I.

2. The rise of income inequality in the United States is largely due to the rise of wage or earnings inequality.

3. The current rise in inequality has arisen not from growth in capital's share—and in fact this has fallen—but from an increase in earnings by top earners.

4. The distribution of wealth is likely to become much more unequal without applying remedies. The first three conclusions above may be taken as in accord with evidence and are illustrated below. The fourth requires explanation.

---

65   Piketty uses tax data for top earners. A critic (a politically conservative critic) of Piketty's work uses survey data for top earners, but it is well known such data are unreliable for top earners, and thus the criticism is unwarranted.

Figure 9.2: Inequality of labor Income across Time and Space

Share of groups in total labor force	Low Inequality (Scandanavia 1970s-1980s)	Medium Inequality (Europe 2010)	High Inequality (US 2010	Very High Inequality (US 2030)*
Top 10%	20%	25%	35%	45%
Top 1%	5%	7%	12%	17%
Next 9%	15%	18%	23%	28%
The Middle Class-40%	45%	45%	40%	35%
Bottom 50%	35%	30%	25%	20%
Gini coefficient a measure of inequality from 0 to 1	0.19	0.26	0.36	0.46

* projected

** Note: In societies where labor inequality is relatively low, such as in Scandanavia the top 10% receive about 20% if labor income, the botton 50% about 35% and the middle 40% about most well paid recive about 30%, the middle 40% about 45%.

The United States shows high inequality. This applies not only to labor income inequality as shown above but also to inequality of total income as shown below.

Figure 9.3: Inequality of Total Income

FIGURE 8.5. Income inequality in the United States, 1910–2010

The top decile income share rose from less than 35 percent of total income in the 1970s to almost 50 percent in the 2000s–2010s.

Sources and series: see piketty.pse.ens.fr/capital21c.

Income Shares for All Anglo-Saxon Countries

It is not just the United States. Shares of income for the top 1 percent in all Anglo-Saxon countries rose rapidly from the 1980s onward as shown below. The two world wars and the Great Depression reduced inequality in the first half of the twentieth century. Now the share of income inequality has returned its historical maximum, which is about the same as just before the Great Depression.

Figure 9.4: Inequality in Anglo-Saxon Countries, 1910–2010

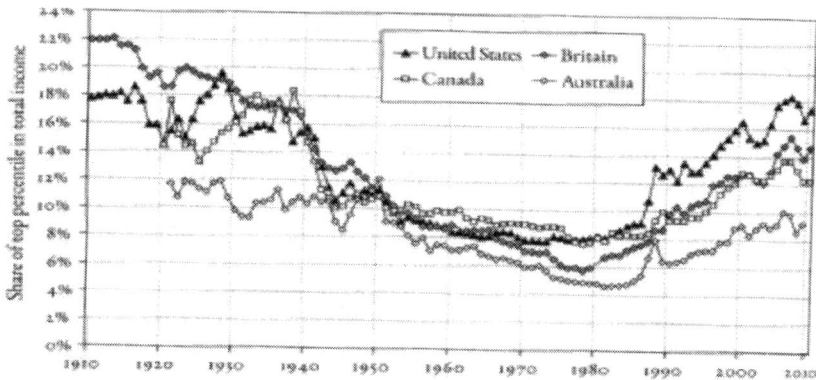

FIGURE 9.2. Income inequality in Anglo-Saxon countries, 1910–2010
The share of top percentile in total income rose since the 1970s in all Anglo-Saxon countries, but with different magnitudes.
Sources and series: see piketty.pse.ens.fr/capital21c.

The graph is similar for the top 10 percent in Anglo-Saxon countries, in contrast to some of Europe and Japan. As the graph shows, wealth (as opposed to income) inequality peaked in 1910 and has fallen a bit in the United States but much less than in Europe.

The Share of Capital in National Income

The share of national income going to capital is about 30 percent in the United States and some European countries. Capital's share of income is defined by the return to capital divided by national income. For the United States, a typical result for capital's share would be about 30 percent. David Burgess and I (2013) found that, r, the rate of return to capital is about 9 percent in real terms. Piketty finds the capital-to-income ratio for the United States to be about four, with 32 percent as the share of income going to capital. In Great Britain and much of Europe, for example, before World War I, the share going to capital was large and even now is higher than in the United States.

Figure 9.5: Wealth Inequality in Europe versus the United States, 1810–2010

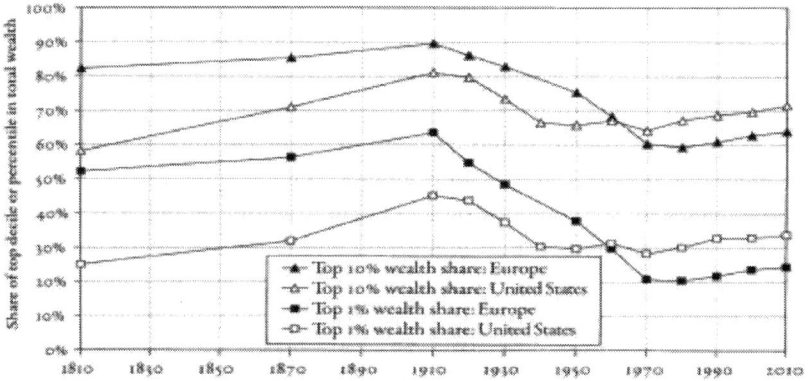

FIGURE 10.6. Wealth inequality in Europe versus the United States, 1810–2010
Until the mid-twentieth century, wealth inequality was higher in Europe than in the United States.
Sources and series: see piketty.pse.ens.fr/capital21c.

The concentration of wealth is always much higher than income concentration. The pattern of changes over time for wealth, however, is the same as for the distribution of income. In the United States, the top 9 percent own a bit more than 70 percent of the wealth. This percentage has been rising. At the beginning of World War I in Europe, 90 percent or more of wealth was owned by the top 9 percent. This has now fallen to about 60 percent. The bottom 50 percent of the population here and in Europe has always held less than 5 percent of wealth. The bottom half in either Europe or the United States owns little wealth (mostly homes) but appreciable income. Piketty and Saez (2003) call those 40 percent, whose wealth share lies between the top 9 percent of wealth holders and the bottom 50 percent, the "wealth middle class" (Piketty

2014, 839). In the United States, this class's share of wealth has varied between 27 percent and 15 percent of total wealth.[66]

A Simple Inequality Calculation for the Future

In the long run, capital's share is determined by the savings rate divided by the growth rate in national income,[67] in symbols K/Y = s/g, where K is capital, Y is income, s is savings and g is the growth rate in national income. The long run (1871–2001) real (after inflation) rate of return to stocks in the United States has been about 6.9 percent per year, with variation as shown below.

Figure 9.6: Key Data Findings: Annual Real Returns

Duration	Stocks Growth	Gold	Bonds	Dividend Yield	Inflation Rate
1871-2001	6.8	-0.1	2.8	4.6	2
1946-1965	10	-2.7	-1	4.6	2.8
1966-19-81	-0.4	8.8	-4.2	3.9	7
1982-2001	10.5	-4.8	8.5	2.9	3.2

This figure above shows that stocks in the long term have returned 6.9 percent per year after inflation, whereas gold has returned -0.1 percent (i.e., failed to keep up with inflation), and bonds have returned 2.9 percent per year in real terms. The equity risk premium (excess return of stocks over bonds) has ranged between 0 and 9 percent; it was 3 percent in 2001. The equity risk premium rose to about 9 percent in 1965; however, that would be unsustainable over the long term. The dividend yield is correlated with real GDP growth. The low stock return and high gold return between 1966 and 1981 were due to very high inflation.

---

66   This is found by taking the top decile share at each point in time as calculated by Piketty and Saez, adding a constant 5 percent as the share of the bottom 50 percent, and attributing the remainder to the middle wealth class.

67   Capital's share will rise as long as the percentage fall in the rate of return is less than the percentage rise in the capital/labor ratio. Experience suggests that the predictable rise in the capital/income ratio will not necessarily lead to a significant drop in the return to capital.

The figures for stocks in figure 9.6 is for a portfolio of normal risk. Now let us suppose something that is not true but that is biased in favor of the bottom 5 percent: that all wealth is in stocks. Total household (and nonprofit) financial capital was on the order of $41 trillion in 2008. The top 9 percent would then own about 70 percent of this, or about $30 trillion; the rest would own about $11 trillion but adding this return to their capital, the bottom 5 percent of the population would at best own about $2 trillion. Now over a fifty-year period, if the top 9 percent make the long- run average in stocks, and they may not, but if they do, and add it to their capital, their total capital in fifty years will be a number larger than I care to report. (Figure it out.)

Let us consider instead numbers to which we can better relate. Suppose total household financial capital is $100, and population is also one hundred. The top 9 percent have $70 in wealth (i.e., 70 percent, as in real life), and the bottom fifty or 50 percent of the population have $5 or 5 percent of the wealth. At a 6.9 percent rate of capital growth per year for fifty years, this would yield $1,877 of wealth for the top 9 percent of wealth holders and $134 for the bottom 50 percent. Both groups have the same percentage of the wealth as before, but the absolute difference in wealth is now much, much larger, as shown in the figure below:

Figure 9.7: The Difference in Wealth per Person over Time for the Top 9 Percent and the Bottom 50 Percent

	Household wealth	Number of people	Current wealth	Wealth per person in 50 years
Total	$100.00	100	$1.00	$26.80
Top 10%	$70.00	10	$7.00	$187.78
Bottom 50%	$5.00	50	$0.10	$2.68

That leads to the following:

Figure 9.8: Differences in Wealth in Fifty Years

	Ratio of wealth of top 1% to bottom 50%	
	2015	2065
Difference in wealth per person	$6.90	$185.10

Originally, the difference in wealth was a bit under $7; now, it is $185, more than twenty-six times as much. I do not know how most people would react to this, but to find out would be interesting.

It is of course possible that as capital grows, its return decreases and that wages grow faster. Piketty regards increasing inequality as a natural result of market economies. He points to the United States, Great Britain, and France, where inequality has increased. This will occur naturally, in Piketty's view, if unconstrained by political forces, as long as the return to capital (r) exceeds the growth rate of the economy (g). This means, says Piketty, that under capitalism, as long as the return to capital exceeds the economic growth rate (i.e., r > g), this implies that wealth accumulated in the past will grows more rapidly than output and wages so that capital's share of the economy will increase relative to labor. This, however, may not true, as it fails to consider that the accumulation of capital could decrease the return to capital, r, even while wages increase so that r > g is not a stable condition. Finally, even if r > g, it is possible for capital's share to decrease as shown below, as long as the return to capital is falling as shown below. In this figure, K is the amount of capital, Y is national income, r is the return to capital, g is the economy growth rate, s is the savings rate, Y^k is the gain from capital, and the final row is capital's share of national income.

A rather likely scenario in my view is that the share of capital in the United States and in much of the developed world, will be

142

roughly constant. In the figure below, capital's share of the GDP (Y) remains constant. Here, the increase in capital is 2.5 percent per period, and there is no change in the return to capital so that the percentage in capital plus the percentage change in r is 2.5 percent, which is lower than the growth rate of 3 percent. This is a wholly realistic scenario, as in developed countries, the growth rate is not generally expected to be above 3 percent, and the savings rate, which determines the increase in capital, is realistic at 5 percent. The average savings rate from personal income for the OECD countries is at 5.6 percent and at 4 percent for the United States.[68]

Thus, at least for the near future, a more realistic assumption might be that the rate of return to capital remains constant. This possibility is captured in the figure below.

Figure 9.9: A Constant Capital Share

Periods	1	2	3	4
K	200	205	210.15	215.45
Y	100	103	106.09	109.27
K/Y (ratio of capital to income)	2	1.99	1.98	1.97
r	9%	9%	9%	9%
g	3%	3%	3%	3%
s	5%	5%	5%	5%
YK (return to capital)	18	18.45	18.91	

It is also possible that the share of capital in national income is falling. Piketty suggests that this will not happen if r > g, but he may be wrong, as shown in the figure below. Here, r > g, but the share of capital in the national income is falling.

68   From http://oe.ed/disclaimer, 2014. OECD Economic Outlook No. 95 (database).

Figure 9.10: The Falling Importance of Capital

Periods	1	2	3	4
K	200	205	210.15	215.455
Y	100	103	106.09	109.273
K/Y (ratio of capital to income)	2	1.99	1.98	1.97
r	9%	8%	7%	6%
g	3%	3%	3%	3%
s	5%	5%	5%	5%
YK (return to capital)	18	16.4	14.71	12.93
Capital's share of GDP	18%	16%	14%	12%

All that is needed in this example is for the rate of return to capital to be falling by more than 2 percent per year. The general rule is that *the share of capital will not increase as long as the percentage increase in capital (here 5 percent) plus the increase in the return to capital, r, (here negative) is greater than the percentage growth rate, g, here 3 percent.* In the above example, capital is increasing by 5 percent per period, r is decreasing by 12 percent, and the growth rate is 3 percent. Thus, the sum of the increases in capital and its return is about negative 7 percent, which is less than the growth rate of the economy. Note that the return to capital could be decreasing at a much lower rate (for example, only 0.2 percentage points per year), and we would still have a declining capital share of GDP. It is also possible that the share of capital is rising, which will happen if the percentage growth of capital plus the percentage change in the return to capital is greater than the growth rate of the economy. (Make up your own example for an increasing share of capital.)

All this may seem as dull as hell, but hey, I am an economist, and it is important. The bottom line is that it is unclear that capital's share will increase going forward. Yet my bet is that it will not decrease absent political action.

Top Earners

Even if capital's share remains roughly constant, as I believe it will, inequality will increase as top earners hold a greater percentage   of the wealth. Currently, a major contributor to inequality is the falling tax rates for the wealthy. This is beyond their ability to shelter money abroad.

The very rich appear to be buying down their tax rates as shown below. In is instructive to look to the top 400 US tax returns, the top 0.00003 percent. IRS data shows the following:

Figure 9.11: Taxes Paid for Top 400[69]

Tax Year	Percentage of Tax Payers in the Top 400 Paying Less Than 25% of Gross Adjusted Income in Taxes	Percentage of Tax Payers in the Top 400 Paying Less Than 10% of Gross Adjusted Income in Taxes
1992	24%	2%
1993	20%	2%
1994	21%	2%
1995	14%	2%
1996	24%	0.8%
1997	57%	3%
1998	73%	3%
1999	69%	3%
2000	69%	3%
2001	63%	5%
2002	60%	3%
2003	67%	6%
2004	69%	7%
2005	74%	6%
2006	76%	8%
2007	82%	6%
2008	74%	8%
2009	60%	6%
2010	78%	9%
2011	79%	10%
2012	86%	8%
2013	60%	3%

In 1992, 24 percent of the top 400 earners were paying less than   25 percent of their income in taxes. In 2009, 60 percent of the top

69   Calculated from https://www.irs.gov/pub/irs-soi/13intop400.pdf.

earners were paying less than 25 percent of the income as income taxes. In 1992, only 2 percent of top earners were paying less than 10 percent of their adjusted gross income in federal taxes. In 2009, 6 percent were paying less than 10 percent.[70] The years 2011 and 2012 were the high-water mark for the rich paying less in taxes, with 86 percent paying less than 25 percent of gross income in taxes in 2012, and 10 percent paying less 10 percent in 2011. This does not lend confidence to the proposition that optimal tax policy will prevail.

Can it be that the very, very rich are purchasing lower taxes? This appears to be the case. This especially seems the case under Trump. They are certainly paying less taxes than they were as a percentage of income. The above figure is for pretax income, and the share of the top 1 percent is a bit less if measured as after-tax income. The Congressional Budget Office notes federal taxes caused the distribution of after-tax income in 2010 to be slightly more even among and between quintiles than was the distribution of before-tax income. Households in the bottom four quintiles received shares of after-tax income that were about 1 percentage point greater than their shares of before-tax income. For example, households in the bottom quintile received 5.1 percent of before-tax income and 6.2 percent of after-tax income, and those in the middle quintile received 14.2 percent of before- tax income and 15.4 percent of after-tax income. In contrast, households in the highest quintile received 51.9 percent ofbefore- tax income and 48.1 percent of after-tax income.[71] Recall that the largest class of top earners are corporate officers. Then we   ask:

---

70   http://www.cbo.gov/publication/44604.

71   http://www.cbo.gov/publication/44604.

Are the Supermanagers Worth It? Or Is There Failure of Corporate Governance?

One defense of the high salaries for top business managers is that they are worth it to the firms they manage. This could be the case, but the evidence does not point in this direction. It is hard to justify management salaries on the basis of management productivity, because it is not easily measurable for managers. Data for publicly traded corporations shows little relationship between executive pay and firm performance. If executive pay were determined by managerial productivity, one would expect its variance to have little to do with external variances (e.g., raw materials prices, exchange rate, etc.), and more to do with nonexternal factors subject to managerial control.

In fact, the opposite is true: when sales and profits increase for external reasons, executive pay rises most rapidly. Bertrand and Mullainhaten (2001) refer to this as "pay for luck."

What has caused the recent increase in the share of the top 1 percent? For the top 1 percent, the answer is probably changes in the top income tax rates. It seems likely, based on the analysis of Averado et al. (2013), that the major reason for the increase of the income share growth of the top 1 percent has been decreases in marginal tax rates for higher income earners. It is instructive to see the changes in tax rates and top income shares for developed countries. This is shown below in figure 9.12.

Figure 9.12

Figure 4

Changes in Top Income Shares and Top Marginal Income Tax Rates since 1960
(combining both central and local government income taxes)

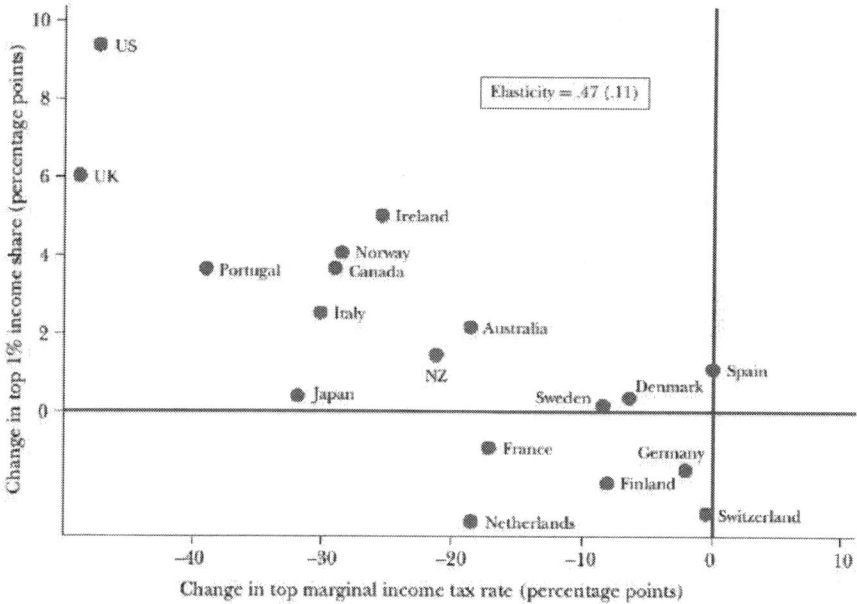

Source: Piketty, Saez, and Stantcheva (2011, revised October 2012, figure 3). Source for top income shares is the World Top Incomes Database. Source for top income tax rates is OECD and country-specific sources.

Notes: The figure depicts the change in the top 1 percent income share against the change in the top income tax rate from 1960–64 to 2005–2009 for 18 OECD countries. If the country does not have top income share data for those years, we select the first available five years after 1960 and the most recent 5 years. For the following five countries, the data start after 1960: Denmark (1980), Ireland (1975), Italy (1974), Portugal (1976), Spain (1981). For Switzerland, the data end in 1995 (they end in 2005 or after for all the other countries). Top tax rates include both the central and local government top tax rates. The correlation between those changes is very strong. The elasticity estimates of the ordinary least squares regression of Δlog(top 1% share) on Δlog(1 – MTR) based on the depicted dots is 0.47 (0.11).

The United States and Great Britain are leaders in the increase of top income shares.

Why the Concentration of Wealth May Increase

The Second Fundamental Law of Capitalism: In the long run, the capital income ratio β is determined by the ratio of the savings rate s to the growth rate g.

Thus, $\beta = s/g$. This equation is an equilibrium condition for the long run. As s and g fall, the capital share will rise over time until the equation is satisfied. As the growth rate of national income falls, the capital income ratio rises for any given savings rate.[72] As Piketty says (166), "in a quasi-stagnant society, wealth accumulated in the past will inevitably acquire disproportionate importance." Moreover, small changes in the rate of growth can have large effects on the capital/income ratio. In more developed countries, the natural growth rate tends to fall, along with the savings rate. Thus, in the long run, we can expect the equilibrium share of capital to rise. With this there is usually an increase in the importance of inherited wealth as Piketty notes.

Piketty's Predictions

What are the concerns? Piketty sees inequality increasing, leading in some sense to a new age of aristocrats. He makes predictions about the evolution of wealth and income distribution in the twenty-first century. High capital/income ratio together with very high concentration of capital ownership may not be healthy for democracy. The importance of concentrated wealth and income may lead to greater political influence for the top holders of wealth and income. Spending to influence elections or to secure special treatment (e.g., tax gimmicks) may increase. Piketty thus predicts a return to patrimonial capitalism with(1) a high concentration of capital ownership through inheritance; (2) oligarchy; and (3) disproportionate influence favoring the high- income, high wealth groups. Does this have to happen?

The increase in wealth share is not inevitable. The significant variations between countries suggest that institutional and political differences played a key role. A recent report by the International Monetary Fund research department

---

72 The growth rate, g, has two components, the growth rate of population and the growth rate of income per capita. That is the growth rate in national income, $G = Pg + lp$. So if the growth rate in per capita income is 2 percent, and the growth rate in population is 1 percent, the economic growth rate would be 3 percent.

("Redistribution, Inequality, and Growth," April 2014, prepared by Ostry, Andrew Berg, Charalambos, and Tsangarides) finds that more unequal societies tend to redistribute more. Thus, as inequality grows in developed countries, redistribution measures may increase. Such redistribution appears generally benign in terms of its impact on growth; only in cases of extreme equality is there some evidence that it may have direct negative effects on growth. Clearly, the simplest redistribution measure is an increase in taxes at top levels.

So What?

David Henderson (2014), in a review of Piketty's book in Regulation, (Fall 2014, vol. 37, no. 3), wonders why Piketty is so worried about growing inequality in societies in which real income for all groups has been growing. Henderson's lack of worry shows he is out of touch with what people care about. People care a lot about their relative income as well as their income level, and they care about the power that money brings. But, they also care a lot about their happiness and relationships. Relative income and wealth have become hot button topics, an interest fueled by the apparent recent rise in inequality in the United States and elsewhere.[73]

So, is greater inequality bad as Piketty and others suggest? Very high equality and very substantial inequality are both associated with lower economic growth rates. Greater inequality is also associated with social unrest, as evidenced by social problems such as gangs, crime, violence, and unhappiness. Although the mechanisms are less clear, it would seem that in terms of economic growth, we again have the upside-down U-shaped curve, in which there is a level of inequality that maximizes economic growth.

---

[73]   Simon Kuznets contributed early (in the 1950s) to determining the changes in the income distribution over time. He thought that competitive capitalistic processes would lead to greater equality over time. His logic appears incorrect and his time series too short. Karl Marx, on the other hand, thought that capitalism would lead to a growth of inequality and finally to intolerable inequality. His logic had holes. Data collection efforts and analyses have expanded since 2000.

Are the Poor Less Happy with Great Inequality?

Yes, according to Pappas (2016), Americans are happier in times when the gap between rich and poor is smaller. The reason, according to research to be published in an upcoming issue of the journal *Psychological Science*, is that when the income gap is large, lower- and middle-income people feel less trusting of others and expect people to treat them less fairly. The study also provides a potential explanation for why American happiness hasn't risen much along with national wealth in the last fifty years. As S. Oishi et al. (2011) note, income disparity has grown a lot in the United States, especially since the 1980s. "With that, we've seen a marked drop in life satisfaction and happiness."

The happiness results apply to about 60 percent of Americans, or those in the low- and middle-income brackets. For wealthier Americans, the larger size of the income gap had no effect on happiness. Economics researchers have long documented growing income inequality in the United States. During the 1960s and '70s, the researchers wrote, the US Gini coefficient was on par with those of many European countries and lower than France's. According to the United Nations Development Program, the US Gini coefficient between 1992 and 2007 was 40.9, higher than France's 32.7. Traditionally happy Nordic countries such as Finland have Gini coefficients in the mid to high twenties.

But it's tough to compare happiness among countries, since Argentina (a country with a large income gap) differs from Finland in many ways other than economics. To get rid of some of those variables, Oishi and his colleagues used the United States–only General Social Survey, which questioned 1,500 to 2,000 randomly selected Americans every year or every other year between 1972 and 2008. More than 48,000 people answered questions on how happy they were, how much they trusted others, and how fair they thought other people were.

Explaining Unhappiness

The results showed that during times when the income gap was large, Americans in the low- and middle-income groups were less happy than during times of lower income gaps. (For wealthier people, the income gap made no difference either way—though another study has found that giving away money, which would seem to lessen that gap, can be very rewarding.) Changes in total household income weren't related to the happiness ups and downs. The results are correlational rather than clearly causal, so researchers can't be sure that the income gap directly caused unhappiness. The best guess is that when the income gap grew, low- and middle-class people became increasingly distrustful of their fellow Americans. They were also less likely to believe that fair treatment from others was the norm. This social fracturing could explain the drop in happiness during these times, the researchers wrote.

If the results hold, the authors wrote, they explain why countries with lower income gaps, including Denmark, France, and Germany, have become happier as their wealth has grown, while Americans have not. "The implications are clear," Oishi said. "If we care about the happiness of most people, we need to do something about income inequality."

Happiness in Relation to Inequality

It seems that the gain in happiness for the poorer part of the population from increased income is worth more to them than to the richer part of the population. As the poor lose relative income, they lose status. As we learn from happiness studies, the increase in emotional happiness from income drops quickly with income increases. Thus, it seems likely that increases in dissatisfaction due to the drop in status outweigh increases in absolute income and would, on net, lead to less happiness for those losing relative income. In this case, there are two ways to change this: increase the relative income of the poor or reduce the magnitude of the effects of income on status.

An increase in equality will increase the status of the portions of society with lower income and wealth and decrease the status of those with higher income and wealth. Economists generally believe that, at least beyond some point, additional income yields less pleasure per unit than previous income. In economic jargon, there is declining marginal utility of income. Would a reduction in the status of the rich decrease their happiness less than the increase in status of the less rich? Are there also decreasing returns to status? I suspect this is the case, but I don't know this. After all, status is just another good, and we find diminishing returns to the purchase of goods in general.

Yet complete income and wealth equality is not only impossible but also undesirable. It is doubtful whether people in a (Rawlsian original) position, in which they vote without knowing what their own future position would be, would vote for complete inequality. There is considerable value to the notion that one can improve one's relative position, which would disappear without advancement opportunities. Thus, I postulate an upside-down U-shaped curve in which a certain amount of inequality is desirable. I do not, however, know this amount. But I am pretty sure we have too much.

Does inequality impede progress? It does if it causes social unrest. Social unrest may occur if inequality provides to be antidemocratic, in the sense that it increases disproportionately the influence of the rich. Economic progress is not simply a product of democracy. It requires only two things: political stability and well-established markets; it does not require democracy. Think of Singapore. Singapore has significant income but wealth inequality. History suggests political stability in the long run seems much more likely to be associated with democracy.

The trick is to find the right level and right kind of government and its level of regulation, along with provisions that keep inequality from being too high or too low. Easier said than done, no doubt.

Structure of Class Inequality in the United States

Mobility

The poor will be happier if they have greater ability to move up in the ranks. Income and wealth inequality is of less concern if the income level and the income rank of persons changes much over time. These changes in economic mobility are of different sorts. Mobility between generations iscalled *intergenerational.* Mobility within a person's lifetime is *intragenerational.* Intragenerational mobility refers to movement up or down over the course of a working career. Intergenerational mobility compares a person's (or group's) income to that of her/his/their parents. Mobility may be absolute or relative. Absolute mobility involves widespread economic growth and answers the question, "To what extent do families improve their incomes over a generation?" Relative mobility is specific to individuals or groups and considers one's position in the economy. It answers the question, "How closely are the economic positions of children tied to those of their parents?" Relative mobility is a zero-sum game; absolute mobility is not.

Intergenerational mobility

According to a 2007 study by the US Treasury Department,

> "There was considerable income mobility of individuals
> [within a single generation] in the US economy during the
> 1996 through 2005 period as over half of taxpayers moved
> to a different income quintile over this period." Another way
> of looking at this, however, is that of the Pew Economic

Mobility Project that 40 percent of children in the lowest income quintile remain there as adults and 70 percent remain below the middle quintile, meaning 30 percent move up two quintiles or more in one generation.[74]

How Much Do Parents Income Influence the Income of Their Children?

This has been estimated. The term β (beta) (a coefficient in a regression analysis) summarizes in a single number the degree of generational income mobility in a society. In this context, β is often referred to as the generational income elasticity. The higher is β, the greater is the economic advantage of children from more wealthy families. A positive value indicates generational persistence of incomes in which higher parental income is associated with higher child incomes; a negative number would indicate generational reversal of incomes in which higher parental income is associated with lower child incomes. If 60 percent of the difference in parental incomes were passed on to the children, β would have the value of 0.6. When β is greater than zero, there is generational mobility of income, such that parents with incomes above the average will have children who grow up to have incomes above the average as well. This is shown in figure 9.13. The United States and Great Britain show the greatest parental influence, with Canada and the Nordic countries the least.

74 Other studies were less impressed with the rate of individual mobility in the United States. A 2007 inequality and mobility study (by Kopczuk, Saez, and Song) and a 2011 Congressional Budget Office study on "Trends in the Distribution of Household Income" found the pattern of annual and long-term earnings inequality "very close" or "only modestly" different. Another source described it as the mobility of "the guy who works in the college bookstore and has a real job by his early thirties," rather than poor people rising to middle class or middle income rising to wealth.

Figure 9.13: Influence of Parents on Their Children's Income"

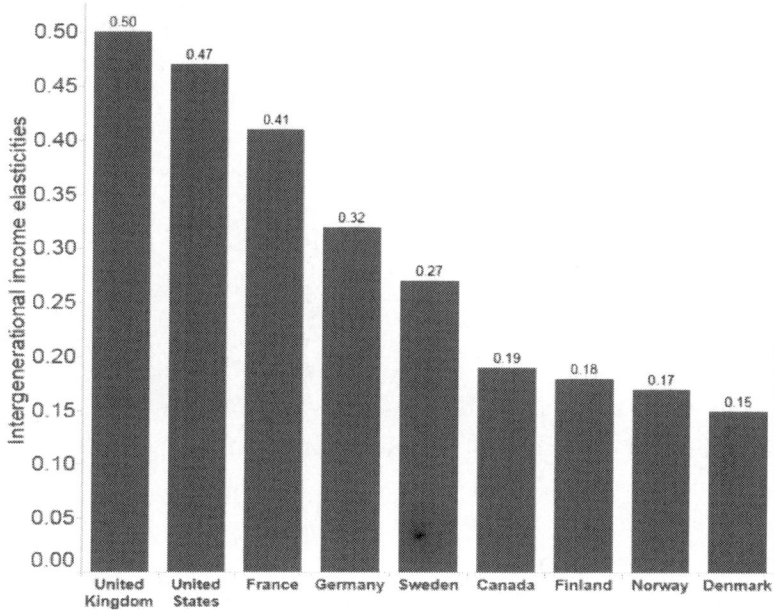

Incomes are much more important in the UK, the United States, and in Scandinavian countries and Finland, fathers' incomes are much less important. There's more social   mobility.

Black and White Families' Incomes

Average income for both white and black families has increased since the 1970s. However, average income for white families with wage earners in their thirties increased from $50,000 to $60,000 from 1975 to 2005, compared to an increase from $32,000 to $35,000 for black families with wage earners of the same age over the same period. So in addition to receiving a lower average income, growth is also less for black families (9 percent growth) than their white counterparts (19 percent growth).

One way this can be explained is that even though marriage rates have declined for both races, blacks are 25 percent less likely to be in a married couple. However, blacks also have less economic

75   Source: Economic Mobility Project, Corak, Miles, 2006. "Do Poor Children Become Poor Adults? Lessons from a Cross Country Comparison of Generational Earnings Mobility." *Research on Economic Inequality* 13(1): 143–168.

mobility and are less likely to surpass their parents' income or economic standing than are whites. On average, two of three white children born into families in the middle quintile have achieved a higher family income than their parents. Conversely, only one of three black children born into families in the middle quintile has achieved a higher family income than his or her parents. On average, black children whose parents were in the bottom or second quintile do exceed their parents' income, but those black children whose parents were in the middle or fourth quintile actually have a lower income than their parents. This shows that, in addition to lower wages, it is less likely for black families to experience upward economic mobility than it is for whites. Social progress in the United States will need to involve relative gains for blacks.

Education and Inequality

Family background and one's socioeconomic status affect the likelihood that students will graduate from high school, what type of college or institution they will attend, and how likely they are to graduate and complete a degree. According to studies, when split into income quintiles including the bottom, second, middle, fourth and top, adult children without a college degree and with parents in the bottom quintile remained in the bottom quintile. But if the adult children did have a college degree, there was only a 16 percent chance that they would remain in the bottom quintile. Education apparently provides an increase in economic status and mobility for poorer families. Not only does obtaining a college degree make it much more likely for individuals to make it to the top two quintiles, but by obtaining an education, individuals with low economic status can increase the income potential and therefore earn more than their parents did and possibly surpass those in the upper income quintiles. Overall, each additional level of education an individual achieves, whether it be a high school, college, graduate, or professional degree, can add greatly to income levels.

Moreover, as we experiment with charter schools and as public schools learn from this experimentation, we should expect some movement toward greater racial equality. The MDRC recently noted that "New findings from MDRC's ongoing study of New York City's small public high schools confirm that these schools, which serve mostly disadvantaged students of color, not only raise graduation rates by 9.4 percentage points, but they boost college enrollment by 9.4 percentage points."[76]

Immigration

According to the US Census Bureau, the number of legal immigrants has been rising steadily since the 1960s, from about 320,000 to almost a million per year. There is a great upward jump in economic mobility from the first to the second immigrant generation because of education. These second-generation immigrants exceed the income levels of the first-generation immigrants, as well as those of some nonimmigrants. Through intergenerational mobility research, the mobility of immigrants from different nations and their children can be measured. In 1970, if immigrants had come from an industrialized nation, then their average wages tended to be more than the average wages of nonimmigrant workers during that time. In 2000, the second- generation workers had experienced a downfall in relative mobility because their average wages were much closer to the average wages of a nonimmigrant worker. In 1970, for the immigrant workers migrating from less industrialized countries, average wages were less than the average wages of nonimmigrant workers. In 2000, the second-generation workers from less industrialized nations experienced an increase in relative mobility because their average wages moved closer to those of nonimmigrants.

76   https://mail.google.com/mail/u/1/#inbox/14918d6d3806ddc6.

Inequality and Social Problems

The relationship between inequality and social problems

Evidence from Wilkinson and Pickett (2009) suggests that countries that are more unequal have significantly greater social problems. These include lack of trust, crime, violence, health problems, mental illness, child mortality, the proportion of the population in prison, and the number of the poor and the fate of children. The relation between inequality and social problems is shown by the diagram below. This figure and the subsequent ones should not be taken as proof, but they are certainly very suggestive.

Figure 9.14: The Simple Relationship between Health and Social Problems by Country[77]

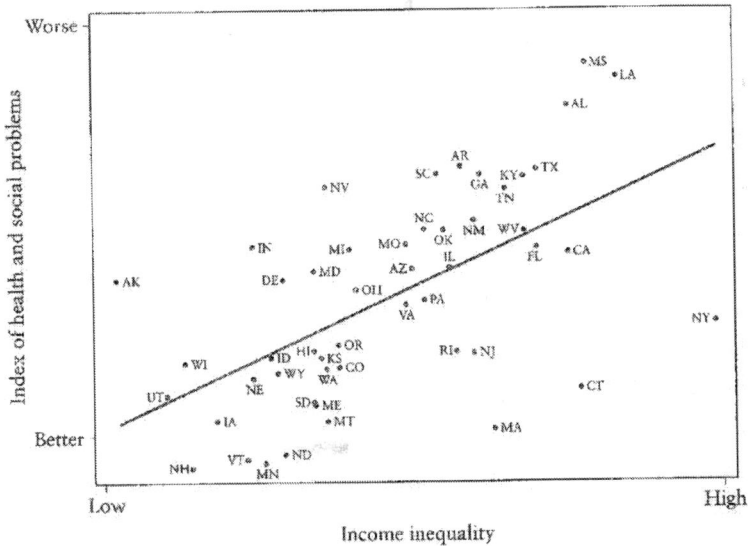

Pickett's inequality test has also been repeated for the fifty American states, asking the question "Do the more unequal states do worse on all these social measures?" The outcome is more or less the same as for differences among countries, as shown below.

Figure 9.15: The Relationship between Health and Social Problems by State[78] *Country*

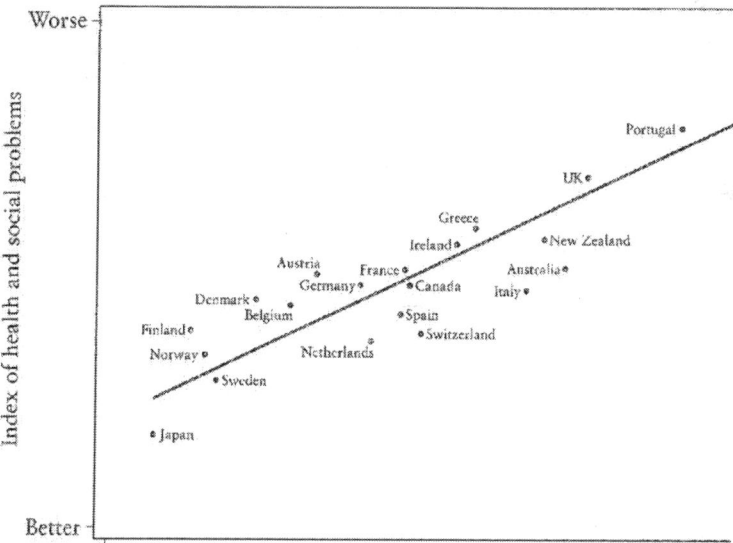

A paper in the *British Medical Journal* that may be found on   the UNICEF index of child well-being suggests that income inequality is inversely related to child well-being. It has forty different components (e.g., whether kids can talk to their parents, whether they have books at home, what immunization rates are like, whether there's bullying at school, and the like). Kids do worse in the more unequal societies, and the relationship is highly significant statistically. The relationship is shown on the next page.

---

78   Id, p. 22

Figure 9.16: The Relationship between Child Well-Being and Income Inequality (from UNICEF)[79]

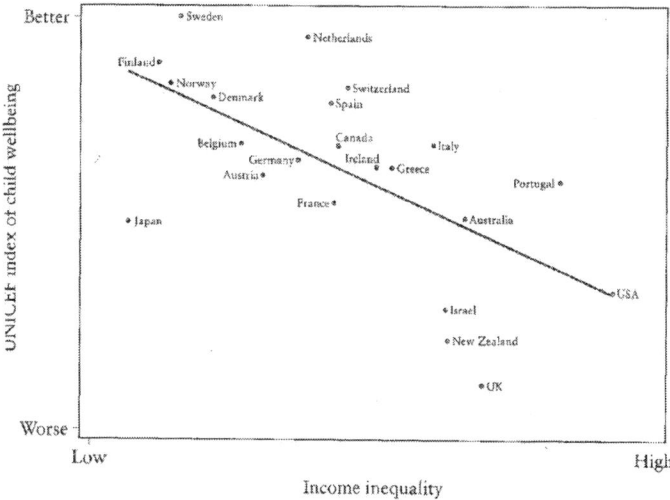

This sort of evidence shows that inequality is associated with social problems. When the level of national income is correlated with these social problems, there is only a quite weak or no relationship. The nature of the nexuses shown awaits a better developed predictive theory and more data. Not surprisingly, there is debate about these results. Criticisms are many and varied.[80]

What Causes the Damage from Inequality?

Wilkinson, who has spent much of his career considering the issues of inequality, believes the answer lies in the psychosocial areas of hierarchy and status. The greater the differential between the haves and have-nots, the greater importance everyone places on the material aspects of consumption; what brand of car you drive carries far more meaning in a more hierarchical society than in a flatter one. The stress effects of this status anxiety find socially corrosive expression in crime, ill health and mistrust.

79   The Spirit Level. p. 23

80   For example, Steirin and Lancee (2011) find the results for trust disappear when the level of national income is included in the equation. This is almost certainly not the case for other variables. The truth of the matter remains to be hammered out in professional articles.

Wilkinson draws on some eclectic illustrations. When monkeys are kept in a hierarchical environment, those at the bottom self-medicate with more cocaine; a caste gap opens in the performance of Hindu children when they have to announce their caste before exams; the stress hormone, cortisol, rises most when people face the evaluation of others; and so on. The result is the same: fear of falling foul of the wealth gap gets under everyone's skin by making them anxious about their status. Stress, as measured by levels of cortisol, a stress-related hormone, among about two hundred subjects was sensitive to social-evaluative threats—threats to self-esteem or social status in which others can negatively judge your performance.

For a while, Wilkinson and Pickett wondered if the correlations were too good to be true. The links were so strong, they almost couldn't believe no one had spotted them before, so they asked colleagues to come up with any other explanations. They looked at the religiosity of a society, multiculturalism, anything they could think of. They even looked at the possibility that they had gotten it the wrong way around, and it was the social problems that were causing the inequality. But nothing else stood up to statistical analysis.

My take is that the inequality story will be found to be essentially correct. In a deeper sense, culture is probably the driver of inequality, and the relationship between inequality social problems is more one of a relationship between culture and social problems. Societies that put more emphasis on money as a measure of status tend to be more unequal. The social problems then result from the "status insecurity," the psychosocial effects of inequality, associated with some cultures.

Summary

Economic inequality has been growing significantly in the United States and part of Europe since the 1980s. This is true of both income and wealth inequality. In the United States, income inequality from 2000 through 2010 regained the record levels observed from 1910 through 1920. (Although the composition of income was now different, with a larger role played by high incomes from labor and a smaller role by high incomes from capital.) There has also been a growing inequality of wealth.

Economists' models suggest that wealth and income inequality will continue to grow unless redistributive steps are taken. Evidence suggests that growth in inequality for developed counties will lead to less overall happiness. The probable cause of the gains of the top 1 percent in the developed world is the reduction in marginal tax rates on higher incomes.

The vast majority (60–70 percent) of the top 0.1 percent of the income hierarchy in 2000–2010 consists of top managers. By comparison, athletes, actors, and artists of all kinds make up less than 5 percent of this group. For developed countries in which inequality is large, the burden is borne by certain groups such as single mothers, blacks, and the less educated.

Some degree of inequality is almost certainly desirable, but what degree this is remains rather unclear. However, it would appear to be less—significantly less—than that currently in the United States.

There is fear that the growth in inequality will lead to political instability and too much political power for the very rich. There is evidence that countries with more inequality have more social problems.

Programs that would help in reducing inequality include (1) higher tax rates on the rich, (2) better educational opportunities for the poor, (3) greater social mobility, (4) more charter schools aimed at the poor, (5) greater recognition based on merit and (6) a reduction in the cultural association between status and income.

Questions

1. Would you rather live in a country with more or less income and wealth equality, assuming your income was the same in both countries? Why?

2. Do you think the United States has too much, too little, or just the right amount of inequality?

3. Do you think your opinion would change is you were very much richer? Very much poorer?

4. Many, probably especially women will, I suppose, object to my claim that in most respects, women's lower wages reflect women's choices. (See Chapter 11) I suggest that you look at the evidence, at basic research and not newspaper accounts and the like. My question is what do you think?

10
Life Expectancy

The common story on life expectancy runs something like this: prehistoric humans, hunters and gatherers, had a life expectancy of about thirty years. Infant mortality was very high, however, so that once past infancy, the life expectancy became much greater. With the advent of agriculture, the quality of food declined but its quantity increased. Life expectancy fell, but population growth increased.[81] The agricultural Greeks in, say, 400 BCE may have had an expectancy as low as about twenty-five to thirty years. Their body and brain sizes were less than those of their hunter-gatherer predecessors, and humans have regained this larger size only in the modern era.

(handwritten: due to more accessible food)

Historic Changes in Life Expectancy

Though life expectancy has increased greatly over time, there have been consistent geographic and temporal differences. The figure below indicates the estimated average life expectancies of various populations.[82] There were, of course, significant disparities among different economic classes and between genders; the average, however, is still illustrative of the general trend.

81   Wilson, Taylor. "Life Expectancy in the Developing World: How Do We Buy Longer Lives?" *The Diplomatic Courier*, August 7, 2014. Available at http://www.diplomaticourier.com/news/ topics/global-health/2326-life-expectancy-in-the-developing-world-how-do-we-buy-longer-lives.

82   Figure replicated from Wikipedia "Life Expectancy." Available at http://en.wikipedia.org/ wiki/Life_expectancy.

Figure 10.1

Era	Life Expectancy at Birth (in years)	Life Expectancy at Older Age
Upper Paleolithic	33	Based on the data from recent hunter-gatherer populations, it is estimated that at age 15, life expectancy was an additional 29 years (total age 54).
Neolithic	20	
Bronze Age and Iron Age	26	
Classical Greece	28	
Classical Rome	20–30	At age 9, expectancy was an additional 35 to 37 years (total age 45–47).
Pre-Columbian North America		25–30
Medieval Islamic Caliphate		35+
Medieval Britain	30	At age 21, life expectancy was an additional 43 years (total age 64).
Early Modern Britain	25–40	
Early 20th Century	31	
2010 World Average	67.2	

One consistent trend across both time and region is that life expectancy increases dramatically with age, as the highest mortality rates occur during childhood. For example, during the 1600s in England, nearly two-thirds of children died before four years of age; in New England at the same time, 40 percent of people died before adulthood.

Take, for example, a male living in medieval Britain. The above figure gives his life expectancy as thirty years. However, were he to survive past the age of twenty-one, his life expectancy rises to sixty-nine—an additional thirty-nine years![83,84] The decrease in child mortality can, in large part, be attributed to the rise in public health. As practices such as proper burial, hospital stays, vaccinations, and sanitary latrines became more prevalent, infectious diseases became less prevalent. For the poorest countries and among children younger than five (the most vulnerable group), the child mortality rate dropped by nearly half

---

83 Wikipedia, "Life Expectancy." Available at http://en.wikipedia.org/wiki/Life_expectancy.

84 For a male member of the English aristocracy living between 1400 and 1500.

between 1990 and 2013.[85] The most spectacular increase in life expectancy has occurred in the reduction of female mortality during childbirth.

Some believe that the increases in life expectancy are reaching an end. But this is not what the data show. For the world during the period from 1840 through 2007, the increase was about three months per year;[86] the increase fits a linear curve. As we saw in the case in John's height in chapter 1, the results of even linear progress will amount to astronomical amounts with enough time. In one hundred years, this rate of increase would take the current life expectancy of 80 to 105 and in two hundred years to an expectancy of 130 years. Great gains can of course realistically be made in countries in transition to development. For example, in South Korea, the gains in life expectancy since about 1986 have been six months per year. Figure 10.2 shows the contribution to increased life expectancy in South Korea for different ages from 1970 to 2005. As with most economies in transition, the greatest improvement is in infancy.[87]

Figure 10.2: Age and Improvement in Life Expectancy in South Korea

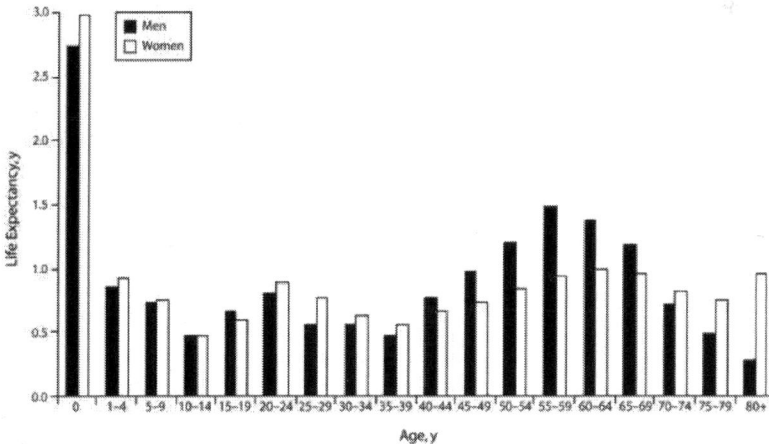

---

85   According to two annual reports by UN agencies, India and Nigeria account for nearly one-third of all the world's deaths among this group.

86   3.3 months per year, as I calculate from http://www.theguardian.com/society/2012/dec/13/life-expectancy-world-rise.

87   http://www.ncbi.nlm.nih.gov/pmc/articles/PMC2853609.

Even in developed countries, life expectancy continues to increase, but the gains are centered not in fewer deaths in infancy, as those are already quite low, but at later ages. For example, in Japan, with the highest expectancy of any major developed country, the three-month increases per year continue to hold.[88] (Monaco has a life expectancy slightly higher than Japan's.[89])

Life Expectancy in the United States

A typical pattern is shown by United States life expectancy at birth for the period from 1900 until 1998. As of 2014, life expectancy was approaching eighty.

Figure 10.3: Life Expectancy in the United States

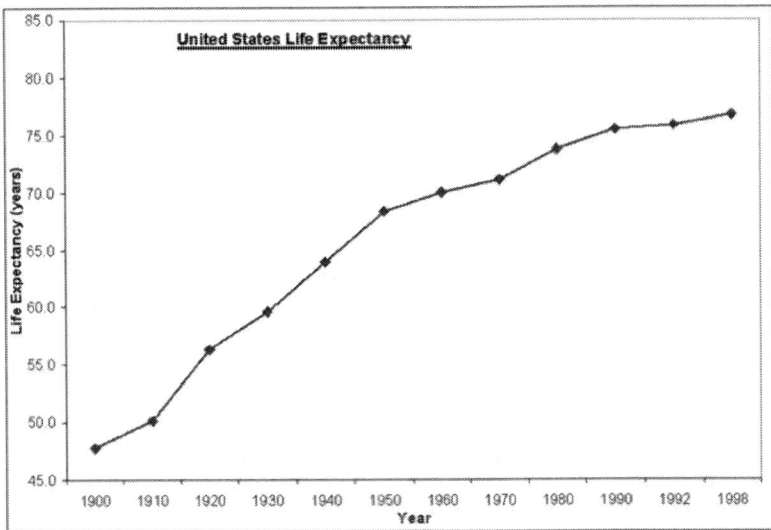

The longer-term limits to life expectancies appear difficult to determine. Some increases at older ages are likely, but any dramatic increases will probably depend on dramatic gains in the understanding of complex physiological interactions and understanding of the use of stem cells. Nevertheless, expectancy has moved up over time at

88 Life expectancy is greatest for women worldwide and is highest for women in Japan, about eighty-seven years.

89 http://www.nia.nih.gov/research/publication/global-health-and-aging/living-longer

every age. The graph below, published by the Old Age, Survivors, and Disability Insurance Program (OASDI, also known as Social Security), compares the survival rate of Americans in 1990, 1950, 2000, and the predicted rates in 2050 and 2100.[90]

Figure 10.4: Survival Rates by Age and Time Period

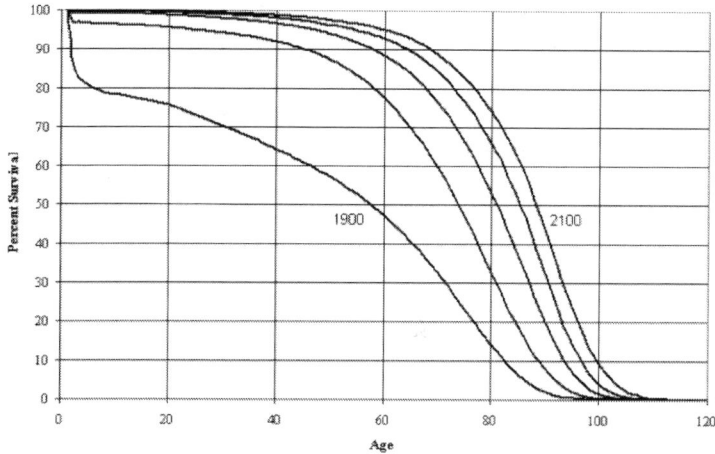

As indicated, child mortality decreased dramatically between 1900 and 2000; additional decrease beyond its current level is unlikely. However, the probability of surviving to older and older ages grows with time. For example, the chances of living to ninety increases greatly from 2000 to 2100. Is there an upper limit to our life expectancy, or will it continue to rise with improvements in medicine and technology? The question is, however, to what end? The 2013 OASDI report explains, "Since mortality rates are found to continue to decline at every age for which adequate data are available, this demonstrates that no absolute limit to the biological life span for humans has yet been reached." Although the OASDI report suggests that such a limit is unlikely to exist, this cannot be known at this time.[91]

---

90   Bell, Felicitie and Michael Miller. "Actuarial Study No. 120: Life Figures for the United States Social Security Area 1900-2100." *Social Security Administration.* August 2005. Available at http://www.ssa.gov/oact/NOTES/as120/LifeFigures_Body.html.

91   Bell, Felicitie and Michael Miller. "Actuarial Study No. 120: Life Figures for the United States Social Security Area 1900-2100." *Social Security Administration.* August 2005. Available at http://www.ssa.gov/oact/NOTES/as120/LifeFigures_Body.html.

Moreover, it does not seem correct. Rather, it seems another example of weakly justified extrapolation. Life expectancy, mainly at older ages, is moving up but at increasing cost per each additional life year. In 1900 the life expectancy at birth was only about forty-seven years. By age sixty in 1900, life expectancy was about seventy-five, a difference of about thirty years. In 1998 the difference between a person age forty in 1900 and one born in 1998 is about the same, being slightly higher for the person age forty in 1900. Old has been about sixty-five for a very long time. A forty-year-old person in 1900 could expect to live to about sixty- seven, and a forty-year-old person in 1998 to about seventy-two,   a difference of about five years. The enormous increase in medical expenditures per person has not had a spectacular effect in increasing longevity.[92] The chart below shows the life expectancy at different ages for different years. It suggests a narrowing of the age gain in expectancy in more recent years.

Figure 10.5

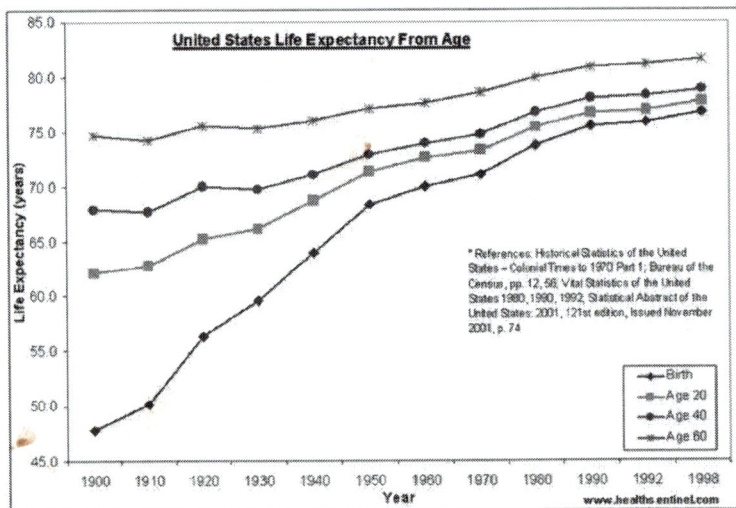

---

92   http://www.caseyresearch.com/articles/why-your-health-care-so-darn-expensive.

Life Expectancy across the World

As expected, there is a strong positive relationship between the
wealth of a country and the life expectancy of its citizens. The
chart below, taken from an article on rising healthcare costs   by
Alex Daley and Doug Hornig, shows a country's per capita GDP
in 2009 in reference to life expectancy in that country in 2009
(Daley and Hornig 2012).

Figure 10.6

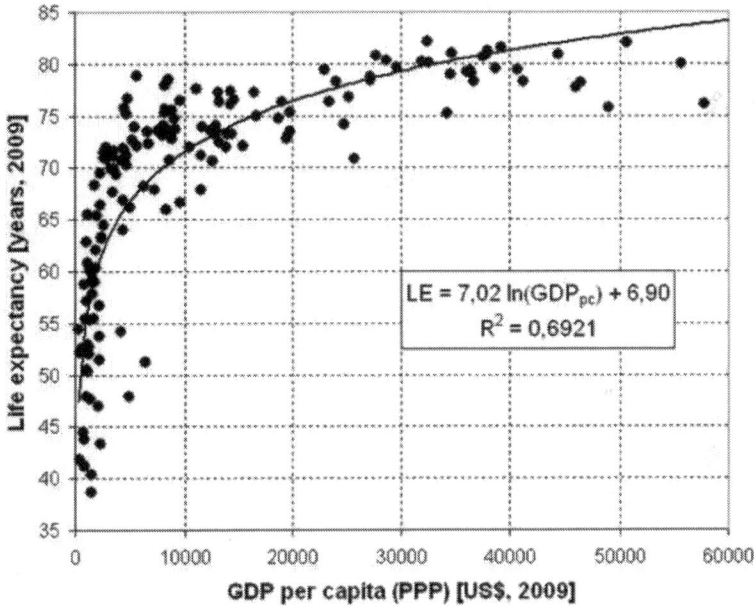

$$LE = 7{,}02 \ln(GDP_{pc}) + 6{,}90$$
$$R^2 = 0{,}6921$$

As indicated, a modest increase in GDP at the lower economic
levels correlates strongly with a dramatic increase in life
expectancy. However, economic increases for wealthier
countries result in very little gain in life expectancy, as marked
by the flattening of the curve. What is notable here is that
increased wealth will do little to raise life expectancy.

However, the trend that people living in more developed or wealthier countries have a greater life expectancy than those living in poorer nations is still persistent. The graph below corroborates this finding (Daley and Hornig 2012).

Figure 10.7

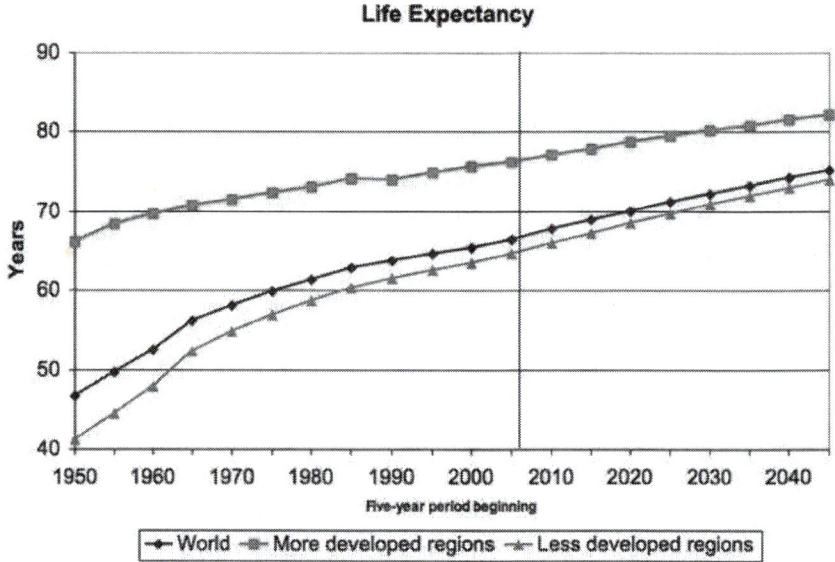

Life Expectancy

Despite its consistent economic growth, the United States is actually losing rank as compared to other developed countries, as shown in the graph below. This trend is especially pronounced for women. According to rankings from the United Nations, American women placed fourteenth in the world for life expectancy in 1985; by 2010, they had fallen to forty-first place. Among developed nations specifically, American women fell from an average life expectancy in 1970 to last place in 2010 (Travernise 2012).

Figure 10.9: US Decline in Rank for Life Expectancy

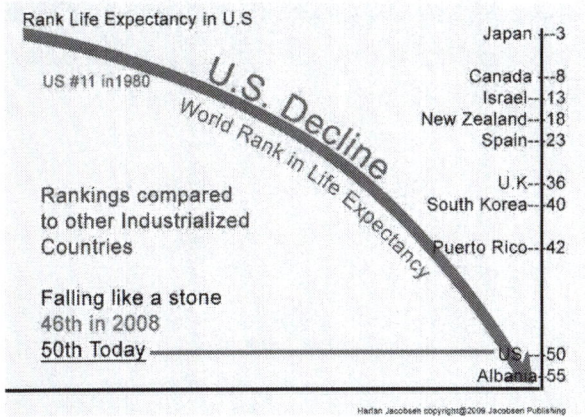

Rank Life Expectancy in U.S

US #11 in1980   U.S. Decline

World Rank in Life Expectancy

Rankings compared
to other Industrialized
Countries

Falling like a stone
46th in 2008
50th Today

Japan---3
Canada---8
Israel---13
New Zealand---18
Spain---23

U.K.---36
South Korea---40
Puerto Rico---42

US---50
Albania---55

Harlan Jacobsen copyright@2008 Jacobsen Publishing

The Cost of Increased Life Expectancy

With increased life expectancy, we now battle different diseases
than those that plagued us centuries ago. For the most part, the
previous harmful diseases would strike a patient once and he or she
would either survive or die. Now that we are living longer, however,
we're subject more to chronic diseases that are more complicated
than their predecessors (Daley and Hornig 2012). The graph below
indicates the diseases to which we are increasingly subject to (Daley
and Hornig 2012).

Figure 10.10: Projected Global Deaths by Source

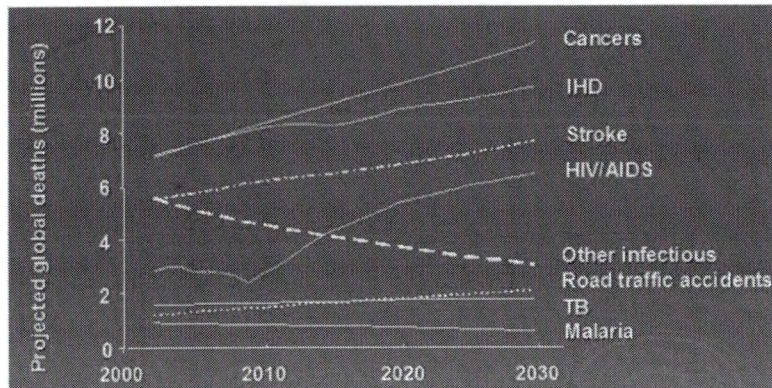

Projected global deaths (millions)

12
10
8
6
4
2
0

2000   2010   2020   2030

Cancers
IHD
Stroke
HIV/AIDS

Other infectious
Road traffic accidents
TB
Malaria

As there is no simple vaccine or one virus to eradicate, these new diseases are often more costly and labor-intensive to treat. Moreover, with current medicine, we're not curing these diseases, but rather finding ways to live with them. The result is that the cost of battling the diseases of adulthood rises dramatically with age. With longer life expectancies comes an increase in healthcare costs. For an individual living in the United States, nearly one third of all healthcare costs will accrue during middle age and one-half when he or she is a senior. Those surviving past eighty five will spend one-third of their total healthcare expenditures in the final years of their lives (Daley and Hornig 2012). Per capita lifetime healthcare expenditure in the United States is $316,600, a third higher for females ($361,200) than for males ($268,700) this difference can be attributed, in large part, to females' longer life expectancy (Daley and Hornig 2012).

Emerging Trends in the United States

Unsurprisingly, life expectancy is not uniform among Americans—there is significant disparity between genders, as well as among racial and social groups. According to the Centers for Disease Control, life expectancy in 2010 for men was 76.2 years, while for women it was 81 years. Across races, the life expectancy for whites was 78.9 years, 75 years for blacks, and 81.2 years for Hispanics.[93]

There has been interesting recent research on the correlation between education and life expectancy. A study conducted at the University of Illinois at Chicago recently found that the life expectancy for women lacking a high school diploma went down five years between 1990 and 2008 (Travernise 2012). The life expectancy for white men lacking a high school diploma decreased by three years, whereas it actually stayed the same for blacks and Hispanics of the same education level.

---

93   "Health, United States, 2013." US Department of Health and Human Services, Centers for Disease Control and Prevention. http://www.cdc.gov/nchs/data/hus/hus13.pdf#018.

According to an article in the *New York Times*, the life expectancy for a white woman lacking a high school diploma is 73.5 years, whereas it is more than ten years greater for white women with a college degree or higher. Even more dramatic is the disparity among white men. Where life expectancy for those lacking a high school diploma is 67.5 years, it is 80.4 for those with higher education (Travernise 2012).

Researchers are unclear as to exactly what is driving the stark disparity. They surmise that it could be due to rising obesity among whites, an increase in prescription drug overdoses, higher rates of smoking among less educated white women, or lack of health insurance among those least educated (Travernise 2012).

Summary

Life expectancy has been increasing in the United States and elsewhere. The United States, however, is falling behind other developed countries. The rate of increase, however, is slowing, especially in the more developed countries. Much of near-term future increases will come in less developed countries. Increases in life expectancy at older ages become increasingly expensive. In the longer term, whether or not dramatic increases in life expectancy can occur must at this time be seen as problematic and will eventually depend on spectacular increases in our understanding of human physiology, aging, and genetics.

11

The Rise of Women

Why Women Have Risen

Why have women in developed countries become more prominent in political and economic circles? Is it the pill? Is it political organization by and/or on behalf of women? Is it the decline of violence or the decline in the importance of physical strength? Is it the rise of morality? Is it the decline in the attempt by men to achieve status by subjugating women? Is it greater survival during childbirth? Is it something else? The answer to these is yes.

However, the fundamental reason is the development of culture. The status of women has risen with civilization and the development of culture, (See chapter 1.) Empathy with women by other women and by men has supported the rise of women. Women in the United States, Britain, and elsewhere obtained the right to vote through the vote of men, just as non-propertied man gained the vote from propertied men. Women in many countries have worked for more opportunities for themselves, for other women, and for future generations of women. The gains in some countries have spread to other countries.

The Patriarchal Bent

The history of mankind has a patriarchal bent. For the majority of recorded history, with little exception, men were the dominant gender in society, with women often assuming second-class citizenship. Early agrarian societies may have held more equal gender roles,[94] but mainly women's gains have paralleled the

---

94   http://www.econ.ku.dk/mehr/calendar/seminars/30112012/Hansen_et_al_2012 pdf.

development of civilization.[95] A reasonable hypothesis is that gains made by women have resulted from the rising importance in our society of communicative, empathic, and cooperative skills, along with the decline of the importance of physical strength. In the twentieth century, starting with universal suffrage, women have been advancing in society to near gender parity with men. The existence of birth control, the rising importance of computer-related work, and the feminist movement of the 1960s all contributed to the advancement and caused cultures across the world to begin confronting the structural inequalities caused by centuries of male favoritism. Today, a country's success is in part associated with its level of gender equality. Countries with greater rights for women are more likely to be stronger economically, though the direction of causality is unclear—it seems to me more likely that stronger economies affect the status of women more than vice versa, though both or either is possible.

Full equality between the sexes still escapes modern society, but there is no doubt that women and men share more of the same benefits than ever before. Every year brings a new measurable milestone of women's achievement in politics, education, business, and culture. These gains should not detract from the remaining work to be done to eradicate the negative effects of an unchecked patriarchal system, but the gains also should not be denied and should be celebrated.

---

95   Some psychoanalysts have suggested that suppression of women resides in both men's and women's fear of resurrecting the necessarily controlling mother. Alexander Dumas (1802–1870) noted, "It is rare that one can see, in a little boy, the promise of a man, but in a little girl one can almost see the threat of a woman." Has this sort of fear always existed? Does it explain the repression of women?

The Closing of the Gender Wage Gap[96]

For time out of mind, women's wages have been lower than men's and still are to this day. In the past few jobs were even open to women. For my mother, the only jobs available were as a secretary, school teacher, or sales clerk. Women's wages in the 1950s were less than 60 percent of those of men. The figure below shows the ratio of women's to men's earning in the United States from 1955 through 2013. As can be seen, there has been substantial growth in the ratio of women's earnings to men's.

Figure 11.1

Figure 1: The Gender Earnings Ratio, 1955-2013, Full-Time Workers

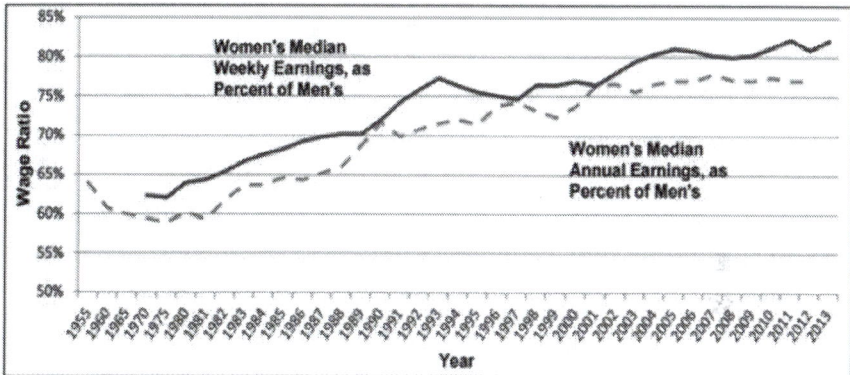

Figure 9.2 breaks down the current income gap by ethnicity. Real earnings (earnings adjusted to constant 2013 dollars so that the effect of inflation has been eliminated) show different stories for women and men.

96 "Differences by Race and Ethnicity: No Growth in Real Wages for Women." April 1997. *American Sociological Review* 62: 209–17.

Figure 11.2: Median Weekly Earnings (Annual Average) and Gender Earnings Ratio for Full- Time Workers, Sixteen Years and Older by Race/Ethnic Background, 2012 and 2013

Race/ethnic background	2013				2012, adjusted to 2013 dollars**			
	Women	Men	Female earnings as % of male earnings of same race/ethnicity	Female earnings as % of white male earnings	Women	Men	Female earnings as % of male earnings of same race/ethnicity	Female earnings as % of white male earnings
All races/ ethnicities	706	860	0.821	-	701	867	0.809	-
White	722	884	0.817	0.817	720	892	0.808	0.808
Black	606	664	0.913	0.686	608	675	0.901	0.681
Hispanic	541	594	0.911	0.612	529	601	0.88	0.593
Asian	819	1059	0.773	0.926	781	1070	0.73	0.876

Notes: These categories are not exclusive because workers who identified themselves as Hispanic/Latino are classified by both ethnicity and race and may be of any race. **Adjustments to 2013 dollars are computed on the basis of the Consumer Price Index for all urban consumers (CPI-U) that is published by U.S. Bureau of Labor Statistics

Source: U.S. Bureau of Labor Statistics, Median usual weekly earnings of full-time wage and salary workers by selected characteristics, annual averages <http://www.bls.gov/news.release/wkyeng.t07.htm>

Women's real earnings grew considerably, from $30,136 in 1980 to $37,146 in 2002. During those same years, men's earnings fell, rose, fell, and rose again, ending in 2000 at $50,388— about the same place they were in 1980 The wage gap narrowed when women's real earnings were growing and men's were not. (These figures are a bit misleading, as they do not show changes in benefits—health insurance, for example.)

Figure 11.3: Women's Median Earnings as Percent of Men's Median Earnings

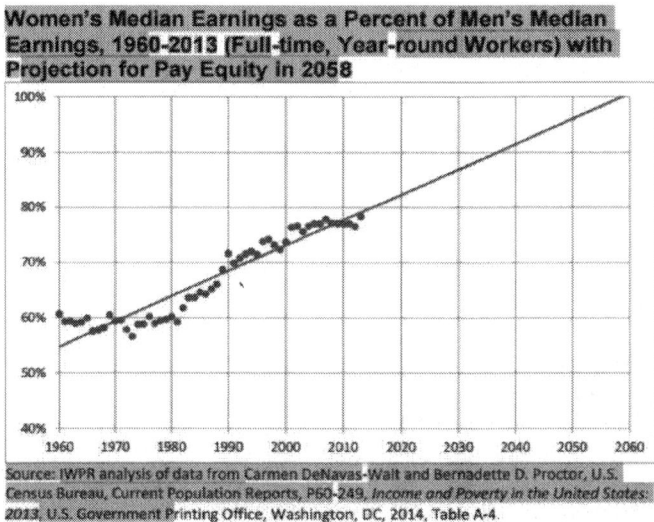

Source: IWPR analysis of data from Carmen DeNavas-Walt and Bernadette D. Proctor, U.S. Census Bureau, Current Population Reports, P60-249, *Income and Poverty in the United States: 2013*, U.S. Government Printing Office, Washington, DC, 2014, Table A-4.

At this rate of growth, the ratio of women's earning to men's would reach parity by about 2058, as shown above. The gap is less for younger women at about 7 percent.[97] The reader will, however, recall from chapter 2 the dangers of extrapolation. However, each cohort of young women finds the pay gap widening as they work longer. To make a meaningful extrapolation, one should know the sources of the current wage gap. If the gap is due to discrimination, social policy is the best option for its mitigation. If, however, it is due mainly to other causes, other remedies can be considered.

Is It Discrimination or Women's Choice?

Clearly some of both. Yet, the men-women wage gap is largely due to the martial effect, the choice of professions, and the fact that more women than men work part time.

This and the following figures can be found at
https://www.youtube.com/watch?v =hRfERVPq2VE.

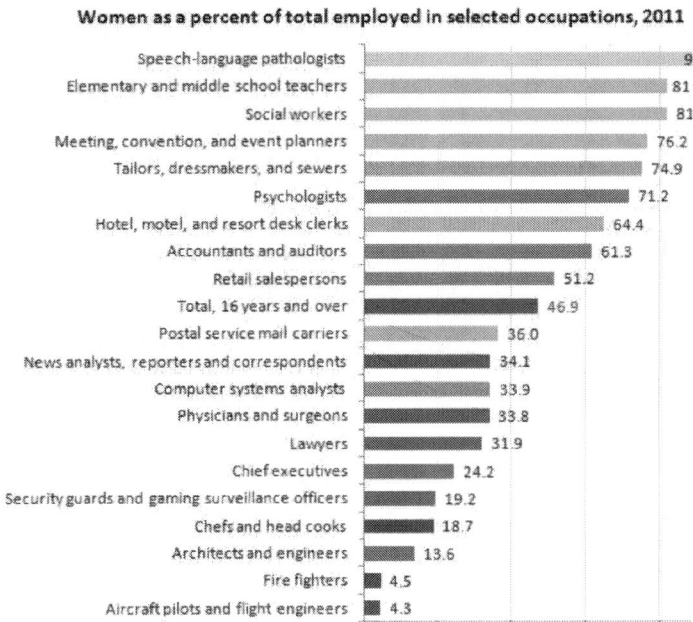

Women as a percent of total employed in selected occupations, 2011

Occupation	Percent
Speech-language pathologists	9
Elementary and middle school teachers	81
Social workers	81
Meeting, convention, and event planners	76.2
Tailors, dressmakers, and sewers	74.9
Psychologists	71.2
Hotel, motel, and resort desk clerks	64.4
Accountants and auditors	61.3
Retail salespersons	51.2
Total, 16 years and over	46.9
Postal service mail carriers	36.0
News analysts, reporters and correspondents	34.1
Computer systems analysts	33.9
Physicians and surgeons	33.8
Lawyers	31.9
Chief executives	24.2
Security guards and gaming surveillance officers	19.2
Chefs and head cooks	18.7
Architects and engineers	13.6
Fire fighters	4.5
Aircraft pilots and flight engineers	4.3

97   http://www.pewresearch.org/fact-tank/2015/04/14/on-equal-pay-day-everything-you-need-to- know-about-the-gender-pay-gap/.

For example, for never-married women and men, the gap is less than 2 percent. Only 28 percent of women work in math and computers, and only 23 percent work as engineers. These professions pay more. Women choose to work in more relationship oriented professions, such as education and health care, where they outnumber men. Women working part time make more than men working part time: $234 per week for women versus $225 per week for men. More men than women, 19 percent or more, work more than forty-one hours per week. This work often involves overtime pay, so this increases the wage gap.

Hanna Rosin, in her *Atlantic Magazine* piece "The End of Men" (which later became a book with the same title), argued that men were more significantly affected than women by the 2008 economic collapse. She states that of the nine million jobs lost during that year, roughly 75 percent were lost by men (Rosin 2010). Many of those jobs were in spheres such as construction and other blue-collar fields that historically have been held by men. The working- and middle-class ideal of a father working a factory job to support his wife and children is vanishing and being replaced by one with two working parents or in some cases with the wife as the primary breadwinner.

As shown by the chart on the previous page, women accounted for 47 percent of total employed Americans over the age of sixteen in 2011. Women are overrepresented in several of the fields listed, including elementary and middle school teachers, where women make up 82 percent of the workforce. It should be noted that women still lag behind men in some of the faster-growing and more lucrative fields, including law, computer science, and business. In 2011, only 24 percent of chief executives were women. This number is even lower among Fortune 500 and Fortune 1000 companies, where in 2014, women held only 5.2 percent and 5.4 percent of CEO positions, respectively.[98]

---

98   http://www.catalyst.org/knowledge/women-ceos-fortune-1000

Yet by now, in the year 2016, discrimination would appear to explain little if any of the wage gap. Gary Becker (1985) predicts that, to the extent that mothers spend more time outside the labor market, the difference in experience will explain much of the wage gap between mothers and other women (Waldfogel 1997). This prediction has been confirmed by a number of studies, which establish that when employment experience is taken into account, the unexplained difference in wages between mothers and other women narrows substantially. The difference in experience also explains the discrepancy in wage rates between working mothers and nonmothers.

Evelyn Witkin, a pioneering geneticist and winner of the Lasker Award, notes that in the 1950s, her boss, Vannevar Bush, came to her when she was pregnant and asked what she needed. She said, "I need maternity leave and to return only part time." He said, "Done, and we're not going to cut your salary because I know you are going to do a full-time job." That act alone, says Ms. Witkin, "made it possible for me to stay with my research." She goes on to say that "I made a decision that if there was conflict between my work and family, the family came first" (*New York Times*, December 15, 2015, D2).

About 14 percentage points of the current gender wage gap of 20 percent appear to be explained by the experience gap resulting from childbirth and care, although the percentage may be as low as 7 percent. This leaves about 6 percentage points, or at most 14 percentage points, to be explained, and all or nearly all of this is explained by the difference between part-time and full-time work. Models combined with data estimate a wage penalty of approximately 9 percent for being employed part-time instead of full-time. This is true for both women and men. Women work part-time more than men. Women earn less because they engage more in part-time work than men do. Differences between mothers and nonmothers on characteristics unobserved in the data were not an important explanatory factor. Do women have more part-time work because they cannot as easily get full-time work? Possibly, but I suspect not. Rather, I suggest that women have a stronger preference for part-time work. It does seem in any event that women give a higher value to time flexibility than do men. Is this preference due to nature or nurture?

This same preference might also explain the "family effect." There is, even after controlling for education and experience, a 4 percent penalty for women with one child and a 12 percent penalty with two or more children. Jane Waldfogel (1994) suggests that one suitable hypothesis is that the work and family conflict, whether in the form of employer perceptions (i.e., discrimination) or employee adjustments (e.g., occupational downgrading, changing jobs after childbirth, etc.), may have a negative effect on the wages of mothers. Some of the remaining pay gap arises because of maternity issues. Jacobsen and Levin (1995), Korenman and Neumark (1992), and Waldfogel (1994) find that controlling for labor market experience eliminates much of the wage effects of children, but unexplained effects of children remained. Studies in Australia (Baxter 1992) and Britain (Joshi and Newell 1989) also found that controlling for employment experience does not account for the entire wage gap between mothers and other women. Further explanations can be sought.

Does the preference for part-time work and the family gap mean that women have a stronger preference than men to take care of children? Maybe, probably, but I don't know.

Time Off for Childcare

The United States is the only developed country without mandated paid childcare leave, lagging behind many less developed countries in providing maternal and childcare. Sweden has extended childcare leave of nearly five hundred days, divided as chosen among men and women and which can be taken any time before the child is eight. Surely some paid leave that could be used by both men and women is desirable, if only in the best interests of children. More paid leave might lower the United States' higher rate of child mortality than is found in other developed countries. This high rate among the poor in the United States is a national disgrace.

Politics

In a few short years, the United States will celebrate its one hundredth anniversary of women's suffrage. In that time, married women have gone from being legally unable to own property to viable contenders for all political offices, including the presidency. Each new election cycle brings higher chances of women gaining legislative seats. While this growth has not always been consistent—"The Year of the Woman" is a phrase that is thrown around by political wonks with little to back it up—it would be hard to say that women in the aggregate are not making tangible gains in political representation.

The most recent election, the 2014 midterms, saw many new gains for women in politics. A total of 108 women serve now in the 114th Congress.[99] The breakdown is as follows: 20 women are in the Senate and 88 in the House. (4 are delegates.). Of those women,   6 are part of the Republican Party, the largest number of women representatives that party has had in the Congress. Joni Ernst is now the first woman veteran to serve in the US Senate, and Mia Love is the first African-American Republican in Congress. There is a record 46 women of color now in the House and 2 in the Senate.

Those numbers are encouraging to some and demoralizing to others. While it is true that women continue to make gains in politics, they still lag far behind their male counterparts. Many studies have attempted to explain this gap. A recent Brookings Institute paper demonstrates that many women lose their drive to enter politics as early as their college years. Do women have a harder time finding funding? To continue closing the gap in political representation, women must have the same drive to enter politics as men. Of course, it is possible that politics is less attractive to women, but we don't know this. (Perhaps because women are more sensible   in staying out of politics.) A gender gap in politics is not in and   of itself a sign that such a gap should not exist. If young men are overwhelmingly more interested in political careers than young women, political representation will remain unbalanced. The issue is that women (and men) should not be barred from doing what they want to do.

Education

Even when women began attending colleges and universities, it was not until the 1960s and 1970s that many institutions were made coeducational. Since then, women have managed to outstrip their male peers. They are more likely to attend college and are more likely to have graduate degrees. This holds true across all racial and socioeconomic lines.[100]

---

100   http://www.whitehouse.gov/administration/eop/cwg/data-on-women#Education

Figure 11.5: College

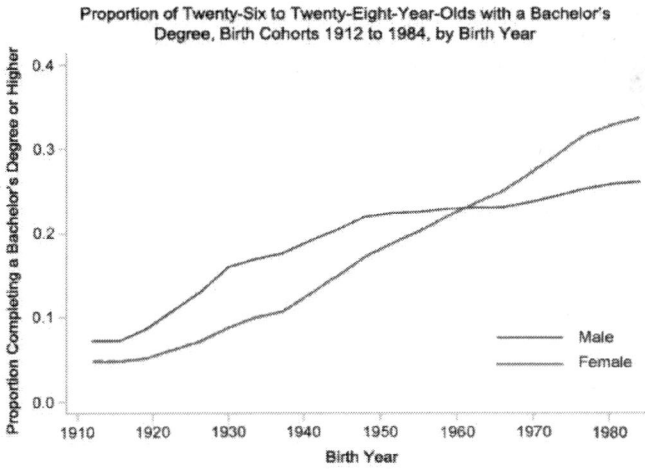

Proportion of Twenty-Six to Twenty-Eight-Year-Olds with a Bachelor's Degree, Birth Cohorts 1912 to 1984, by Birth Year

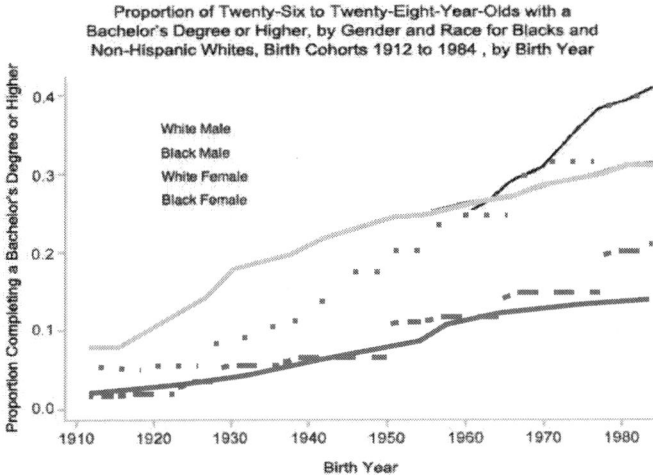

Source: Author's compilation based on IPUMS census data, 1940 to 2000 (Ruggles et al. 2010); American Community Survey (U.S. Census Bureau 2010).

Figure 11.6

Proportion of Twenty-Six to Twenty-Eight-Year-Olds with a Bachelor's Degree or Higher, by Gender and Race for Blacks and Non-Hispanic Whites, Birth Cohorts 1912 to 1984 , by Birth Year

White Male
Black Male
White Female
Black Female

Source: Author's compilation based on IPUMS census data, 1940 to 2000 (Ruggles et al. 2010); American Community Survey (U.S. Census Bureau 2010).

While women have higher representation in undergraduate and graduate programs than men, men still dominate the fields of science, technology, engineering, and math (STEM). Those numbers, like the political representation numbers, are improving each year. Blame for the lack of women in STEM fields is often put on the unfriendly atmosphere those environments have toward women. For whatever reasons, the fact still remains that women are underrepresented in the fastest growing fields of study.[101] Does this have to do with the atmosphere or with women's interests? This is an unpopular question; the answer is still elusive.

Economic realities mean that an undergraduate degree, even just a few years of college, constitutes a leg up in finding reliable employment. If women outpace men in attending higher education, it holds then that women would trump men in employment numbers as time goes on. Since the Great Recession in 2008, women's wage and employment gains have finally started to catch up, or even surpass, their male peers, adjusting for the differences in part-time work.

Maternal Deaths

The development of more effective birth control and increased education especially among women have led to women's greater ability to work as well as to a decrease in maternal deaths during childbirth. In the recent era, this has been most impressive. Mainly for this reason, women have gained more life years than men from the rise of modern medicine. A striking finding within this data, however, is that the death rate changed little in England and Wales from the early eighteenth century until about 1935. These death rates were perhaps as high as 2 percent, or higher, per birth in the seventeenth and eighteenth centuries. If a woman attempted to give birth to many children, which was often the expectation, her chances of eventually dying in childbirth were fairly high. Before her eighth or ninth child, the cumulative probability of her death was 9.6 percent, as I have calculated below.[102]

---

101   *New York Times and Slate* article.

102   The historical novelist Catherine Delors suggests that "in the 17th and 18th centuries one woman out of two died in childbirth. Staggering." Too staggering, as I find no evidence of this. At such a rate, the cumulative probability of death for the mother of 9 children would be 99.9 percent. This was not the case, so her 50 percent is incorrect.

Figure 11.7: Calculation of Cumulative Probability of Death in Children by
Number of Children with 1% Probability of Maternal Death per Child

Number of Children	Cumulative Probability
1	0.01
2	0.02
3	0.03
4	0.039
5	0.049
6	0.059
7	0.068
8	0.077
9	0.086

The death rate from 1700 through 1750 was slightly over 1 percent, as shown above. Since these calculations include only live births, they underestimate the total number of maternal deaths, as they do not include instances in which the fetus also dies. With current death rates of roughly 0.1 percent, the cumulative probability of death after nine children would be 0.9 percent.

The current maternal death rate is about 1 in 50,000 (or about .002 percent) in countries with the lowest rates. It is about 1 in 4,400 to 1 in 7,800 in the United States but about 1 in 16,400 to 1 in 29,000 in Canada. That the death rate is higher in the United States than in other developed countries is a national disgrace and arises in large part from the extensive income inequality in the United States.[103] The maternal death rate now is higher than during the years from 1979 to 1986, rising from about .009 per one thousand births in the earlier period to about 0.018.5 deaths per one thousand live births in 2013.

---

103   At a country level, India (19 percent or 56,000) and Nigeria (14 percent or 40,000) accounted for roughly one-third of the maternal deaths in 2010. The Democratic Republic of the Congo, along with Pakistan, Sudan, Indonesia, Ethiopia, United Republic of Tanzania, Bangladesh, and Afghanistan comprised between 3 and 5 percent of maternal deaths each. These ten countries combined accounted for 60 percent of all the maternal deaths in 2010, according to the United Nations Population Fund report. Countries with the lowest maternal deaths were Estonia, Greece, and Singapore.

What Do Women Want?

As with Freud, I have no answer to this question. But the question of what we mean by equality does have an answer. Equality involves equal opportunities and an equal right to make choices. Perhaps given equal opportunity and freedom of choice, women and men will be equally represented in all occupations. I find this unlikely because what women want may differ from what men want. But the rights of choice and of opportunity are fundamental bases for a mature culture for every group.

It is reasonable to expect that a culture that supports women will be stronger, as supporting both parts of your society leads to greater harmony and productivity than merely favoring one segment over another. This explains why feminism in one form or another has become a dominant philosophy in most countries and why gender equality is a good marker for the continued success of a culture. Progress is still needed, but the obvious benefits that the rise of women in society bring to the world will hopefully ensure that this progress continues to grow.

Are Women and Men Different?

In case you hadn't noticed, and as the French legislature said, "*Vive la difference.*" Some personality differences have been noted from analysis, using the five-factor model (FFM), which considers five personality traits: (1) neuroticism (N), (2) extraversion (E), (3) openness to experience (O), (4) agreeableness (A), and (5) conscientiousness (C) (Chapman, Duberstein, Sörensen, and Lyness 2014).[104] Women score higher than men on neuroticism and agreeableness. These differences hold for both younger and older women. These are not the only differences that exist—or example, women have been found to be generally more pragmatic and men more principled (conformity with abstract ideals). These

104 [104]Other classifications, and perhaps better ones, have been suggested under the rubric of lexical ordering. See Lockehoff et al., *Journal of Cross-Cultural Psychology* 2014, Vol. 45(5) 675–694. DOI: 1177/0022022113520075

differences have been found to be fairly consistent across age groups, developmental trends, and cultures.

Compared with men, women tend to score higher on all facets   of openness except openness to ideas and higher on all facets of consciousness except competence and deliberation. For facets of E, men tend to score higher on assertiveness and excitement seeking, whereas women score higher on warmth, gregariousness, and positive emotions.

Figure 11.8

Neuroticism	Extraversion	Openness to Experience	Agreeableness	Conscientiousness
Anxiety	Warmth	Fantasy	Trust	Competence
Angry Hostility	Gregariousness	Aesthetics	Straight-forwardness	Order
Depression	Assertiveness	Feelings	Altruism	Dutifulness
Self-Consciousness	Activity	Actions	Compliance	Achievement Striving
Impulsiveness	Excitement-Seeking	Ideas	Modesty	Self-Discipline
Vulnerability	Positive Emotions	Values	Tender-Mindedness	Deliberation

Any conclusion about the implications of these differences must be speculative. To my knowledge, this has not been explored in terms of public policy, but it seems that those characteristics most associated with female gender are also more associated with those qualities of culture that promote cooperation and empathy. Such qualities may have more value in a world of less violence and a more humanistic culture. This would be consistent with the rise of women and with their further rise.

Summary

Since about 1900 but especially in more recent times, women have made great gains in the growth of opportunities available to them. These have been both economic and political. They have also made income gains relative to men. Women now constitute a greater portion of college students than men. They are quite underrepresented in the STEM subjects in college for reasons that are not entirely clear but that probably reflect women's choices.

The gender earnings gap for young women as compared to men appears to be due to differences in experience and in a stronger preference of women for part-time work. Having children appears to increase the gap even aside from the experience effect. There is evidence to suggest that women bear a price to gain more flexibility in their work—for example, in working more part-time. The increasing power and respect gained by women is a cultural advance.

Questions

1. Is it possible that in the future, women may play a dominant role relative to men?

2. If so, what would the world look like? (Check out the sci-fi novel Glory Season by David Brinn.)

3. What would be the advantages in a world run by women?

4. Would there be any disadvantages?

5. Why are mother-child relationships often problematical? (My wife, a psychoanalyst, has an answer.)

6. Yet don't we owe a lot to our mothers?

7. I ask again: Many, probably especially women, will, I suppose, object to my claim that in most respects, women's lower wages reflect women's choices. (See Chapter 11). My question is what do you think?

12

The Decline and Persistence of Racism

The Decline of Racism

I wish to make here only a couple points. First, racism has declined dramatically in my lifetime. Second, tribalism as a kind of racism is always with us but will decline with cultural maturity. Let us consider the latter point first.

What if we all were hybrids in the United States and elsewhere in terms of color? That is the direction in which we are moving, and in the long run, we all will all be hybrids in terms of color. American "blacks" are all shades of skin tone. Will having an entire society of mixed skin tones and physical characteristics lead to the end of racism? Probably not; however, it may reduce it.

Humans are all one species, mainly meaning that they can all have sexual congress and produce children. In the chapter on morality, we maintained that all humans deserve the same treatment in terms of human dignity. The end of racism or xenophobia will occur only when the culture attains psychological maturity, which is difficult, as there is a natural tendency to form groups and to disparage groups to which you do not belong. Furthermore, the number of possible different groups is virtually infinite: black, brown, white, yellow, male, female, Catholic, Protestant, Jewish, Islamic, Buddhist, short, tall, and the list can go on. These tendencies to belong to a group, it would seem, are built into our genetic structure. The middle ground is hard to hold; the extremes are simpler and thus more attractive.

Racism has declined much since the '30s, '40s and '50s, in which I grew up. I am older than most of you, and let me tell you, there has been progress in race relations, in women's rights, and in removal of anti-Semitism. Any scientific opinion poll or census of jobs and attainments will show it. Children of today have little idea of the circumstances that existed a mere sixty or seventy years ago, a time that still exists within living memory. By 35 percent to 23 percent, more Americans believe US race relations have gotten better rather than worse with Barack Obama's election as president.

However, a contrasting viewpoint maintains that racism is as strong as it ever was. I find this to be nonsense. This idea is that previous racism was "old-fashioned racism." There is agreement and data and experience that suggests that this sort of racism is considerably less than it was. Yet it is held that the form of racism has changed. Racism to be sure is more subtle today. The academic literature (Conahay, Hardee, and Batts 2012) tends to say that whether or not racism has declined

> *depends on how prejudice is measured and who does the measuring. To the extent that the assessment is made using old-fashioned items and under conditions that engender socially desirable answers, as in most public opinion polls, the decline will appear to be much greater than with ideologically ambiguous measures and less pressure for social desirability.*

The New Racism

So it is held that there is a new racism that is simply a layer underneath the old. Its existence shows that racism has declined, yet it still persists. Taylor et al. (1978) reported a dramatic decline in prejudiced responses to four out of five items that have been asked regularly by the National Opinion Research Center since 1963. The fifth item has fluctuated over the years but has declined very little. The four that have declined measure old-fashioned racism. They deal with school desegregation, inviting blacks home to dinner, the right to keep blacks out of neighborhoods, and anti-miscegenation laws.

The item that is held to not show a decrease in prejudice is the agreement to one of the modern racism scale statements: "Blacks shouldn't push themselves where they're not wanted." Is agreement with such a statement racist? Racism as a deep evil has its basis in status seeking. Is it morally acceptable not to want certain types of associations with people of a different color? For women to eschew men in women's only clubs and vice versa, for sports fans to separate from non-sports fans and so forth? Such an attitude may be a sign of individual and cultural immaturity, a narrow-minded indicator that additional cultural progress is needed. However, it also may show evidence of status seeking, and not all status seeking is immoral. Status can be linked to memberships and can be about belonging. This shows a lack of cultural maturity and is an evil, but is it deep evil?

Whites tend to think racism is a thing of the past. Hence, whites perceive the continuing efforts and demands of blacks as unjustified, while blacks see whites' resistance to these efforts as tangible proof of racism and hypocrisy. Hence, the cycle of conflict continues. Discrimination may reflect not prejudice but bias, where bias is formed by experience. Consider:

Suppose that you are a jeweler in New York City. You have a store in which there is entrance only by permission, controlled by a door that must be buzzed open. A young, black man wearing gang colors and tattoos is awaiting entrance. You know from recent available FBI crime numbers, black male teenagers are nine times more likely to commit murder than are their white counterparts. You guess that the disproportionality is even greater in large cities and at least as great for robbery. Do you admit him? If not, you are breaking the law. Is your failure to admit him discrimination on the basis of age, of color, of gang colors? Does the jeweler's failure to admit the youth show racism?

Suppose that the jeweler does not admit the man. He is acting illegally and with bias, and many will see his action as racism. The young, black man may see the failure to admit him as racism. This sort of interaction is best met not just by law but by cultural progression that changes experience. Both parties here may or may not possess social good will. We cannot and should not ignore experience and related bias. To further progress, focus on congressional candidates who are able to work and compromise with others. Discourse and understanding are the signs of a mature culture. To have blacks and whites more accepting of each other promotes their positive interactions. Listen up, universities.

To get political, my view as an independent, middle-of the-road voter is that Obama has been a great president. He has served during substantial opposition in Congress. He took office during the deepest postwar recession. His legacy is found first in a growing economy, although of course presidents should not get too much credit or blame for what the economy does. Second, his legacy is found in the Affordable Care Act, a program for greater equality. Third, his restraint in dealing with the Middle East is highly commendable. Fourth, his work toward passage of the trade act is in the long run best for the world and the United States, in spite of Democratic opposition. Three of the great issues that remain are climate change, greater income equality, and better access to education. I am herewith announcing my campaign for the Republican nomination for president. You say I am not qualified? I ask, have you looked at the other candidates?

Summary

There has been substantial progress in reducing racism, especially old-fashioned prejudice (pre-judging). The new racism is more the result of bias than prejudice and is less pernicious than the old. The chances of reducing racism further seem pretty good, but there remains a long way to go. Greater cultural maturity requires that we attain a higher level of integration and a greater ease of acceptance of all colors of people.

Questions

1. Describe the new racism.
2. You are black. You see a group of young blacks coming down one side of the street and a group of young whites coming down the other side street. Which side of the street do you choose? Why?
3. Same question as above, but assume you are white.
4. What is the difference between prejudice and bias? Which is the most harmful?

13

Population Growth

There is no exception to the rule that every organic being naturally increases at so high a rate, that if left unchecked, the earth would soon be covered by the progeny of a single pair.

—Charles Darwin On the Origin of Species (1859)

The Current and Historical Picture

In 2015, the world population was about 7 billion people. With a growth rate of about 1.14 percent per year, the average population change is currently estimated to be at around 80 million per year. Annual growth rate reached its peak in the late 1960s, with a population of 3,039,451,023 and a growth rate of about 2 percent. Starting with the current population of 7 billion at a growth rate of 1.14 percent per year, in another one hundred years, the population will be about 28 billion, or about four times the current population. Such is the power of exponential growth.

Figure 13.1: Historical Population Growth

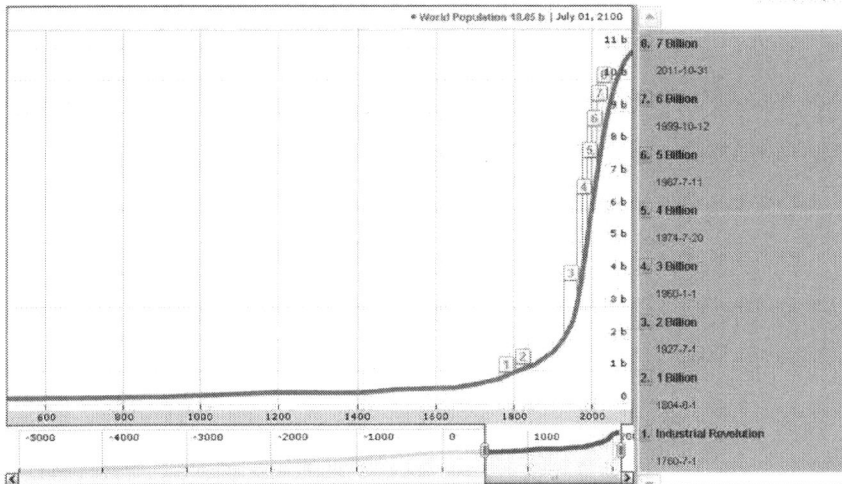

We are experiencing exponential growth, which cannot continue forever. Consider the following figure. Consider first the growth curve for bacteria in a closed environment as shown below. The exponential phase appears linear in the graph below as in vertical axis is in logs.

Figure 13.2: Phases of Life

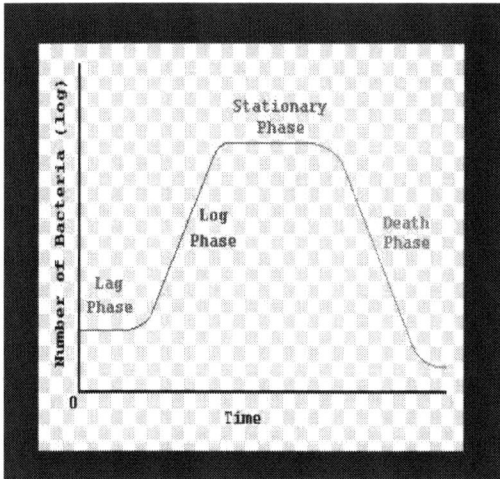

After a lag, there is a period of rapid growth, then stagnation, then death. Is this the future of the human population? In the following figure, we see the power of exponential growth.

Figure 13.2: Exponential Growth

Exponential growth starting with one	Years	Grow rate pe yea
398,264,651.66	1000	0.0
158,614,732,760,369,000.00	2000	0.0
63,170,641,290,655,500,000,000,000.00	3000	0.0
25,158,633,448,643,400,000,000,000,000,000.00	4000	0.0
10,019,794,386,618,500,000,000,000,000,000,000,000.00	5000	0.0
3,990,529,921,072,670,000,000,000,000,000,000,000,000,000.00	6000	0.0
1,589,287,008,947,340,000,000,000,000,000,000,000,000,000,000,000.00	7000	0.0
632,956,837,003,199,000,000,000,000,000,000,000,000,000,000,000,000,000.00	8000	0.0
252,084,334,203,709,000,000,000,000,000,000,000,000,000,000,000,000,000,000,000.00	9000	0.
100,396,279,550,111,000,000,000,000,000,000,000,000,000,000,000,000,000,000,000,000.00	10000	0.

At 9,000 years, a population undergoing exponential growth of 2 percent per year is $100e^{84}$, more than the number of atoms in the universe.

Population growth is, in a way, like traffic congestion. When deciding on having a child, most parents do not take into account its effect on others, just as those entering the traffic stream consider only the average time for their own trip without considering their contribution to the congestion. This is an example of the collective action problem previously described in chapter 1. The classic way of handling such a problem is through creating property rights where feasible and charging for use. For example, if government owns the highways, it should charge congestion tolls. Applying this model to childbirth, parents would have to pay for each additional child they have. The immediate effect of such a proposition would be that richer people could, if they wished, pay for more children. For such a basic right to be considered property would incur resistance from the general population, even though the policy implications might be seen by many as quite attractive. Alternatively, there could be a limit placed on the number of children each family could have and a penalty levied for violations—the approach that China has taken. This would be similar but not identical to the first option but might meet less resistance. The most benign way of reducing the birth rate would be to promote education, especially of females, and wealth growth, as such programs reduce birth rates. This latter is a solution that is most attractive to most mature people.

It is difficult to say what the future is for population growth, and previous attempts at population prediction have done poorly. Future population projections are notoriously inaccurate; a difference of just 0.1 percent between predicted and actual growth rates translates into hundreds of millions of lives. (See Measuring Scale: Ecological Footprint.) The standard picture, however, may be one that is simply painted—that population will continue to grow in the developing world, and that growth in developed countries will be stagnant or decrease. The presiding fear is that growth will overwhelm resources; however, there are hopes that through measures such as education (especially that of women), growth will stop or decline in about 2050.[105] The figure below shows a current projection.

Figure 13.3: World Population Projection

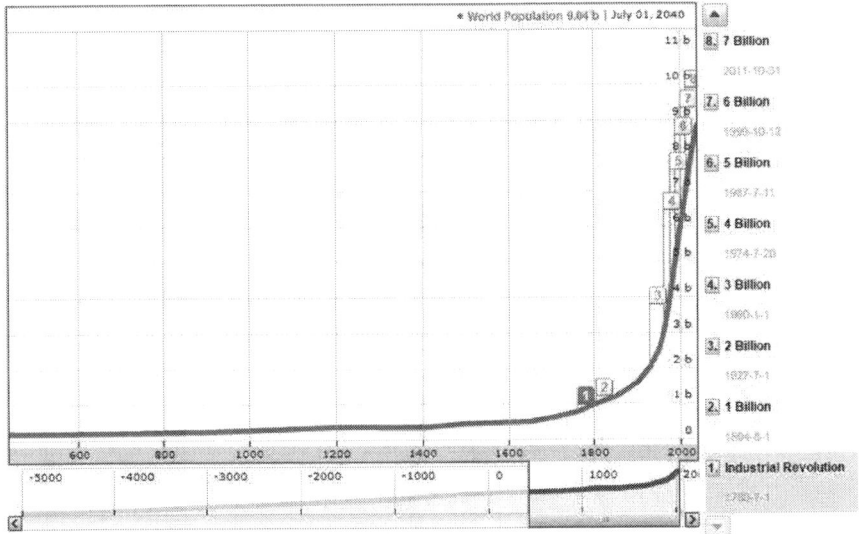

From the beginning of agriculture in about 8000 BCE, the world population was about 5 million. Over the next eight centuries, it grew to about 200 million. It took all of previous human history to reach the first billion in about 1800, about 130 years to reach the second billion, less than 30 years to reach the third, about 15 years to reach the fourth billion, and only 13 years to reach the fifth billion in 1987. Note the great growth after about 1800 that parallels the growth in per capita income (chapter 3).

Though population numbers are expected to grow, the rate at which population is expected to grow is expected to decrease, as it has since the 1970s. Current, perhaps optimistic, expectations are that the human population will level off at about nine billion people

---

105   Income growth is associated with population decline, but this is probably in part because income growth is associated with greater rights for women and with more education.

by 2050 and stabilize or slowly decline thereafter. The globally declining population growth rate is due to a number of factors:

Increased sanitation and health care (by reducing mortality)

Increased education and employment opportunities for women

Later age at first parturition

Availability of family planning and contraception

A phenomenon known as the "demographic transition" also is thought to contribute to a decline in growth rates. In the past, as societies became more prosperous, there was an increase in levels of sanitation, nutrition, and health care, each of which contributed to a decrease in the death rate. The birth rate, however, generally continues upward for several decades before declining. The result of increased prosperity therefore initially results in an increase in population but eventually leads to a decrease. This was the pattern for what are now the major industrialized countries. The factors leading to decline appear to be a decreased need for more children as a source of old-age insurance as wealth grows, the effect of particularly women's education, and a shift in strategy from many children to devoting more researches to fewer children as educational possibilities grow.

The difficulty in predicting future populations is shown by the following graph of different populations levels by the United Nations. In the graph below are current alternative projections of the numbers of people into the future.

Figure 13.4

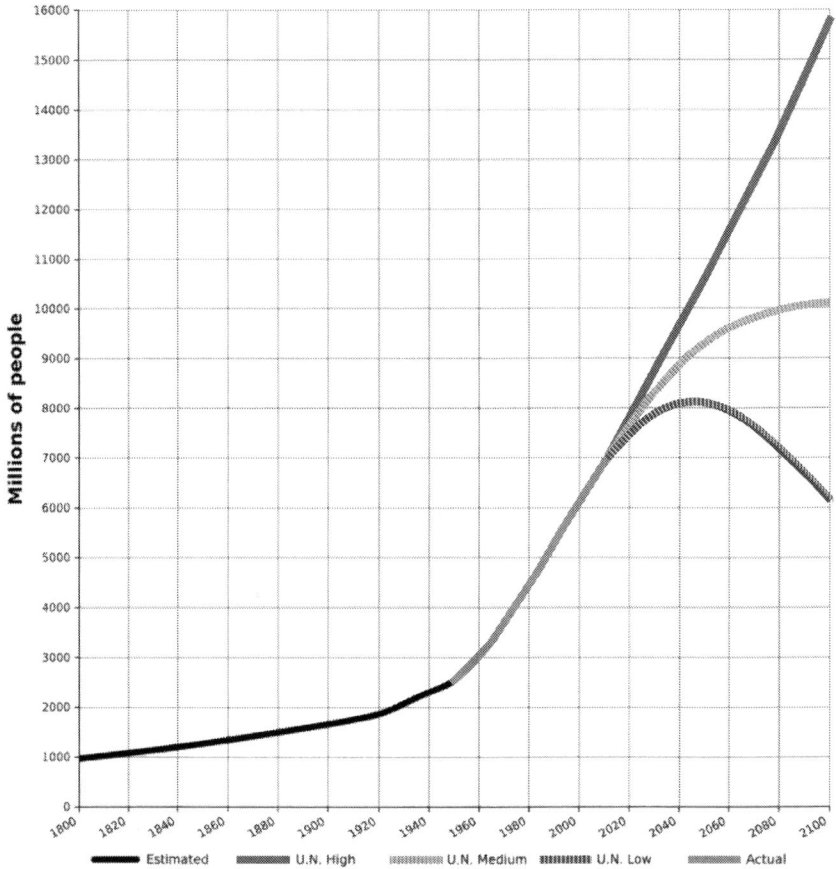

The lines based on data from the UN Long-Range World Population Projections (1991) gives five estimates of world population growth from the present through 2150, assuming that total fertility rates decline from the 1991 value of 3.4 to something approaching 2.06 children per female . A value of 2.06 will produce a stable population of about 9.5 billion, a value 5 percent below that (1.96) will cause the population to drop back to close to 6.1 billion, while a value of only 5 percent above (2.17) would produce a population of more than 20 billion and rising.

A Consensus?

The several agencies that are trying to predict future population seem to be moving closer to a consensus that

The world population will continue to grow until after the middle of this century.

World population will reach a peak of some 9.6 billion and then perhaps decline in the waning years of the century.

Despite the decline in overall population growth rate, the absolute size of the human population will continue to increase over the next several decades, even if population growth rates fall.

Currently, nearly one-third of the world's population is under fifteen years of age. Because this demographic group is so large   in absolute numbers, even if each woman has fewer children than in the past, there will still be a significant increase in global population over the next several decades because the current base is large.

Most of the population growth over the next several decades is expected to occur in developing countries where growth rates are generally higher than for developed countries (1.5 to 2.1 percent versus 0.2 percent for the most affluent countries). The United States is an exception, with one of the most rapidly growing populations of any developed nation. (Do we have a percentage for the United States?)

Figure 13.5: Population Projection by Socioeconomic Level[106]

Growth by Current Socioeconomic Level

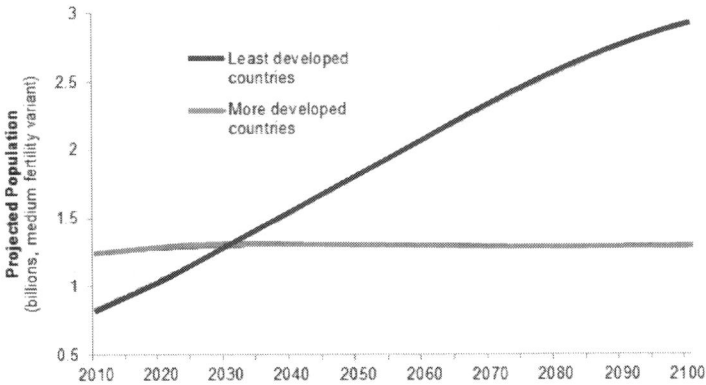

Summary

Population growth faces a collective action problem. Actions by one will affect others in ways that may not be taken into account in the decision process. Accurate estimates of population growth are difficult to make. Most population growth is occurring the developing countries. Projections suggest that this is where future growth will continue to occur. Exponential growth in population cannot continue forever. More education, especially for women; greater work opportunities for women, especially in the developing world; and reduced infant mortality will contribute to a reduction in population growth.

Questions

1. How would you define an optimal population?

2. Justify your answer.

3. What programs currently contribute to reducing population growth? Google this in forming your answers.

4. What programs would you suggest? Why?

---

106 http://users.rcn.com/jkimball.ma.ultranet/BiologyPages/P/Populations.htmlhttp:// and history-world.org/civilization.htm.

14

The Current Extinction

Did you know we are experiencing a mass extinction of Earth's species? Is this a sign of regression? Do we have a moral obligation to reduce extinctions? We noted in chapter 1 that there is considerable agreement that moral progress is associated with recognizing equal human dignity. In The Descent of Man (1871, 1874), Darwin observed that the history of man's moral development has been a continual extension of the objects of his "social instincts and sympathies." Originally, each man had regard only for himself and those of a narrow circle. Later, he came to regard "not only the welfare but the happiness of his fellowmen... his sympathies extending to men of all races, to the imbecile, maimed, and other useless members of society, and finally to the lower animals."[107]

Darwin also believed man would sink into indolence if severe struggle was not continuous and thought that "there should be open competition for all men; and the most able should not be prevented by laws or customs from succeeding best and rearing the largest number of offspring" but noted also that the moral qualities of man were advanced much more by habit, reason, learning, and religion than by natural selection.

To what extent should the concepts of dignity, fairness, empathy, and the Golden Rule be extended to animals other than us? Doesn't having dominion over life on Earth imply a moral duty to this life? Suppose that advanced aliens visit Earth. Surely we would hope they would treat us well, and not as the scientific writer Liu supposes in the The Three Body Problem series. We would hope they had evolved to have reached an extensive Golden Rule level. But I would not count on it.

---

107   This is a redacted version taken from Stone (1972).

As shown in the figure below, there have been until now five great extinctions of life on Earth:

Figure 14.1 Five Mass Extinctions

Cretaceous	65 mya
Triassic	208 mya
Permian	245 mya
Devonian	360 mya
Ordovian	438

Each of these extinctions was caused by climate change brought on by various causes, and each occurred long before the existence of humans. Nevertheless, there were several periods in which humankind nearly died out, reduced to perhaps a few thousand people. Now are we in the process of killing ourselves or at least changing ourselves through human-caused climate change?

We are entering, indeed are in the midst of, the sixth extinction, one that will very likely be labeled the Anthropocene. The irony of our own possible extinction is that the very idea that there could be any species extinction was not recognized until about 1800. The current species extinction differs from the others in its human cause. Within the history of our own species, we can count the loss of the mastodon, the mammoth, the saber tooth tiger, the passenger pigeon, the Great Auk, and so on as part of a list whose length is substantial and whose growth is accelerating rapidly. The current Anthropocene extinction is due to habitat loss, hunting, climate change, and ocean acidification, which is itself a product of climate change. How we deal with this extinction may be a test of our own future, including determining whether or not we will have one. The question of humankind, for us, is whether or not cultural maturity will expand sufficiently to extend to other creatures and in fact to ourselves. I suggest in this regard that readers might appreciate E.O. Wilson's *The Social Conquest of Earth* and the law review article by Christopher Stone, *"Do Trees Have Standing?"* and subsequent books on this topic by Stone.[108]

Will this extinction continue? Surely it will unless we develop the level of mature to empathize and sympathize with other species. It will recognize the level of dignity associated with various habitats, as in the public outcry over the Seattle Zoo's elephants being shipped to another zoo (Oklahoma City) rather than to an elephant sanctuary where they would have more room to roam and to interact with other elephants. Could we expand our morality to apply William Talbott's Expanded Original Position (2010) to other animals? Such an extension could happen only if we can gain greater traction in dealing with our collective action problems such as climate change.

---

108   (1972) 45 Southern California Law Review 450.

Summary

There have been five major extinctions. We are in the middle of a sixth. If we do not gain the maturity to reverse this perhaps we will also be unable to prevent out own.

Questions

1. We are in the midst of a sixth extinction of species. How will our own species be affected?

2. Explain the relationship between collective actions problems and climate change.

3. How could we implement Talbott's Expanded Original Position?

4. Darwin struggled to understand the extent to which cultural selection can change us. What is your view?

15
Climate Change[109]

Snow had fallen, snow on snow, snow on snow,
In the bleak midwinter, long ago."
—Christina Rossetti, In the Bleak Mid-Winter

Introduction

The climate change literature is a mess for those that are not climate scientists. Many opinions, uncertain facts, ideological rants. Here I try to cut through this. The questions I ask are how much should we spend to limit climate change and how should it be spent? Should we spend a huge fraction of our GDP each year to control or attempt to control climate change? Clearly, we should spend more wisely than we are now. Given proper responses, climate change is likely to be substantial but tolerable for most, rather than catastrophic. Currently, the discussion of these issues varies from alarmist to denial. Dissent from an alarmist attitude is viewed with moral disfavor and high dungeon. By 2100, fears are that unchecked world temperature increases might be as much as nine degrees Fahrenheit. This would not be good at all not be good at all. However, the relevant question is what are the costs and benefits of various levels of control? The world will get too hot only if we ignore simple and relatively inexpensive approaches to curb temperature rises. Of course, there are climate change skeptics on the one hand and alarmists on the other, as well as the sensible middle ground, which I try to hold to here.

---

109 Nice summaries of climate change economics are found in chapters 18 and 19 of Harris and Roach, *Environmental and Natural Resource Economics: A Contemporary Approach* (2014), and at http://www.ase.tufts.edu/gdae/education_materials/modules/the_economics_ of_global_climate_change.pdf.

Has Climate Change Been Caused by Humans?

Yes it has. The only place where this is not recognized appears to be on Fox News and in the White House.[110] The evidence for it is clear enough. Weather extremes are changing from human influence. Scientists are certain that average temperatures will increase over most land areas. It is true that no evidence used for prediction is ever completely beyond dispute (the sun may not rise tomorrow), as it is always a question of probabilities. However, if we dismiss evidence because its conclusions come with probability bounds, we must dismiss all evidence. The George W. Bush administration was a master of using uncertainty to do what it wanted to do and to not do what it did not want to do. This is not a rational, scientific approach. Climate change uncertainties should not keep us from acting, and these uncertainties should be incorporated into policy planning.

Although there has been controversy about whether there is a human contribution to climate change, this is no longer the case. Scientists have established that the warming trend has been caused by human activity, primarily burning fossil fuels, with a smaller contribution from deforestation. CO_2 emissions from fossil fuel combustion and industrial processes contributed about 78 percent of the total GHG emission increase from 1970 to 2010, with a similar percentage contribution for the period 2000–2010. CO_2 remains the major anthropogenic GHG, accounting for 76 percent in 2010. CO_2 emissions were the highest in human history from 2000 to 2010.

Climate Change Skeptics

There remain a diminishing number of climate change skeptics. An opinion piece in the *Wall Street Journal* in January 2012 by a group of sixteen scientists, entitled "No Need to Panic about Global Warming" summarizes the skeptics' claims. William Nordhaus, whom they cite, is a noted climate change economist.

---

110   The series is produced by the UK Hadley Center, the US Goddard Institute for Space Studies (GISS), and the US National Climatic Data Center (NCDC). A similar series is produced by Nordhaus (2012).

He note, however, that the basic message of the opinion piece is that Earth is not warming, that dissent voices are suppressed, and that delaying policies to slow climate change by fifty years will have no serious consequences. Nordhaus goes on to note, that in regard to the key issues, the sixteen scientists provide incorrect or misleading answers. Consider the claim that the planet is not warming. The dissident scientists suggest that "the...most inconvenient fact is the lack of global warming for well over nine years now" (Nordhaus 2012). This is not inconvenient but a mere detail and now no longer true. It is a detail in looking at only ten years when the relevant periods are longer.

The following graph shows the long-term trend.

Figure 15.1[111]

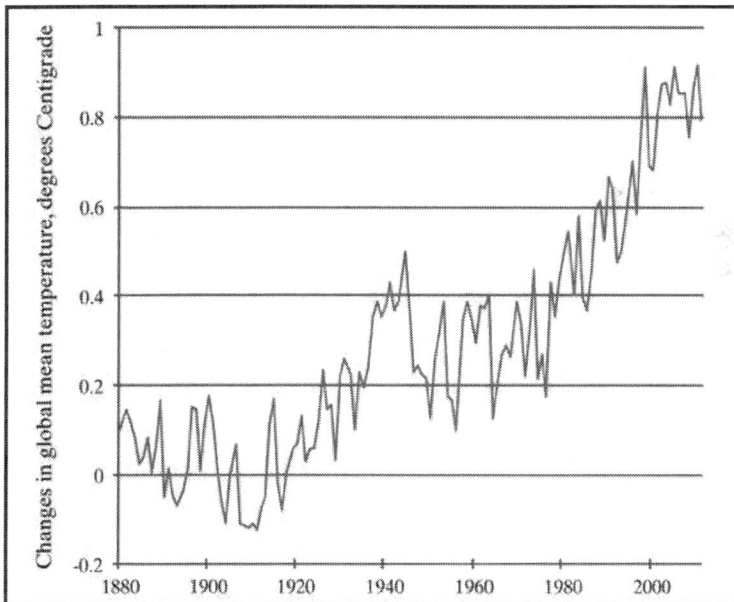

This is a highly volatile series so that calculations over a mere ten years are highly misleading. Temperatures in the period from 1880 through 1980 are rising at 0.0042 degrees Celsius per year, while in the period from 1980 through 2000, they are rising at 0.135

111   Source: Synthesis Report, IPCC, p. 3.

degrees Celsius per year. Nordhaus notes that the likelihood that this difference would happen by chance is less than one in a million.

A second argument raised by the skeptics is that "the smaller than predicted warming over the 22 years since the UN's Intergovernmental Panel on climate Change (IPCC) began issuing projections— suggests that computer models have greatly exaggerated how much warming additional CO_2 can cause." The standard test, Nordhaus notes, is to perform an experiment in which modelers predict the temperature path using human and natural sources of CO_2 with a model in which human sources are not included. This sort of experiment has been performed many times using climate models. An example of such an experiment is used in the Fourth Assessment Report of the IPCC (2013). This experiment shows that the projections of temperature changes are consistent with recorded temperatures over recent past decades only if human sources of CO_2 are included. The IPCC report concluded that no climate model using natural warming factors alone has reproduced the observed global warming trend in the second half of the twentieth century. On the whole the predictions have well tracked the trends, but not on a year to year basis.

Climate Change Doubters

Of course, some still doubt man made climate change, and they mostly seem to reside on Fox News. No sensible analysis supports this doubt. A 2014 statement by the US Global Research Program said,

Evidence for climate change abounds, from the top of the atmosphere to the depth of the oceans. Scientists and engineers from around the world have meticulously collected this evidence, using satellites and networks of weather balloons, observing and measuring changes in location and behaviors of species and functioning ecosystems. Taken together, this evidence tells anunambiguousstory: the planet

*is warming, and over the half century, this warming has been
driven primarily by human activity. [Emphasis added.]*[112]

This sort of opinion is supported by almost all climate scientists and
most particularly by the dominant coordinated effort embodied in
the International Panel on Climate Change, IPCC. The rise of human
generated emissions of CO_2, is shown below. The CO_2 emissions
parallel all GHGs.

Figure 15.2: The Growth in Human-Caused CO2 Emissions[113]

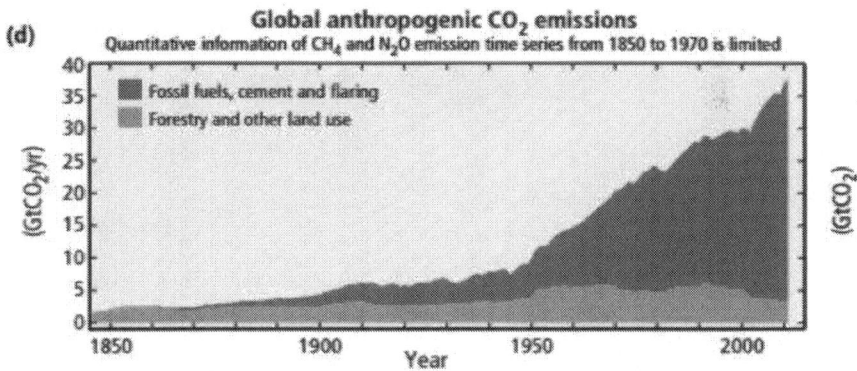

The increase in human-caused GHG emissions has soared since
1950.

Probably temperatures will rise at least 2.5 degrees Celsius (or 4.5
degrees Fahrenheit) regardless of what we do. The IPCC 2013 report
projects a temperature change by 2100 of between 1.5 degrees
Celsius (2.7 degrees Fahrenheit) and 4.8 degrees Celsius (9.6
degrees Fahrenheit). The figure below shows the relation between
human contribution to GHS and global warming since 1850. The
numbers in the pink area show the range of human- caused CO_2
emissions in parts per million.

---

112   Source: US Global Change Research Program, Third National Climate Assessment, May 2014,
Overview and Report Findings, p. 7.

113   Source: The Synthesis Report of the IPCC, 2014, p. 2.

Figure 15.3: Temperature and Emissions[114]

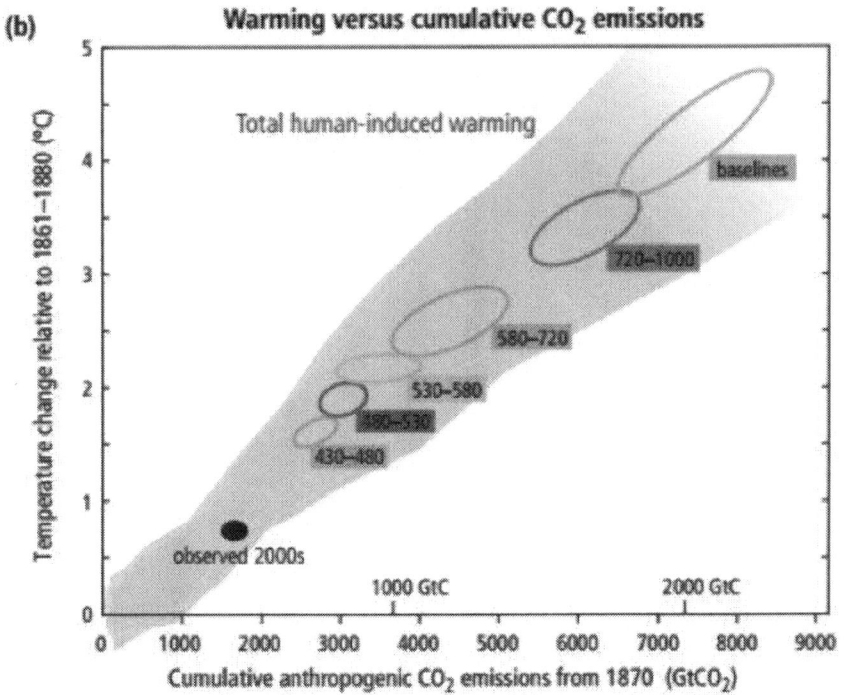

(b)

Warming versus cumulative CO$_2$ emissions

Total human-induced warming

baselines

720–1000

580–720

530–580

490–530

430–480

observed 2000s

1000 GtC   2000 GtC

Temperature change relative to 1861–1880 (°C)

Cumulative anthropogenic CO$_2$ emissions from 1870 (GtCO$_2$)

The surface temperature of Earth is projected to rise over the twenty-first century, even if emissions of GHS fall. A global temperature rise of around 2.4 degrees Celsius is associated with emissions of about 580 parts per million, which we are approaching. One guess is that we will hit 3.0 degrees Celsius by the end of the century.

The Social Cost of Carbon

The social cost of carbon (SCC) is an estimate of the monetized damages from a small increase in carbon dioxide emissions in a given year. This is not a constant number. It is, however, an important number as it is used to direct climate change policies. For example, the EPA uses an SCC figure for such things as car emissions. The SCC number now used by the EPA and other federal agencies is

---

114   IPCC Climate Change 2014 Synthesis Report Summary for Policy Makers, p. 9. http:// www. dailyclimate.org/tdc-newsroom/2012/12/ipcc-prediction-fact-check.

either twelve dollars, forty-two dollars or sixty-two dollars per ton. These different figures represent discount rates of 5 percent, 3 percent and 2.5 percent, respectively (Johnston 2016). Using a more reasonable rate of 7 percent, the SCC drops to about six dollars per ton per year. It seems quite doubtful if a figure that allows for risk would be greater than thirty dollars per ton per year. Can we pass a carbon tax in the U.S.? Certainly not for a while.

The British government appointed a civil servant, Nicolas Stern, to determine the potential cost of climate change into the future. Stern comes up with scary numbers, such as a loss of 5 percent to 20 percent of world GDP every year forever, with the 5 percent being more likely. At 5 percent, this would have a present value of $108 trillion, about 1.42 times world GDP. This is a large and scary figure.

But wait, as the ads say. What about the costs? The economist Richard Tol called the Stern Report alarmist, incompetent, and preposterous. He is right. First, Tol finds that reducing emissions by 80 percent by midcentury to meet the goal of limiting temperature rise to under 2 degrees Celsius by 2100 would avert about $3 trillion per year in damages but that achieving this would cost about $40 trillion per year with current technology. So the Stern Report is not to be relied upon. Second, even with the 5 percent loss that Stern postulates, world GDP in one hundred years will be about $898 trillion, or twelve times current world GDP, with a growth rate of 2.5 percent. Thus, the first conclusion to make is that even Stern's extreme figures will not be such a disaster, even at 5 percent loss of GDP each year. The second is that we should think carefully about how much we should invest now to benefit those richer persons almost a hundred years from now. The third conclusion is that a significant investment to reduce temperature rise early is worthwhile. (Note that I assume net growth will be 2.5 percent per year over and beyond the loss of 5 percent of GDP.) This may be too optimistic.

Consider another problem with the Stern Report. It uses real (inflation-adjusted) discount rates of 2.1 percent for the twenty- first century, 1.9 percent for the twenty second century and 1.4 percent for subsequent centuries. This is equivalent to a constant rate of 1.9 percent per year (geometric mean). The rate that David Burgess and I, and Arnold Harberger and Glen Jenkins, have recommended for discounting generally is between 6 and 9 percent real, with our best estimate at 7 percent real. The use of unjustifiably low discount rates increases the present value of damages over the next three centuries by a factor of about 3.5, so that, as Matt Ridley points out, this would give the same value in spending now to reduce the risk of death of a relatively rich person in 2200 as spending to reduce the risk to someone now. The decision to do this would be nonsense. Why? Because, you are putting a much greater value on the life of a person in 2200 than one now. Yet we can invest a much smaller amount now to save the future person than we would have to spend now to save a person now. Suppose you have two friends. One is in danger of dying now at age fifty, and you can extend his life for nine years for $1,000. You also have a friend whose life could be extended nine years when she reaches fifty, which will occur in thirty years, for an expenditure of $1,000 in thirty years. You save both of their lives: the first by an expenditure now of $1,000 and the second by an expenditure now of $412, even if your investment returns as little as 3 percent per year. This is what is meant by valuing the lives differently; in reality, you value them the same.

What Stern has done, what others also do, and it is wrong, is to incorporate into the discount rate other things, such as ethical or moral sentiments. This is extremely confusing, as it disguises the value attached to such sentiments. We might ask with Nigel Larson, "How great a sacrifice is it either reasonable or realistic to ask the present generation, particularly the present generation in the developing world, to make, in the hope of avoiding the prospect that the people of the developing world in a hundred years' time may not be 9.5 times as well off as they are today, but only 9.5 times?" All the IPCC's scenarios, Ridley notes, assume that the world will experience so much economic growth that the people alive in 2100 will be on average four to eighteen times as wealthy as we are today. The reader may recall that in chapter 2, I suggest a growth rate in per capita income of at least 1.9 percent per annum. This gives a per capita income in 2100 greater than 6.5 times today's.

The bottom line is that we can cope with climate change. The loss of GDP from climate change consists of the sum of the costs of mitigation and the damage from climate change. As long as the sum of these costs does not growth more rapidly than world GDP or GDP per capita, we can cope. In chapter 3, I suggested a steady state rate of growth in per capita income of 1.9 percent per year. If the problem of climate change, net of the climate change costs, reduces income grow to, say, only 1 percent per year, it is still the case that current per capita income will double in seventy years.

Mitigation and Taxes

The strategy of the now-famous Paris Agreement will cost a fortune but do little to reduce global warming. Bjorn Lomborg shows, using the same climate model used by the United Nations, that widely hailed major policies of Paris Agreement signatories will have a negligible temperature impact. He shows that the Paris Agreement strategy, even if fully implemented, which is unlikely, results in a temperature reduction by the end of the century of only 0.08 degrees Fahrenheit. Lomborg notes that if it is generously assumed that the promised cuts for 2030 are not only met (which itself would be a United Nations first) but also sustained throughout the rest of the century, temperatures in 2100 would drop by 0.3 degrees—the equivalent of postponing warming by less than four years at the end of the century. The costs of the Paris climate pact are likely to run from $1 trillion to $2 trillion annually throughout the rest of the century, using the best estimates from the Stanford Energy Modeling Forum and the Asia Modeling Exercise. As

Lomborg correctly notes, spending more than $100 trillion for such a feeble temperature reduction by the end of the century does not make sense.

Lomborg suggests that the Paris Agreement is the wrong solution to a real problem. We should focus more on green-energy research and development, he says, like that promoted by Bill Gates and the Breakthrough Coalition. The most straightforward and simplest solution is a carbon tax. Such a tax will spur research and development of alternative means of reducing emissions. Even a tax as low as about five dollars per year per ton of carbon emissions will both cut emissions and provide an inducement to create carbon substituting technology. There is uncertainty about the best level for such a tax. A tax of between twenty-five and thirty dollars per year will increase gasoline prices by about thirty cents. It will raise the price of electricity generation by about three cents per kilowatt hour for coal. This will induce a switch from coal to natural gas.

Isabel Galina and Chris Green (2010) analyze the costs of a technology-led climate policy as a response to climate change as part of the Copenhagen Consensus on Climate Change. In their report, they find that expenditures of about 0.2 percent of GDP per year on green research and development would be sufficient to control the climate change issue by the end of the century. This cost is about $152 billion per year. Every dollar spent in this way would save about nine dollars, according to Bjorn Lomborg (https://www.ted.com/talks/bjorn_lomborg_sets_global_ priorities?language=en). The research and development could be funded by a low carbon charge of about five dollars per ton of CO2e that would gradually rise. These numbers are of course guesstimates, but they show the order of magnitude. Lomberg is somewhat too optimistic about the size of the necessary taxes, but he's right that we can handle the problem if we will.

The emphasis on technology forcing from a tax is sound policy in a world in which restricting the use of carbon would be very expensive and impossible to implement politically. Impossible because developing countries are not going to restrict their own development in the interest of the rest of the world. As Galiana and Green show, you cannot cap carbon emissions unless there are good, non-carbon-emitting substitutes. Technology-based research and development will dominate brute force policy by a benefit-cost ratio of nine to eighteen to one, regardless of the assumed level of climate damages.

Even with a tax as high as $30 per ton per year, we can cope. The world now produces about nine billion tons of CO2 per year. A tax of $30 per ton would cost $330 billion per year worldwide, assuming carbon production remains the same. This is only about 1.5 percent of global GDP. Such a tax will induce private sector research and development to develop carbon substituting technology. Currently solar, wind, and the like are insufficient.   In the United States, the cost of such a tax would be about 0.23 percent of GDP. This is a large number, $46 billion, but it pales in the face of the gain from two years' growth in US GDP, which is about $1 trillion, at a growth rate of $1 trillion per year.

Having said this, it is nevertheless important to recognize how shaky the SCC figures used by the EPA are. The correct figures will be steadily revised as estimates of the effects of global temperature rise are revised with further work by both economists and physical scientists. From a policy perspective, it will be important that federal and state agencies allow for these revisions and not be locked into current estimates or that courts require the use of such revisions as they occur.

Already such taxes have been introduced around the world but generally not at the level of $30 per ton of equivalent CO2.

The figure below from the World Bank shows location and size of the tax. Mostly these taxes are on CO_2e, where the e means

CO_2 equivalents. British Columbia and Denmark have taxes at the level of around $30 per ton, as suggested here. The British Columbia tax is revenue neutral; people pay more for energy but less in personal and corporate taxes. Note that the carbon tax, even if revenue neutral, will still provide the incentives to cut carbon use. A similar approach is cap and trade. This involves setting a limit to total emissions, selling permits up to the cap limit, and allowing the permits to be traded. This is also an efficient approach. California, and soon Ontario and Manitoba, will provide a cap- and-trade system. The highest taxes are in Sweden at $168 per ton and Switzerland at $68 per ton on CO_2e. These taxes have been implemented in the main by the richer nations.

Figure 15.4: Carbon Taxes around the World

	Country/Jurisdiction	Type	Year Adopted	Overview/Coverage	Tax Rate
1	British Columbia	Sub-national	2008	The carbon tax applies to the purchase or use of fuels within the province. The carbon tax is revenue neutral; all funds generated by the tax are returned to citizens through reductions in other taxes.	CAD30 per tCO2e (2012)
2	Chile	National	2014	Chile's carbon tax is part of legislation enacted in 2014. The country is to start with measuring of carbon dioxide emissions from thermal power plants in 2017 and begin the tax on CO2 emissions from the power sector in 2018.	USD5 per tCO2e (2018)
3	Costa Rica	National	1997	In 1997, Costa Rica enacted a tax on carbon pollution, set at 3.5 percent of the market value of fossil fuels. The revenue generated by the tax goes toward the Payment for Environmental Services (PSA) program, which offers incentives to property owners to practice sustainable development and forest conservation.	3.5% tax on hydrocarbon fossil fuels
4	Denmark	National	1992	The Danish carbon tax covers all consumption of fossil fuels (natural gas, oil, and coal), with partial exemption and refund provisions for sectors covered by the EU ETS, energy-intensive processes, exported goods, fuels in refineries and many transport-related activities. Fuels used for electricity production are also not taxed by the carbon tax, but instead a tax on electricity production applies.	USD31 per tCO2e (2014)
5	Finland	National	1990	While originally based only on carbon content, Finland's carbon tax was subsequently changed to a combination carbon/energy tax. It initially covered only heat and electricity production but was later expanded to cover transportation and heating fuels.	EUR35 per tCO2e (2013)
6	France	National	2014	In December 2013 the French parliament approved a domestic consumption tax on energy products based on the content of CO_2 on fossil fuel consumption not covered by the EU ETS. A carbon tax was introduced from April 1, 2014 on the use of gas, heavy fuel oil, and coal, increasing to €14.5/tCO2 in 2015 and €22/tCO2 in 2016. From 2015 onwards the carbon tax will be extended to transport fuels and heating oil.	EUR7 per tCO2e (2014)
7	Iceland	National	2010	All importers and importers of liquid fossil fuels (gas and diesel oils, petrol, aircraft and jet fuels and fuel oils) are liable for the carbon tax regardless of whether it is for retail or personal use. A carbon tax for liquid fossil fuels is paid to the treasury, with (since 2011) the rates reflecting a carbon price equivalent to 75 percent of the current price in the EU ETS scheme.	USD10 per tCO2e (2014)

Country/Jurisdiction	Type	Year Adopted	Overview/Coverage	Tax Rate
			particular, by using a CO₂ emission factor for each sector, the tax rate per unit quantity is set so that each tax burden is equal to US$2/tCO₂ (as of April 2014).	
10 Mexico	National	2012	Mexico's carbon tax covers fossil fuel sales and imports by manufacturers, producers, and importers. It is not a tax on the full carbon content of fuels, but rather on the additional amount of emissions that would be generated if the fossil fuel were used instead of natural gas. Natural gas therefore is not subject to the carbon tax, though it could be in the future. The tax rate is capped at 3% of the sales price of the fuel. Companies liable to pay the tax may choose to pay the carbon tax with credits from CDM projects developed in Mexico, equivalent to the value of the credits at the time of paying the tax.	Mex$ 10 -50 per tCO2e (2014)* * Depending on fuel type
11 Norway	National	1991	About 55 percent of Norway's CO₂ emissions are effectively taxed. Emissions not covered by a carbon tax are included in the country's ETS, which was linked to the European ETS in 2008.	USD 4-69 per tCO2e (2014)* *Depending on fossil fuel type and usage
12 Portugal	National	2014	Portugal's carbon tax of €5 per tCO2e went into effect in 2015 as part of a wider package of green tax reforms. It applies to non-EU ETS sectors and covers approximately 26 percent of the country's greenhouse gas emissions.	€5 per tCO2e (2015)
12 South Africa	National	2016	In May 2013 the South African government published a policy paper for public comment on introduction of a carbon tax. The paper proposes a fuel input tax based on the carbon content of the fuel. It was agreed that emissions factors and/or procedures are available to quantify CO2-eq emissions with a relatively high level of accuracy for different processes and sectors. The carbon tax will cover all direct GHG emissions from both fuel combustion as well as non-energy industrial process emissions and is expected to start in January 2016.	R120/tCO2 (Proposed tax rate for 2016)* *Tax is proposed to increase by 10% per year until end-2019
13 Sweden	National	1991	Sweden's carbon tax was predominantly introduced as part of energy sector reform, with the major taxed sectors including natural gas, gasoline, coal, light and heavy fuel oil, liquefied petroleum gas (LPG), and home heating oil. Over the years carbon tax exemptions have increased for installations under the EU ETS, with the most recent increase in exemption starting from 2014 for district heating plants participating in the EU ETS.	USD168 per tCO2e (2014)
14 Switzerland	National	2008	Switzerland's carbon tax covers all fossil fuels, unless they are used for energy. Swiss companies	USD 68 per tCO2e
Country/Jurisdiction	Type	Year Adopted	Overview/Coverage	Tax Rate
			can be exempt from the tax if they participate in the country's ETS.	(2014)
15 United Kingdom	National	2013	The U.K.'s carbon price floor (CPF) is a tax on fossil fuels used to generate electricity. It came into effect in April 2013 and changed the previously existing Climate Change Levy (CCL) regime, by applying carbon price support (CPS) rates of CCL to gas, solid fuels, and liquefied petroleum gas (LPG) used in electricity generation.	USD15.75 per tCO2e (2014)

Only human failure to work together can prevent a reasonable solution to climate change. As *The New York Times* said in an editorial on January 19, 2016,

> *China's announcement last year that it would set up a national cap-and-trade system was hugely encouraging—the world's largest emitter agreeing to tax itself to help solve a problem that,*

only a few years ago, it barely acknowledged. Yet Congress has refused to act even as it becomes clear that putting a price on greenhouse gas emissions is the most.

A Higher Tax

Suppose, however, that it turns out that 1 percent per year of GDP investment is required—the Nordhaus estimate—and that this requires a tax of about $30 per ton of CO_2 equivalent. Is the world rich enough to afford such a tax? It is. World GDP is currently estimated by the IPCC to grow at about 2.4 percent per year. I would give it a range from 1.9 percent to 3.4 percent. At the low end of this range, the world economy will be about 6.5 times richer then now in one hundred years. If the cost of climate change is 1 percent of GDP per year, this reduces our future wealth only to about 6.0 times greater than it is now.

Currently the world GDP is about $76 trillion, which at 7.2 billion people is about $9,555 per person. The most pessimistic growth rate used by the prestigious IPCC panel in non-climate world GDP of about 1.34 percent per year. At this 1.34 percent growth rate, world GDP will be about $251 trillion in 2100. At a reasonable estimate of nine billion people in 2100, per capital income will be about $25,000. That is, under a pessimistic scenario people ninety years from now will be more than twice as rich as we are now. How much should we spend now to reduce harm to these relatively rich people? The high estimate of the Stern Report is that GDP in 2100 will be, at the extreme, 20 percent lower than it would be without climate change. This gives a per capita global income of $20,000, more than twice as much as current per capita income. These are understandable and large effects but far from a need for panic.

But what about the risk of catastrophe?

Climate Change   223

Is There Risk of Catastrophe?

The climate change models say there is a very, very small risk of catastrophe. By risk I mean probability. By uncertainty I mean the uncertainty of the risk. A true coin has a probability of 0.5 of landing heads. It has no uncertainty, as the risk probability is well known. A coin that may or may not be true has uncertainty, since the level of risk is not well known, as the coin may be biased, and the level of bias may be unknown. A biased coin that yields heads 40 percent of the time has risk but not uncertain if the 40% probability is known. Climate change has both risk and uncertainty about the probabilities. We can estimate probabilities, but we put error bounds around these probabilities to represent uncertainties. The wider the error bounds are, the greater the uncertainty.

Some of the climate change models have what are called fat tails, meaning that the uncertainties of disaster are rather large. According to the report from *The Economist*,

Climate change is a long-term, probably irreversible problem beset by substantial uncertainty. Crucially, however, climate change is a problem of extreme risk: this means that the average losses to be expected are not the only source of concern; on the contrary, the outliers, the particularly extreme scenarios, may matter most of all.

The economist Martin Weitzman shows that there is some small risk of a climate change catastrophe, according to the climate change models. He suggests that normal economics does not apply when the disaster could be so huge.

Yet normal economics certainly do apply to economic models of allocating resources. Catastrophic climate change is not the only possible disaster, and finite funds need to be allocated among them—asteroids, North Korean missiles, nuclear war, plague, Russian and or Chinese aggression. Each risk is unlikely, but we still have to choose how to allocate spending to prevent among the possibilities. None deserve vast spending to prevent at this time, but they all do deserve some for insurance.

The uncertainties are not a reason for drastic action. All phenomena are uncertain; even the past is uncertain. (Think about it.) This does not mean that uncertainty should be ignored. The phenomena of climate change are complex and difficult to model, with several feedback loops and interrelationships among variables. The major uncertainty is, however, over the regional distribution of effects, not so much for the global picture. Nearly everything we have any confidence in when it comes to climate change is related to global patterns of surface temperature, which are primarily controlled by thermodynamics. In contrast, we have less confidence in atmospheric circulation aspects of climate change, which exert a strong control on regional climate. That is, the global predictions are more accurate than the regional ones. A carbon tax of about thirty dollars per ton is a strong insurance policy for climate change.

Discount rates are boring but terribly important. They determine how much should be spent today to reduce climate change damage in the future. This depends crucially on the rate of discount of the future, on the growth of world GDP, and on the yearly damage from global warming. World GDP is about \$107.5 trillion. Say this increases by 2.5 percent per year for a long time. Suppose the yearly damage from climate change is .01 percent of GDP per year forever. This gives a present value of damage from climate change of \$116 billion. The present value is the amount that could be invested now to offset the 0.01 percent risk. This is a very small number. The GWP at a growth rate of 2.0% per year and a risk of .01 % would yield a GWP of about 290 trillion about close to 3 times the current GWP.

Suppose instead the yearly damage is higher as shown below. If the loss per year from climate change is equal to the growth rate, GWP never gets higher. Consider Table 15.5 below

Table 15.5: World GWP in 50 years at different risk levels, assuming a 2% growth rate in GWP without climate change.

Risk per year	GWP in 50 years	Richer by a factor of:
0	290.00	2.70
0.01%	276.00	2.57
0.10%	275.50	2.56
1.00%	176.80	1.64
2%	107.50	1.00
5%	23.44	0.22

Wow this is interesting, isn't it. Even at a yearly level of risk of 1% per year, which is high, and a 2% growth rate, which is a bit low, the world will be 64% richer in 50 years. However if the yearly damage were to be as high as 5% per year while the growth rate remained at 2% we would be in terrible shape. The GWP would only be 22% of the current world GWP. Hence the argument for spending to control climate change as insurance.

The Center for American Progress estimates that over the three- year period from 2011 through 2013, the federal government spent $136 billion dollars for disaster relief and recovery, or almost $400 per year for each US household. Much of this was for disasters related to climate change. This is 0.76 percent of GDP. By spending wisely through a carbon tax per ton of CO_2 equivalents and raising this tax as GDP increases, we can materially reduce
the effect of climate change and limit the possibility of catastrophe.

Effects of Climate Change

The fifth International Policy Climate Change report (IPCCz) (2013) stresses that the elevation of global temperature will very likely be above 2 degrees Celsius. James Hansen, a prominent climate scientist, thinks the warming will be well above this level. Since the fourth report in 2007, annual global GHG emissions have continued to grow and reached 49.5 billion tons of carbon dioxide equivalents (CO_2eq) in the year 2010, higher than any level prior to that date. The current trajectory of global annual and cumulative emissions of GHGs is inconsistent with widely discussed goals of limiting global warming at 1.5 to 2 degrees Celsius above the preindustrial level. Temperature levels are likely to rise above the levels experienced during the period of much modern development, the Holocene. The Holocene is the geological epoch that began approximately 10,000 years BCE and continues to the present. This period can be considered an interglacial period, part of the long-term move toward an ice age. (The increase in temperature of 2 to 3 degrees Celsius, which is the most likely range of temperature increases, is equal to 3.6 to 5.4 degrees Fahrenheit.)

In its fifth report, the IPCC estimates impacts by continent over the coming decades. The figure below summarizes the list of probable impacts at different levels of temperature increases.

Figure 15.6: Effects of Temperature Rises

Type of Impact	Eventual Temperature Rise Relative to Pre-Industrial Temperatures				
	1°C	2°C	3°C	4°C	5°C
Freshwater Supplies	Small glaciers in the Andes disappear, threatening water supplies for 50 million people	Potential water supply decrease of 20-30% in some regions (Southern Africa and Mediterranean)	1-4 billion more people suffer water shortages Serious droughts in Southern Europe every 10 years	Potential water supply decrease of 30-50% in Southern Africa and Mediterranen	Large glaciers in Himalayas possibly disappear, affecting ¼ of China's population
Food and Agriculture	Modest increase in yields in temperature regions	Declines in crop yields in tropical regions (5-10% in Africa)	150-550 million more people at risk of hunger Yields likely to peak at higher latitudes	Yields decline by 15-35% in Africa Some entire regions out of agricultural production	Increase in ocean acidity possibly reduces fish stocks
Human Health	At least 300,000 die each year from climate-related diseases Reduction in winter mortality in high latitudes	40-60 million more exposed to malaria in Africa	1-3 million more potentially people die annually from malnutrition	Up to 80 million more people exposed to malaria in Africa	Further disease increase and substantial burdens on health care services
Coastal Areas	Increased damage from coastal flooding	Up to 10 million more people exposed to coastal flooding	Up to 170 million more people exposed to coastal flooding	Up to 300 million more people exposed to coastal flooding	Sea level rise threatens major cities such as New York, Tokyo, and London
Ecosystems	At least 10% of land species facing extinction Increased wildfire risk	15-40% of species potentially face extinction	20-50% of species potentially face extinction Possible onset of collapse of Amazon forest	Loss of half of Arctic tundra Widespread loss of coral reefs	Significant extinctions across the globe

Sources: Stern, 2007; IPCC, 2007.

Benefit-Cost Analysis

Benefit-cost analysis compares the present value of benefits to the present value of costs. The present value is the value one would need to invest today to gain the future cash flow (net benefits) calculated. For example, if we invested $100 at 9 percent interest, at the end of a year we would have $110. The $110 is the future value, and the $100 is the present value. Clearly, the present and future values will depend on the interest rate involved. Suppose that the rate is 5 percent rather than 9 percent. One hundred dollars (present value) invested today would be worth $105 one year from now. If we were offered $110 in one year and the interest rate was 5 percent, the present value would be $100/1.05 or $95.24. This would be the present value, and we could invest this amount for a year and gain $100, for a net gain of $4.76. If we were to be offered $100 after one year and the interest rate was 9 percent, the present value would be $100/1.9 or $90.91. The present value goes down as the rate goes up, as at higher rates, invested money grows more rapidly.

Professor William Nordhaus of Yale, the leading American expert on climate economics, concludes that the economically optimal policy involves only a modest rate of emission reduction, and in this case, the damages might be limited to something around 2 to 3 percent of world GDP. His conclusion ignores certain classes of damages and thus is an underestimate of damages from climate change. But it is probably our best estimate now. The Nordhaus estimate of meeting the requirements of the Copenhagen Accord is shown below. Figures are in billions of US dollars. The Copenhagen Accord resulted from a meeting of world leaders in 2009. The provisions of the accord call for the United States and 185 other nations to reduce emissions, invest in clean energy technology and practices, and help people adapt to the effects of climate change. The accord also, for the first time, acknowledges that staying below 2 degrees Celsius may not be sufficient and includes a review in 2015 of the need to potentially aim for staying below 1.5 degrees Celsius. The accord states that the parties "shall" enhance their cooperative actions to combat climate change, while recognizing the scientific view that an increase in global temperatures be kept below 2 degrees Celsius. We are now too late to obtain the 2-degree limit.

Table 15.7 Estimates of Costs and Benefits of Meeting the Copenhagen Accord by Country in Billions of 2005 USD.[115]

Region	Change in Damages	Abatement Costs	Permit Purchases	Net Costs
US	-51	328	228	505
EU	-56	160	171	276
Japan	-12	44	64	96
Russia	-5	92	-176	-89
Eurasia	-4	62	-150	-92
China	-52	655	-260	335
India	-54	185	-1	130
Middle East	-47	123	-134	-57
Africa	-41	0	0	-41
Latin America	-33	127	154	248
Oceania	-18	96	48	126
Other	-42	188	64	209
World	-413	2060	0	1647

This table illustrates the region asymmetry of the Copenhagen Accord. The estimates take the present value of abatement cost and averted damages and uses the capital weighted international real interest rate.

Still the total costs are 1.5% of world GWP and below our assumed growth rate of 2.0%. From estimates by Nordhaus, Stern, and others (Haneman), it is safe to say at least that the better estimates of net benefits from reductions of greenhouse gases from a carbon tax would be worthwhile. Of course, these and any figures for net benefits must be regarded as rough and should be taken with a considerable measure of doubt.

The take-home message is that reasonable control may be reasonably attained. The real question is whether or not we have the will and whether or not the collective action problem can be solved.

115   Source: William Nordhaus, *Handbook of Computable General Equilibrium Modeling*, 2013, 1069–1131.

What Can Be Done?

From experiences with eliminating pollution in the United States and in determining how to limit the catch in fisheries, it is clear that the best rational approach would be to either set a carbon tax or set a worldwide cap on the production of worldwide gases and then set a quota for reduction for each country (cap and trade). These quotas would be tradable so that one country could buy a permit to admit from another country, with the total amount of the quotas remaining fixed. This sort of approach has been used to reduce pollution in the United States and elsewhere. It has been successfully used to limit the catch from fisheries that would otherwise have been depleted. This is just our old collective action problem again. Agents acting individually will not preserve the fishery in the expectation that others will continue to overfish. A fisher will not pass up a catch that might otherwise be taken by someone else. In the context of pollution and fisheries, this is called the tragedy of the commons. The tragedy is that social wealth (fish, for example) is used and used up too quickly, so that total wealth is less than if the commons is properly managed.

The major problem that arises and which now prevents the Paris negotiations from developing such a scheme is how to assign the amount of greenhouse gas reduction among countries. Developing countries argue that developed countries have been the biggest polluters and users of fossil fuels, which has been a major source of their wealth, and that it is unfair for developing countries to be denied access to such fuels now. This could be handled by granting to these countries larger polluting permits, which they could use or sell. This, of course, sounds simple, but the negotiations would be complex. A second problem would be enforcement. Some third party such as the United Nations would need to have enforcement authority and powers. Trade sanctions could be imposed on cheaters. This brief treatment here does not do justice to the problems. A good extended discussion is found in Tietenberg (2002).[116] The point is, the more action we can take now, the less severe will be the temperature changes in the near and far future.

What Is Likely to Happen?

I don't know. But the best guesses are that over the long term, continuing emissions of heat-trapping gases will inevitably cause the planet's surface temperatures to rise anywhere from 2.7 degrees Fahrenheit to 7.2 degrees Fahrenheit by 2100, relative to pre- 1900 conditions. The warming will be unevenly distributed, with more warming over land and even greater warming at the poles. Temperature increases such as these, even at the lower end, could increase the chances of not only extreme heat waves and drought but also flooding due to heavy rains. They will probably raise sea levels in areas where hundreds of millions of people reside.

Globally, economic and population growth will continue to be the most important drivers of increases in CO2 as noted above. Clearing forests releases large amounts of CO2, and worldwide deforestation means that we don't have as many trees to absorb the extra CO2. This means more CO2 stays in the atmosphere, trapping more heat. The contribution of population growth between 2000 and 2010 remained roughly identical to the previous three decades. The contribution of economic growth has risen sharply. Between 2000 and 2010, both drivers outpaced emission reductions from improvements in energy intensity. Without additional efforts to reduce GHG emissions beyond those in place today, emissions

---

116   Much of the material on climate change in this chapter is drawn from the 2014 Climate Change Synthesis Report, released by the United Nations' Intergovernmental Panel on Climate Change (IPCC). This report, published every five to seven years, is the work of several hundred scientists from around the world, who summarize the current understanding of all aspects of climate change research. Thousands of scientists review the summary, after which the IPCC publishes a comprehensive report, which synthesizes findings from thousands of research studies. Almost two hundred countries are involved in the process. The IPCC also publishes reports that provide potential options for climate change mitigation and adaptation. The creators of the fourth IPCC report were collectively awarded the Nobel Peace Prize in 2007.

growth is expected to persist, driven by growth in global population and economic activities.

Human success here will depend on our ability to cooperate. And this will depend on the maturity of the world's culture, as explained in chapter 1. (As an aside here, I would like to mention the interesting, if overly bloody, sci-fi trilogy by Ramen Naan, in which cooperation is enhanced by the development of technology that allows mind reading.)

Summary

Climate change is real and is human caused. There is a wide range of possible adverse effects from climate change, including the possibility of catastrophic effects. A carbon tax perhaps as high as thirty to forty dollars per ton of equivalent carbon emissions should be sufficient to reasonably mitigate the rise of temperatures. Effects will be case and site specific. Mitigation efforts and associated costs vary among countries in mitigation scenarios. In globally cost-effective mitigation scenarios, the majority of mitigation efforts take place in countries with the highest future emissions baseline scenarios (e.g., the United States and China). Mitigation policy will devalue fossil fuel assets and reduce revenues for fossil fuel exporters, as most mitigation scenarios are associated with reduced revenues from coal and oil trade for major exporters. The sooner we undertake effective mitigation and the more efficient are our efforts, the less severe will be the effects of climate change.

16
Human Evolution[117]

Evolution can occur at the level of the gene. It can occur above that level, at the epigenetic ("above genetics") level and through group selection. These paths can interact. Genes can change through mutation. The vast majority of mutations are harmful and die out, but some are very important. Changes in the basic genetic makeup through mutation that improve our fitness as a species takes place rarely and change also takes place slowly through natural selection, in which populations change toward individuals that are better suited for survival.

Epigenetics is different. You heard it here: *Epigenetic manipulation will be huge in the future*. Well, probably! Changes can take place at a level above the gene, the epigenetic level. The recent study of epigenetics has resulted in a biological revolution, overturning fundamental principles of biology, including the understanding of evolution. Epigenetics refers to the ability to shut down or turn on different genes. DNA, which carries genes, is wrapped around a coil of proteins called histones. A protein has been found that makes a specific change in the chemical histone and is able to shut down or turn off the activity of genes. Different forms of a creature can be created out of the same genome through epigenetics. These changes can be inherited. Thus changes in humans can occur much more rapidly so that natural selection can operate much more rapidly than was supposed by focusing on natural selection alone.[118]

---

117   I wish to thank Patricia Kramer, a biological anthropologist, of the University of Washington's department of anthropology for information and suggestions. Any errors or speculations are, however, my own.

118   See D. Mukherjee (2016).

Genetic changes can also take place at the level of group selection. E.O. Wilson believes now that group selection, not kin selection, is the major driving force of human evolution.[119] That is, in my terms, culture can determine destiny. Biologists define culture as the collection of traits that distinguishes one group from another. Such trait differences are to be found among groups of chimpanzees and bonobos. A culture trait is a behavior for animals and humans that is either first invented within a group or else learned from another group, then transmitted among members of the group. Whether or not culture favors cooperation, for example, may influence the survival of the culture and of the people in it. As Wilson notes, for land animals, environments are dominated by species with the most complex social systems. The most complex systems are those possessing eusociality (true social coperation). The most successful human societies now are cooperative and humanitarian ones. Are the people in such societies lucky and/or are they more genetically disposed toward cooperation than others? Are less stressful societies more likely to incorporate epigenetic changes that promote cooperation? Evidence suggests that at least for insects and possibly for humans, a gene for altruism may lead to a more successful society and to altruism as an inheritable trait (E. O. Wilson 2008). It should not be surprising for us or you to see rapid changes in human traits due to the interaction of these forces.

Is Smarter Better?

The evolving brain

The human brain is evolving. Robin Smith (2013), a scientist at the National Evolutionary Synthesis Center in Durham, North Carolina, notes in a blog that in the six to nine million years since the ancestors of humans and chimps went their separate ways, the human brain has more than tripled in size, while brains of chimps have remained the same. Our brains are not only larger but also

119   Wilson seems not to give credit to, for example, Ernst Mayr for this insight. I believed Mayr was right back in the 1970s when Wilson was promoting kin selection. Kin selection supposes that one's decisions are made to favor those related to us and that others are more favored depending on their genetic relatedness

different. As culture continues to change, our brains are evolving to keep pace. "Our environment and the skills we need to survive in it are changing faster than we ever imagined," noted Professor Lahn; he goes on to say that, "I would expect the human brain, which has done well by us so far, will continue to adapt to those changes" (Decker 2013).

Many animals are smarter than humans in particular areas. De Wahl (2016, 110) notes that Ayumu is a young chimpanzee that puts humans to shame. He can recall a series of random numbers from one through nine and tap them in the right order after seeing them for one-fifth of a second. No human has been able to do this. Ayumu took on a British memory champion known for his ability to memorize an entire stack of cards. Ayumu won. Corvids, crows and parrots have better eidetic (seeing things in space) memories than humans. Let crows and humans see where you hide objects. Let them come back later. The crows will remember where more of the objects are.

Would it be progress if the human race were to become more intelligent? Surely we would regard it so. From an evolutionary point of view, however, it is unclear that greater intelligence would be beneficial. Humans are an outlier in terms of brain size when compared with other animals. Is this suggesting that humans are more likely to survive if less smart? Maybe. It is nevertheless the case that up until now being smarter has benefited human survival.[120]

In biology, the relevant concept is *fitness*, which is defined by how well a species or an individual is equipped to survive in a specific environmentally. More intelligence might make us less fit as a species in the long run. "Just because these genes are still evolving, doesn't necessarily mean they make you any smarter," explains Professor Bruce Lahn, a professor of human genetics at

---

120 Professors who are more religious and more politically extreme are more likely to have lower IQs and to be in the social rather than in the physical sciences. In self-defense, I note that my undergraduate major was in the physical sciences, and as a social scientist, I am an economist, which group has higher IQs than many of the social scientists. http://www. religjournal.com/pdf/ijrr10001.pdf.

the University of Chicago. Evolution favors whatever increases survival probabilities. When informed of the probability of other life in the universe, the great physicist Enrico Fermi is reported to have asked, "Where are they?" He then speculated that beings capable of technology sufficiently advanced to communicate with us may not last long, as their technology destroys them. Think hydrogen bomb and global warming.

So, is our choice to be fit and alive or smart and dead? Or is there another choice? Can we be both smarter and alive and well?

Morality and Survival

Evolution has not always favored traits that increased morality. We've evolved genes for selfishness, violence, cruelty—all of which are in place because they may make survival easier (Decker 2013). If so, how? Will these qualities become less important in the future? Will morality itself increase survivability or decrease it? Might we end up immoral and alive or moral and dying? Or could morality be important for our long-run survival?

The Human Story

Hominids became hominins. And from hominins came *Homos* and from *Homos* came us, *Homo sapiens*. A mere twenty years ago, the human story was seen as much simpler than it is seen now. It was commonly believed at the time that the first hominins split off from apes about 4.4 million years ago (mya), followed by the genus Homo a bit more than 2 mya. Hominids left Africa about 1 mya. Neanderthals died out about 30,000 mya, leaving Homo sapiens as the last man standing, except that we carry some Neanderthal genes.

This account has been changed beyond recognition in the last twenty years, as new discoveries are made. The hominoid classification has been divided into two parts as follows: Hominid—the group consisting of all modern and extinct great apes (that is, modern humans, chimpanzees, gorillas, and orangutans, plus all their immediate ancestors). Hominin—the group consisting of modern humans, extinct human species, and all our immediate ancestors, including members of the genera *Homo, Australopithecus Paranthropus, and Ardipthecus*[121]

Now the story has changed substantially. There are many more hominin than formerly thought. Sex between archaic hominin and *H. sapiens* appear to have benefited *H. sapiens* according to Wong (2010). Neanderthals were much more technological than formerly thought; we are part Neanderthal, so that the genomes of non-African people are up to 3 or 4 percent Neanderthal. (Wong suggests that the sum total of Neanderthal genetic material in today's humans is at least 20 percent.) The figure below shows the evolution of human traits. Recently it has been proposed that humans and/or Neanderthals were in the Americas very much earlier than supposed.

Figure 16.1: The Appearance of Human Traits

Time period for appearance of human traits	Trait
7 mya	Forwardly placed opening for spinal cord; small canine teeth
4.1 mya	Strong knee joint
3.7 mya	Arched foot; short toes
3.2 mya	Short, broad pelvis; long thumb
2 mya	Twisted humerus; low shoulders
1.9 mya	Enlarged femur; long legs
1.6 mya	Barrel-shaped rib cage
1.4 mya	Strong wrist
1 mya	Large brain
200,000 ya	Chin retreat

---

121   The hominins are a class between family and genus. See more at http://australian museum.net. au/hominid-and-hominin-whats-the-difference#sthash.6O18YJuF.dpuf.

Why Did Our Brains Get Larger?

Why did larger and smarter brains make Homo and its progeny more fit?

Behind this question is another: Why did a branch of hominins develop into *Homo*? The short answer is climate change. There is near consensus among archaeologists and paleontologists that climate change put pressure on hominins' survival. The climate went from bad to terrible, resulting in scarcity of traditional food sources. The transition from hominins to *Homo* occurred during a period of cycling from wet to dry climates and then back again. The two prominent cycling periods occurred about 3 mya and about 2 mya (de Menocal 2013). The cycling of climate from forest to grassland and back favored hominins that could consume both meat and vegetation, so hominins that consumed only grass died out. This cycling is thought to have rewarded greater brain flexibility and ability to plan, resulting in an increase in forebrain size. Climate change required the ability to include larger amounts of meat and marrow in the diet.[122] In order to secure meat, the *Homo* branch of hominins learned to hunt cooperatively, which favored larger brains and the development of teeth and guts able to better utilize meat. That is, cooperation favored larger brains.[123] Larger brains developed amazingly fast during that period. Meat and marrow are calorie-dense resources with essential amino

---

122 The strongest evidence for meat and marrow eating are butchery marks found on bones. Pounding a bone with a large stone to break it open and extract the marrow inside can leave percussion marks. Cut and percussion marks together are called butchery marks, may be the result of skinning, disarticulation, and bone breakage for dietary and nondietary reasons (Blumenschine and Pobiner 2006). Experimental and prehistoric evidence for human chewing on bones has only recently begun to be explored (e.g., Landt 2007; Delaney-Rivera et al. 2009; Fernandez-Jalvo and Andrews 2011; Pickering et al. 2013).

123 The carnivory of hominins is unique among primates in three ways: (1) use of flaked stone tools to access animal resources; (2) acquisition of resources from animals much larger than the hominins themselves; and (3) procurement of animal resources by scavenging. Chimpanzees, our closest living relatives, routinely hunt, capture by hand, and eat meat from colobus or other smaller monkeys (e.g., Mitani and Watts 2001). However, meat is a small proportion of their diet because they cannot efficiently digest carrion (Ragir et al. 2000), and they rarely scavenge (Watts 2008). How this novel source of food was first recognized by hominins remains unknown. Hominins would likely not have been able to directly exploit grass as grassland expanded habitats across Africa, but an increase in large (grazing) animal resources would have been useful for any species that could procure and digest them (Plummer 2004).

acids and micronutrients, and their aquatic fauna offer nutrients needed for brain growth. Increasing the consumption of animal foods appears to have allowed hominins to increase their body size without losing mobility, agility, or sociality (Milton 1999). Climate change produced more dead animals. Assuming opportunistic encounters with carcasses about 2 mya, hominids that could adapt to eating more meat had an advantage. (Blumenschine and Pobiner 2006 and references therein). And it was this group that became *Homo*. The evolving *Homo* found that stone tools were a great asset in hunting. The shaping of stone tools requires complex mental processing—how to strike to make an edge or point, which stones are best to use, and where they are located. Thus, *Homo* arose about 2.9 mya to 2.4 mya from a stew of other hominins. A combination of adaption to increased meat consumption, the necessity to be strong hunters with cooperative hunting practices, and the ability to develop tools for hunting which led to brains with greater adaptability or plasticity that allowed us to survive. It seems that each recently cited documentation that it was the advantages of cooperation that lead to our using a crucial portion of the new energy from meat energy for brain development and that made us human.[124]

The earliest evidence for hunting technology, in the form of hafted spear point, dates back about 500,000 years. Complex projectile weapons appeared only 71,000 years ago. Not coincidentally, it is also around this time that we start to see the first evidence of archaeologically visible accumulations of stone tools. The earliest well-documented evidence of persistent hominin carnivory in association with large concentrations of stone tools is about 2.0 mya.

---

124   The earliest evidence for hunting technology, in the form of hafted spear points, dates back to about 500,000 years ago. Complex projectile weapons only appear 71,000 years ago. Modern human gut proportions and size are unique among great apes, and studies have found signatures of selection in genes in modern humans that may have played a role in adaptations to dietary changes. Many zoo archaeologists think it likely that at least some animal carcasses were obtained by scavenging. It is likely that these modes of carcass procurement—hunting and scavenging—ere not mutually exclusive behaviors but were both employed, depending on a variety of behavioral and ecological variables (e.g., available hominins in the group for carcass procurement, butchery, and transport; prey size, age, and species; habitat; other available food resources; and presence of other predators).

Only in the *Homo*, especially in *Homo erectus*, do we see biological features linked to meat eating, such as a decrease in tooth and gut size and an increase in body and brain size (e.g., McHenry 1992, Aiello and Wheeler 1995, Anton 2003, and Braun et al. 2010).

Brains are metabolically costly. In the normal course of evolution, in order to gain more intelligence, we would have to give up something else. What did we give up? Apparently, we gave up stronger muscles and in certain respects brains. For example, chimps of equal size are much stronger than we are, and crows (corvids) and some other animals have better eidetic memories.[125] Relative to humans, more of the chimp's energy is devoted to development of its body than its brain. While the rise of agriculture and the switch from hunting and gathering to farming for *Homo sapiens* provided us with larger quantities of food, although such food was of much lower quality. The result was a striking decrease in physical size and probably brain size that was only reversed in the United States about 120 years ago.

Simply put we developed larger brains because larger brains increased our fitness. The simple answer to why we evolved larger brains is that this had survival value for us. Evolution's focus is on survival, not on intelligence. Our brains have evolved to support aggression, murder, violence, and war because these turned out to be good for survival. Will they still be good for survival in the future?

About 500,000 years ago, the first evidence is found of archaeologically visible accumulations of stone tools. The earliest well-documented evidence of persistent hominin carnivory in association with large concentrations of stone tools is at about 2.0 mya. In addition to terrestrial animals, evidence from one site at Koobi Fora shows that hominins began to incorporate aquatic foods like turtles, crocodiles, and fish into their diets by about

---

125   For more information, see the work of John Marzluff at the University of Washington.

1.95 mya (Braun et al. 2010). Multiple localities at Olduvai Gorge, Tanzania, dating to 1.9 mya also show evidence of on-site butchered mammal remains, ranging in size from hedgehogs to elephants.

Only in the *Homo* lineage, especially in *Homo erectus*, do we see biological features linked to meat eating, such as a decrease in tooth and gut size and an increase in body and brain size (e.g., McHenry 1992, Aiello and Wheeler 1995, Antón 2003, Braun et al. 2010). We also see in *Homos erectus* substantial signs of cultural advancement.[126] What happened to other hominins? Some accounts speculate that we exterminated them; however, the evidence for this is not substantial. A more likely scenario is that a failure to adapt combined with pressure on the food supply brought about by humans paired with climate change led to their demise.

A Unique Dietary Strategy among Hominins

The carnivory of hominins is unique among primates in three ways:

(1) use of stone tools to access animal resources;

(2) acquisition of resources from animals much larger than the hominins themselves, and

(3) procurement of animal resources by scavenging. Chimpanzees, our closet living relatives, routinely hunt, capture by hand and eat meat from colobus or other smaller monkeys (e.g., Mitani and Watts 2001) but meat is a small portion of their diet because they cannot efficiently digest carrion (Ragir et al. 2000), and they rarely scavenge (Watts 2008). How this novel source of food for primates was first recognized by hominins remains unknown. Hominins would likely not have been able to directly exploit grassland habitats across Africa, but an increase in large grazing

---

126   We do not know when the switch from twenty-four to twenty-three chromosomes occurred; we do not know the number for *Homo erectus*.

animal resources would have been useful for any species that could procure and digest them.

What Determines Intelligence?

I thought once that intelligence was determined by an animal's brain-to- body-mass ratio. This turns out to be too simple. True, a human's brain- to-body ratio is huge compared to that of an elephant or other "smart" mammals, (about 1/40 versus 1/560); but the ratio is the same as that of a mouse and is actually *smaller* than the ratio you encounter in some small birds (1/12).

There appear to be three ways of becoming smarter: having a larger brain, having a more efficient brain or both, though a larger brain is no guarantee. For humans, it seems to have been both. Although having a larger head does not mean that one is smarter than someone with a smaller head, there is a weak correlation. Increasing brain size much would require larger heads and, consequently, make natural birth more difficult. For brains to become more efficient, we would have to channel more energy to them. This would mean that either we channel less energy elsewhere or we become able to generate energy. To do this, our mitochondria (our cell energy powerhouses) would have to evolve to be more efficient—which they did at least one time in our past.

Predicted Brain Mass

There is a statistical relationship among brain sizes that gives an average across all animals. This is called predicted brain mass. Predicted brain size is given by

$$BM(e) = 1.77 * (W^{0.76}),$$

where BM(e) is predicted brain mass, and W is actual body mass in grams. This indicates that predicted brain mass does not increase proportion to body mass. In comparing the brain mass of two animals with body masses of 100 and 1000, the predicted brain masses will be 58.6 and 337.3, respectively; the larger animal with ten times the body mass of the smaller has a predicted brain mass only 5.7 times as large. The difference between the predicted and actual brain mass is one measure of brain mental capacity but not a perfect one mass.

The above equation defines a relationship between expected brain size, BM(e), and a measure of body size. The mathematical relationship above is nonlinear, as is apparent from the presence of the exponent.[127]

The Encephalization Quotient

Encephalization quotients (EQ) represent the positive or negative residual value of brain mass, compared the predicted mass and are calculated by

$$EQ = BM(0) \div BM(e)$$

where BM(0) = actual brain mass, and BM(e) = predicted brain mass for body size. EQs are shown below for a range of organisms.

---

127   A short, easily readable introduction to this topic is provided by Martin (1992).

Figure 16.2: Species, Weight, and the EQ

Species	Weight (kg)	Brain (g)	EQ
Human	75.00	1400.00	6.56
Whale dolphin	73.00	1162.00	5.55
Bottlenose dolphin	119.96	1535.00	5.26
Commerson's dolphin	43.00	732.00	4.97
Macaque	4.89	108.87	3.15
Baboon	9.88	155.44	2.81
Chimpanzee	45.00	398.60	2.63
Capuchin	3.10	66.94	2.63
Gorilla	120.50	512.92	1.75
Coyote	8.51	84.24	1.69
African gray parrot	0.33	5.70	1.00
Lion	142.82	240.60	0.73
Tiger	184.50	263.50	0.68
Hippopotamus	1351.00	732.00	0.50
Blue whale	58059.00	6800.00	0.38

The coefficient of the equation for BM(e) is close to 0.75, almost exactly the same as the relationship between body size and basal metabolic rate (BMR). Max Kleiber (1961) showed that there is a fixed ratio between brain size and basal metabolic rate, BMR, and that the size of an individual's brain is closely linked to the amount of energy available to sustain it (Milton 1988, Parker 1990).

Kleiber, a Swiss anthropologist, showed that the metabolic rate R for all organisms, including plants, follows exactly the three-quarter-power law of the body mass (i.e., $R = M3/4$). An interesting consequence of this is that all animals are given more or less the same number of heartbeats, and the faster the beat, the shorter the lifespan—for example, mice have a fast heartbeat and only live about a year, while elephants and humans have a slow heartbeat and are long lived.

Why should so many species, with their variety of body plans, follow the same rules? Recently, Amos Maritan and Andrea Rinaldo[128] provided an answer: the three quarter-power law is a feature of

128   See http://www.umdrightnow.umd.edu/news/how-evolution-shapes-geometries-life.

any optimally efficient network. The law is explained by the fact that the relationship embodied in Kleiber's law has survival value. That is, it is consistent with fitness.

The big question, however, is not so much evolution as human-induced life and life modification. Humans have now created life artificially. If we can change our genetic structure or create new life in the lab, what sort of decisions should we make? We are very far from answering this. Consider the possibility of greater intelligence.

Would Greater Intelligence for Humans Be Desirable?

The short answer is yes, if such greater intelligence has survival value. This might take a long time: several hundred thousand years or longer. Another approach to take would be to ask if we ourselves could take actions to increase our intelligence. Our scores on IQ tests have been going up (when they are unnormalized from an average of one hundred), although IQ does not capture all types of intelligence and is mainly a measurement of abstract thinking. Children's IQs tend to change with their environment. But in fact, our brain size has diminished in recent geologic years. This increase in IQs is a bit peculiar, since average brain size has decreased over the last nine thousand to twenty thousand years (Hawks). The average male brain has decreased from 1,500 cubic centimeters to 1,350—a loss of roughly the size of a tennis ball.[129] The female brain has shrunk by about the same percentage. It is unclear why but we can mention several possibilities.

One suggestion for the decline is that average body size has also decreased, at least until recently, from that of hunter-gatherers, thus reducing the size of the neural network required to run it. Why has body size decreased? Warmer weather is one reason—colder weather favors bulkier bodies because they better conserve heat

---

129   This is a significant loss.

(Stringer 2014, 74). A second reason is that males don't have as much need for larger size to compete with each other or to fend off predators, so males have gotten a bit smaller. Finally, it could be that we don't need as much intelligence as early man.

A third suggestion is that we are losing brain size as we become physically lazier. I favor this explanation. Larger brains are energetically expensive and, if they are not needed, will become smaller. For example, domesticated animals such as cats or dogs have smaller brains than their wild counterparts, as they don't require the extra brain power to evade predators (Stringer 2014). Finally, it may be that while the human brain has been getting smaller, certain mutations to our DNA may have increased the efficiency of our minds. What seems to be happening in fact is that the type of intelligence we have is changing, becoming more abstract and less situational. This is suggested by the IQ test results mentioned earlier.

Of particular interest in explaining brain changes are changes in microcephalin and ASPM, two genes that regulate brain size. Based on studies conducted by University of Chicago researchers, it appears that a new variation of microcephalin first appeared about 37,000 years ago, while one for ASPM occurred only about 5,800 years ago. While these are hardly short spans of time, they are a mere blip in the 200,000-year reign of modern man (aka *Homo sapiens*). Apparently, natural selection favored these changes, since the microcephalin variant is present in about 70 percent of humans today and the ASPM variant in about 30 percent.

Interestingly, each of these gene mutations occurred when human culture was leaping forward. Microcephalin was changing as art, music, religion, and advances in toolmaking appeared in the human timeline. The ASPM mutation had its roots in the establishment of Mesopotamia in 7000 BC, the oldest documented civilization. Does this mean that brain size began to decrease as life became easier, in the way domestic cats, for example, have smaller brains than their wild predecessors? Or did our brains become more efficient, allowing them to become smaller?

What Is the Future of the Evolution of Intelligence?

Suppose that instead of the climate going from bad to terrible for early humans and their predecessors, it had gone from bad to much better. Humans probably would not have developed large brains. Maybe *Australopithecus Robustus* would be widespread. In nature, it is either evolution or death.

In evolution, the global best solution is never available, only local adaptations. Evolution builds on what it has at the time. Evolution must work with the Legos in the toy box. It is constrained by the past. Once we became bipedal, for example, this influenced our further evolution. The great human invention was not brain size per se, important as this has been, but the development of greater plasticity or adaptability.

To what extent can we develop new forms of life other than by evolution? Craig Ventor and his lab have created artificial life or something close to it.[130] They were able to insert a man-made, custom-built chromosome into brewer's yeast to not only create a life form but one that also passes down its man-made genes to its offspring.

This future is beyond our imaginations. Of course, we may develop some sort of machine life, perhaps digital machine life. Could we have life as fast as cheetahs, as strong as gorillas, with the eyesight of eagles or buzzards, and the intelligence of supercomputers and with consciousness? The speed of cheetahs arises from their body shape and their very flexible spines.

Roger Penrose the brilliant physicist suggests that consciousness is based on quantum phenomena. So, machines of the sort we currently know could never have consciousness maybe. Can we develop machine "life" that incorporates consciousness? After

---

130   http://sploid.gizmodo.com/scientists-have-created-first-ever-man-made-chromosome-1553312707.

all, we have quantum computers. No one yet knows. The best treatments of this are in science fiction.[131]

Summary

Brains became larger for the *Homo* line of hominoids as they turned to meat eating to survive in a difficult period. The *Homo* line was the only hominids that did this.

The availability of meat meant greater energy so that early humans (*Homo erectus*) were able to divert some of this energy to larger brains. Even with more energy available for brains, energy for other body functions were drained for the brain. The result is a loss of body strength, as compared, say, with chimps, and loss of some brain function, specifically eidetic memory, as compared with chimps. For the last 9,000 to 20,000 years, our brains have been shrinking. This is probably due to the decline in average human size, the development of more efficient brains, or a decreasing need for some brain functions that earlier may have been important for survival (fitness) but are no longer so useful. The development of greater human intelligence will depend on how, and how efficiently, the body and brain can evolve to use energy more efficiently.

Questions

1. To what extent is our intelligence limited by our brain size and therefore by our head size?

2. Hybrid vigor is the tendency for the progeny of hybrids to be enhanced. Might this operate among Americans? Does the greater athletic success of African American-white hybrids rest, at least in part, on this?

3. What about white-Asian hybrids or black Asian hybrids?

4. Who is Jeremy Lin?

---

131 See, for example, Robert Harris's *The Fear Factor*, Hogan's *The Two Faces of Tomorrow*, and Isaac Asimov's robotic series.

17

A PositiveFuture?

Now is the winter of our discontent made glorious summer
—William Shakespeare

We are drowning in information while starving for wisdom
—E.O. Wilson

Introduction

The growth in technology, medical science, life expectancy, and wealth is apparent. The world growth rate in per capita GDP is at a peak. Per capita violence is declining, life expectancy is increasing, the rate of obesity is finally starting to fall in developed countries, and divorce rates among the educated appear to be falling. Fuel cells will probably soon be used to power automobiles and to remove carbon from the atmosphere. Innovations and advances in the biological sciences are growing rapidly, with some astounding possibilities appearing: the end of cancer, slowing of aging, stem cell regrowth, and increases in life expectancy.

Yet we are clearly in a period of transition. From analog to digital. From treatment of disease to regrowth of parts with stem cells. From lesser inequality to greater. From men in power to women in power. From nation states to globalization. From a slower rate of change to a faster one.

Possibilities

The short-term future

Nicolas Kristoff, a *New York Times* columnist whom I much favor, notes that a recent survey found that two-thirds of Americans believe the proportion of the world population living in extreme poverty has almost doubled over the last twenty years. Another

29 percent believe that the proportion had remained the same. This 95 percent are quite wrong. The proportion living in extreme poverty has fallen by more than half between 1993 and 2011. In 1990, more than twelve million children died before the age of five, and this number has dropped by half. A larger percentage of children are becoming educated. (October 1, 2015, A27).

Will there also be growth in emotional intelligence? This is a harder topic to describe than the growth in technology, but think of the most mature and wise person you know—he or she does not lie or cheat; is helpful, happy, and productive; takes satisfaction in his or her contributions to others; and give thanks for the wise parenting he or she received. Steps toward a society of such individuals would involve more emphasis on wise childcare and treatments for illness and drug abuse, less emphasis on punishment, and more on preventive measures to reduce the development of criminal behavior.

Carl Sagan famously said that the universe is neither hostile nor benign, it is indifferent. In a fundamental sense, this is clearly not true. We are part of the universe, and we are often not indifferent, not about each other and not about the fate of our world or the universe. Though more difficult to predict and measure, we have also seen progress in emotional growth and in cultural maturity. One measure of cultural maturity is the level of care of both the very young and very old, which has increased. Another is movement toward an acceptable level of economic equality, which has grown at least for the world if not for important parts of it. It is easy to see in the present wonderful and exciting possibilities.

Innovation

In 1899 Charles H. Duell, commissioner of the US patent office, is reputed to have famously said, "Everything that can be invented has been invented."[132] Just think of the world then and now. Think of the world to be. The figure below gives some indication of the pace of

---

132   This quote may be apocryphal.

per capita innovation.[133] The number of per capita patents granted is
increasing rapidly.[134]

Figure 17.1: Patent Growth in the United States[135]

PATENTS PER MILLION PERSONS

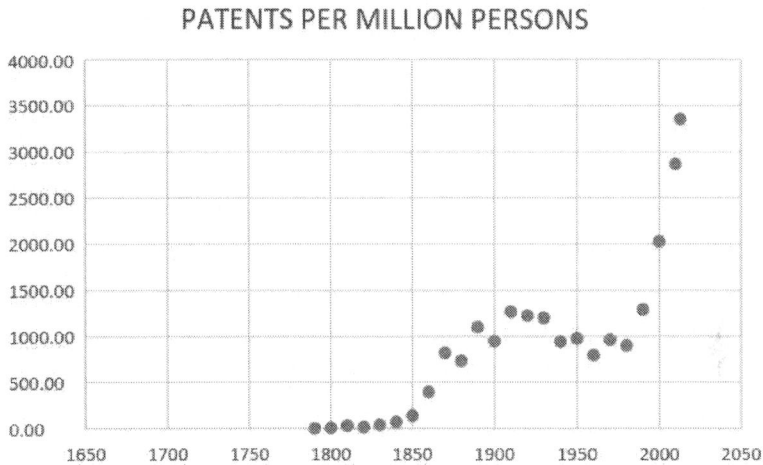

Figure 17.2: Patents per Million Persons in the United States

Year	U.S. population in millions	Patents per million persons
2013	318	3352
2010	309	2868
1980	227	897
1960	179	792
1940	132	940
1920	106	1225
1900	76	944
1880	50	732
1860	31	395
1840	17	71
1820	10	15
1800	5	8
1790	4	0.75

133   Patents per capita are also subject to how difficult it is to obtain a patent in different eras and
other factors.

134   From US Patent Activity by Calendar Years 1790 to the Present and the Statistical Abstract of
the United States, 2012–13).

135   Calculated from data posted on December 9, 2014 in business and innovation, energy, oceans,
policy and politics, science and technology, and from census data.

The average yearly number of patents per person has grown at a rate of about 3.9 percent per year since 1790. This has occurred despite the fact that federal defense spending on research and development has been falling.

Since 1976, government research and development spending has had a downward trend and for the first time is below 1 percent   of GDP. In the meantime, research and development spending by the Chinese government has been increasing. This trajectory is perhaps disturbing. The trend is shown below in figure 17.3.

Figure 17.3: Trends in Federal R&D as Percent of GDP

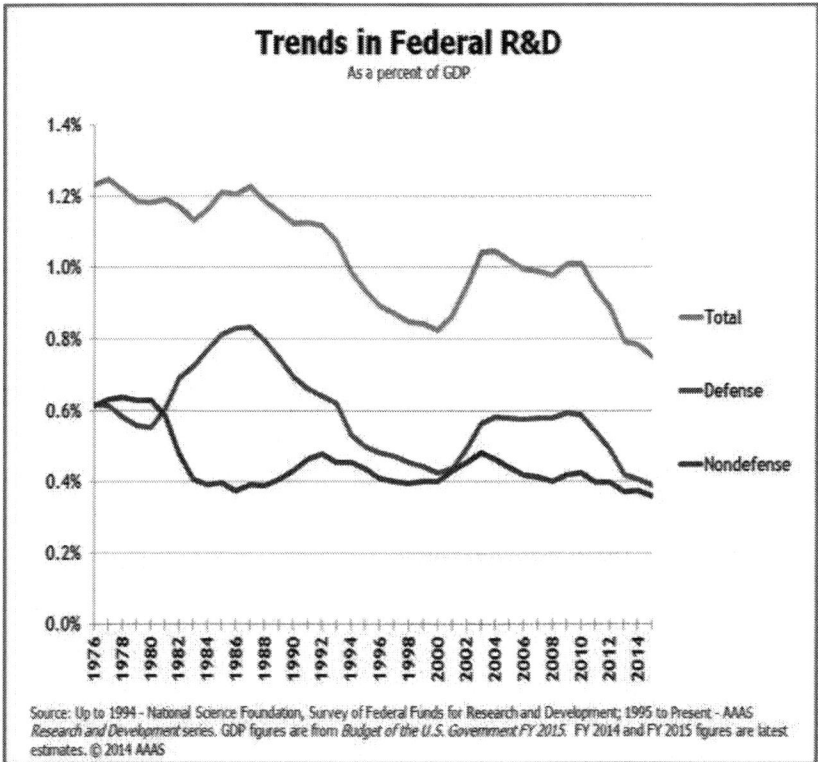

Its consequences if it continues will not become apparent for years. In the meantime, China doubled its research and development spending between 2008 and 2012, a growth rate of almost 18 percent per year. Within five years, China could surpass the United States in absolute innovation. Consider the growth of China's solar energy production.

Solar Energy as an Example of Technological Progress

Arecent article in the Yale Environmental Review notes that, despite recent progress, solar power accounts only for about 1 percent of the world's energy mix. However, the US Department of Energy's SunShot Vision Study projects solar power will provide 14 percent of American electricity by 2030. The International Energy Agency (IEA) says that solar energy, most of it generated by decentralized "rooftop" photovoltaic systems, could well become the world's single biggest source of electricity by midcentury.

This increase will be due to innovations, creating a new generation of superefficient, low-cost sunlight harvesters. New designs and novel solar materials have been setting efficiency records. In addition, innovators are making steady progress in creating a new generation of materials that can harvest the sun's energy far more efficiently than traditional silicon photovoltaic cells. The leading candidates are multijunction cells with layers of light harvesters that gather energy from a separate slice of the solar spectrum, superefficient semiconductor materials like perovskite and gallium-arsenide, and cells made with tiny but powerful solar- absorbing "quantum dots."

Technical hurdles remain. Today's solar panels achieve about 16 percent efficiency. Yet already new materials in testing have achieved 20 to 24 percent efficiency. Overall, solar innovation is being held back by the low priority countries place on clean energy research and development, according to the IEA. The agency reports that on average, governments in developed countries spend at least six times more on defense research than on energy research. Figure17.4 below shows growth of newer energy sources in recent years.

Figure 17.4: Growth of Alternative Energy

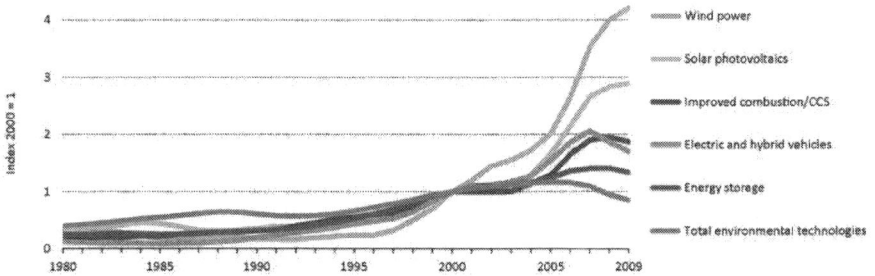

Futures

The immediate future

Nicholas Kristoff also notes (*Seattle Times*, April, 20, 2015) that in 1971, among college graduates, there were about two business majors for every English major. Now that are seven times as many. He quotes Larry Katz, a labor economist at Harvard, that returns to pure technical skills are flattening with the highest financial returns (not to mention emotional returns) going to those who combine soft humanities with technical skills. An understanding of others and the ability to empathize with them and to appreciate ethical issues is fostered by the humanities. As we mentioned earlier in the book, much of happiness is based on interactions with others; these will be richer and more rewarding with an understanding of literary arts.[136] Kristoff goes on to note how much progress

---

136 A recent best-selling science fiction book, *The Three Body Problem*, is a technological tour de force. As with much of science fiction, though not in fantasy literature, there is a great void of human interaction, empathy, commiseration, and understanding. This is understandable in science fiction, but this sterile sort of picture has been growing while the phenomenal growth of the paranormal in scientific fiction and fantasy also gets away from what it is to be maturely human. Will we become merely digital creatures? Contrast this sort of work with the recent excellent fantasy work by William Rothfuss, *The Sound of the Wind*, or the wonderful retelling of fairy tales by Robin McKinley. It is not my purpose to detail how to achieve such goals, nor could I. Rather the purpose of this chapter is simply to appeal to your imagination of what a bright future would look like and to suggest that obtaining it will have much to do with the ability to obtain cultural maturity and with your vision for it.

there has been: the decline in violence, the increase in life expectancy, the growth in income and the diminution in poverty. Yet these gains are not generally recognized. Peoples estimate that poverty has grown, that violence has increased. Looking ahead for the next several years, it is easy to imagine that these positive trends will continue. Of course.

When I was in working in Canada in the 1960s, I wrote an article about future possibilities and suggested the next century would be the age of the interaction of computers and biology. I talked about increasing choice in selecting the characteristics of one's children, computer life, and the like. No one wanted to publish it, understandably, as it was regarded as too speculative. Tooting my own horn, I would say it was prescient. We are at the dawn of the digital age and perhaps digital life.

The Long Term Future

Is the longer-term future: the end of natural man? Perhaps man has future. Natural man was created by natural selection. Man is now creating animals and plants by intelligent design. Harari (2015) notes the creation of a florescent rabbit by using rabbit and jellyfish DNA. To some unknown extent, future life will be created by intelligent design. This life can be organic life created by biological engineering, part organic life created in part by biological engineering and machine parts (cyborgs) or machine life, or digital life in the form of intelligent robots. Harari notes that not only can we create new life but are close to being able to genetically determine its behavior and thus its social structure. We will soon be able to create superhumans. Would such superhumans be evolutionarily fit? That is, would they be able to adapt to new physical or social environments? If we create our own environments, we will be able to create creatures to fit those environments. Perhaps the superhumans will be able to create and control their environments to an extent we *Homo sapiens* seem not to be able to. Will this be a Brave New World that has such creatures in it?[137] We are entering a world in which we will have in Venter's (2013) words, "Life at the Speed of Light."

The idea of direct communication between human and computer "brains" is an old one. Now it is a potentially realizable one. If we are all connected to the same computer reservoir, will we become eusocial creatures such as ants and bees like the bugs in the book Ender's Game, in which there is one main mind governing all. Or like the superhumans in Ramen Naam's trilogy, Nexus. Is machine consciousness possible? Roger Penrose suggests that consciousness is a quantum phenomenon and would not be easily replicable artificially and perhaps not replicable at all. Yet we are slowly creating quantum computers. Will some form of future computer like life or cyborg be able to reverse entropy and say "let there be light"?

I quote from Harari:

> Yet the real potential of future technologies is to change
> Homo sapiens itself, including our emotions and desires...
> What is a spaceship compared to an eternally young cyborg
> that does no breed and has no sexuality, who can share
> thoughts directly with other beings, whose abilities to focus
> and remember are a thousand time greater than our own, and
> who is never angry or sad, but has emotions and desires that
> we cannot begin to imagine.

If the curtain is indeed about to drop on Sapiens' history, we members of one of the final generations should devote some time to answering one last question: what do we want to become if anything?

---

137   See A. Huxley.

Extraterrestrial Life

What is the probability of intelligent life in the galaxy or the universe? There are about nine billion Earthlike planets in our galaxy, and one hundred billion in the known universe. This gives us nine billion chances of extraterrestrial life in our galaxy and one hundred billion for our universe. For there not to be extraterrestrial life, the chances of it arising would be less than one in one hundred billion. It took about 3.5 billion years for life on Earth to arise. *Homo sapiens'* ancestors have been around for about 6 million years. Or only a small fraction of Earth's years. A rough estimate, then. based on these figures is that intelligent life requires about 4 billion years to evolve. The age of the known universe is about 14 billion years, so there would seem to have been enough time for intelligent life to exist. Moreover, many of the Earthlike planets are far older than Earth. Thus it would seem that there has been enough time for intelligent life to appear. Consider the following; Bostrum has calculated that it would take 29 million years for an intelligent species to completely colonize the Milky Way galaxy if it could travel at 1 percent the speed of light. My calculations below show the number of years to colonize the galaxy if the space travelers could travel only at 0.015 percent of the speed of light—100,000 miles per hour:

Figure 17.5: Years to Calculate All Earthlike Planets in Milky Way Galaxy

Speed in Miles per Hour	Number of Years for Colonization
One Percent of Speed of Light	29 million
100,000	1.9 billion

Where are they, then, the great physicist Enrico Fermi's question? There would seem to be three possibilities: (1) the probabilities of life arising are very, very, very small; (2) intelligent life, when it reaches a certain level of technological complexity, destroys itself (Fermi's idea), and (3) at the level of complexity sufficient for space travel, they go elsewhere. Where? So, where are they?

Low Probability of Intelligent Life[138]

Ernst Mayr pointed out that *Homo sapiens* were very close to extinction a number of times. Yet this would seem to be offset by the great number of chances that exist in the galaxy and by current research on how life can form. This explanation does not seem likely. Advanced life destroys itself.

The Bible in Genesis notes,

> "after he drove the man out, he placed on the east side of the Garden of Eden cherubim and a flaming sword flashing back and forth to guard the way to the tree of life."

This suggests first that there is a tree of life, so that immortality may be possible, and that God (nature) did not want mankind finding it or at least not easily. Why not? Perhaps God is a jealous God who did not want man or superman as a rival. Perhaps God created a barrier until mankind developed sufficient maturity that he or she or it could be proud of his or her or its creation. Perhaps mankind could not develop such maturity if immortality was achieved too early. Perhaps!, God knows? It is not difficult to imagine us destroying ourselves; there are so many possibilities: war, pestilence, climate change, anarchy, and the destruction of institutions that have led to our ascent and artificial life that eliminates us.

Liu Cixin's recent Hugo Award–winning book *The Three Body Problem* considers a world in which a godlike prime directive resets civilization when it reaches a sufficiently high level and human destroy themselves. Fermi is not alone in suggesting this possibility.

---

138 The three-body problem in physics involves tracing the path of three bodies exerting gravity on each other. It has never been completely solved. (See, e.g.,http://www.math.umn. edu/~rmoeckel/ presentations/Presentations.html).

They Went Away

Perhaps beyond our galaxy, perhaps to another universe, maybe of their own creation, perhaps to a life form that exists as a sort of cloud. Perhaps they know of us but are not interested, at least until, if ever, we develop a higher level of cultural maturity.

Summary

The growth in technology, medical science, life expectancy, and wealth is apparent. The world growth rate in per capita GDP is at a peak. Per capita violence is declining, life expectancy is increasing, the rate of obesity is finally starting to fall in developed countries, and divorce rates among the educated appear to be falling. Fuel cells will probably soon be used to power automobiles and to remove carbon from the atmosphere. Innovations and advances in the biological sciences are growing rapidly with some astounding possibilities appearing: the end of cancer, slowing of aging, stem cell regrowth, and increases in life expectancy.

Yet we are clearly in a period of transition. From analog to digital. From treatment of disease to regrowth of parts with stem cells. From lesser inequality to greater. From men in power to women in power. From nation states to globalization. From a slower rate of change to a faster one.

And yet, and yet we are reaching the end of Moore's law. Big breakthroughs will await new approaches, perhaps quantum computing. If extraterrestrial life in our galaxy has existed for long, it should have spoken. In the future, will *Homo sapiens* be replaced by machine life? Is machine life an oxymoron?

References
(Not all references are mentioned in text)

Adler, Moshe. 1985. "Stardom and Talent." *American Economic Review*., vol. 75, issue 1, pages 208-12

Aiello, L. C., and P. Wheeler. 1995. "The Expensive-Tissue Hypothesis: The Brain and Digestive System in Human and Primate Evolution." *Current Anthropology* 36:199–221.

Alvaredo, Facundo, Anthony B. Atkinson, Thomas Piketty, and Emmanuel Saez. 2013. "The Top 1 Percent in International and Historical Perspective." *Journal of Economic Perspectives* 27(3): 320.

Anderson, C. Leigh, and Janet W. Looney. Making Progress: Essays in Progress and Public Policy. (2002).

Andrews, P., and L. Martin. 1991. "Hominoid Dietary Evolution." *Philosophical Transactions of the Royal Society of London B: Biological Sciences* 334: 199–209.

Antón, S. C. 2003. "Natural History of Homo erectus." *Yearbook of Physical Anthropology* 46: 126–170.

Axelrod, Robert M., and W. D. Hamilton. 1984. The *Evolution of Cooperation*. New York: Penguin.

Babbitt, C. C. 2011. "Genomic Signatures of Diet-Related Shifts during Human Origins." *Proceedings of the Royal Society B: Biological Sciences* 278: 961–969.

Barzun, Jacques. 2000. *From Dawn to Decadence*. Harper Collins.

Bellomo, R. V. 1991. "Methods of Determining Early Hominid Behavioral Activities Associated with the Controlled Use of Fire at FxJj 20 Main, Koobi Fora." *Journal of Human Evolution* 27: 173–195.

Bertrand, Marianne, and Sendhil Mullainathan. 2001. "Are CEOs Rewarded for Luck? The Ones without Principals Are." *Quarterly Journal of Economics* 116 (3): 901–932.

Binford, L. R. 1981. Bones: *Ancient Men and Modern Myths*. New York: Academic Press.

Binford, L. R. 1988. "Fact and Fiction about the *Zinajnthropus* Floor: Data, Arguments, and Interpretations." *Current Anthropology* 29: 123–135.

Blumenschine, Robert J. 1986. "Carcass Consumption Sequences and the Archaeological Distinction of Hunting and Scavenging." *Journal of Human Evolution* 15: 639–659.

Blumenschine, Robert J. 1987. "Characteristics of an Early Hominid Scavenging Niche." *Current Anthropology* 28: 383–407.

Blumenschine, Robert J. 1988. "An Experimental Model of the Timing of Hominid and Carnivore Influence on Archaeological Bone Assemblages. *Journal of Archaeological Science* 15: 483–502.

Blumenschine, Robert J. 1995. "Percussion Marks, Tooth Marks, and Experimental Determinations of the Timing of Hominid and

Carnivore Access to Long Bones at FLK Zinjanthropus, Olduvai Gorge, Tanzania." *Journal of Human Evolution* 29: 21–51.

Blumenschine, Robert J., and Briana Pobiner. 2006. "Zooarchaeology and the Ecology of Oldowan Hominin Carnivory." *In Early Hominin Diets: The Known, the Unknown, and the Unknowable,* edited by P. Ungar, 167–190. Oxford: Oxford University Press.

Blumenschine, Robert J., and M. M. Selvaggio. 1988. "Percussion Marks on Bone Surfaces as a New Diagnostic of Hominid Behavior." *Nature* 333: 763–765.

Blumenschine, Robert J. et al. 2007. "Vertebrate Taphonomic Perspectives on Oldowan Hominin Land Use in the Plio-Pleistocene Olduvai Basin, Tanzania." *In Breathing Life into Fossils: Taphonomic Studies in Honor of C. K. (Bob) Brain,* edited by T. R. Pickering, N. Toth, and K. Schick, 161–180. IN: Stone Age Institute Press

Boehm, Christopher. 2012. *Moral Origins: The Evolution of Virtue, Altruism, and Shame.* New York: Basic Books.

Bossard, James H., and Eleanor Stoker Boll. 1966. *The Sociology of Child Development, 4th ed.* Harper & Row.

Brain, C. K., and A. Sillen. 1988. "Evidence from the Swartkrans Cave for the Earliest Use of Fire." *Nature* 336: 464–466.

Brantingham, P. J. 1998. "Hominid-Carnivore Coevolution and Invasion of the Predatory Guild." *Journal of Anthropological Archaeology* 17: 327–353.

Braun, D. R. et al. 2010. "Early Hominin Diet Included Diverse Terrestrial and Aquatic Animals 1.95 Ma in East Turkana, Kenya." *Proceedings of the National Academy of Sciences* USA 107: 10,002–10,007.

Brin, David. 1984. *Otherness*. Bantam.

Broadberry, Stephen and Mark Harrison. 2005. *The Economics of World War I.* New York: Cambridge University Press.

Broadhurst, C. L. et al. "Brain-Specific Lipids from Marine, Lacustrine, or Terrestrial Food Resources: Potential Impact on Early African *Homo sapiens."* *Comparative Biochemistry and Physiology Part B: Biochemistry and Molecular Biology* 131(4): 653–673.

Brockman, Hilke, Jan Delhey, Christian Welzel, and Hao Yuan. 2009. "The China Puzzle: Falling Happiness in a Rising Economy." *Journal of Happiness Studies.*

Brown, K. S. et al. "An Early and Enduring Advanced Technology Originating 71,000 YearsAgo in South Africa." *Nature* 491, 590–593.

Bunn, H. T. 1981. "Archaeological Evidence for Meat-Eating by Plio-Pleistocene Hominids from Koobi Fora and Olduvai Gorge." *Nature* 291: 547–577.

Bunn, H. T. 1986. "Patterns of Skeletal Representation and Hominid Subsistence Activities at Olduvai Gorge, Tanzania and Koobi Fora, Kenya." *Journal of Human Evolution* 15: 673–690.

Bunn, H. T. 1991. "ATaphonomic Perspective on the Archaeology of Human Origins." *Annual Review of Anthropology* 20: 433–467.

Bunn, H. T., and Ezzo, J. A. 1993. "Hunting and Scavenging by Plio-Pleistocene Hominids: Nutritional Constraints, Archaeological

Patterns and Behavioural Implications." *Journal of Archaeological Science* 20: 365–398.

Bunn, H. T.& Kroll, E. M. 1988. "Fact and Fiction about the *Zinajnthropus* Floor: Data, Arguments, and Interpretations." *Current Anthropology* 29: 135–149.

Bunn, H T. et al. "Was FLK North Levels 1–2 a Classic 'Living Floor' of Oldowan Hominins or a Taphonomically Complex Palimpsest Dominatedby Large Carnivore Feeding Behavior?" *Quaternary Research* 74(3): 355–362.

Burks, Stephen. 2009. "Performance Pay and the Erosion of Worker Cooperation: Field Experimental Evidence." *Journal of Economic Behavior and Organization* 70(3): 458–469.

Cahill, Thomas. 2006. *Mysteries of the Middle Ages: The Rise of Feminism, Science, and Art from the Cults of Catholic Europe.* N.A. Talese.

Cahill, Thomas. 1998. *The Gifts of the Jews: How a Tribe of Desert Nomads Changed the Way Everyone Thinks and Feels.* N. A. Talese.

Campbell, Joseph. 1983. *Historical Atlas of World Mythology.* A. Van Der Marck Editions.

Cannadine, David. 1998. *Class in Britain.*

Cannadine, David. 1990. *The Decline and Fall of the British Aristocracy.* New Haven, CT: Yale University Press.

Capaldo, S. D. 1995. "Inferring Hominid and Carnivore Behavior from Dual-Patterned Archaeofaunal Assemblages." PhD diss., Rutgers University.

Capaldo, S. D. 1997. "Experimental Determinations of Carcass Processing by Plio-Pleistocene Hominids and Carnivores at FLK 22 (*Zinjanthropus*), Olduvai Gorge, Tanzania." *Journal of Human Evolution* 33: 555–597.

Carneiro, Robert. L. 1970. "A Theory of the Origin of the State."

Science 169: 733–738.

Carr, Nicholas G. 2010. *The Shallows: What the Internet Is Doing to Our Brains.* New York: W.W. Norton.

Cavallo, J. A., and Robert J. Blumenschine. 1989. "Tree-Stored Leopard Kills: Expanding the Hominid Scavenging Niche." *Journal of Human Evolution* 18: 393–399.

Chapman, Benjamin P, Paul R. Duberstein, Silvia Sörensen,

and Jeffrey M. Lyness. 2014. "Gender Differences in Five Factor Model Personality Traits in an Elderly Cohort: Extension of Robust and Surprising Findings to an Older Generation." *Personality and Individual Differences* 43(6): 1594–1603. http://doi.org/10.1016/j.paid.2007.04.028.

Chida Y, and A. Steptoe. 2008. "Positive Psychological Well- Being and Mortality: A Quantitative Review of Prospective Observational Studies." *Psychosomatic Medicine* 70: 741–756.

Chirot, Daniel. 1994. *How Societies Change*. Sage Pine Form Press.

Claessen H. J. M. 2000. "Problems, Paradoxes, and Prospects of Evolutionism." In *Alternatives of Social Evolution*, edited by N. N. Kradin,

A. V.Korotayev, D. M. Bondarenko, V.de Munck, and P.K. Wason, 1–9. Vladivostok, Russia: FEB RAS.

Clark, Andrew, Paul Frijters, and Michael A. Shields. 2008. "Relative Income, Happiness, and Utility: An Explanation for the Easterlin Paradox and Other Puzzles." *Journal of Economic Literature* 46(1): 95–144.

Clark, Gregory. 2007. *A Farewell to Alms: A Brief Economic History of the World.* Princeton, NJ: Princeton University Press.

Coase, R. H. 1974. "The Lighthouse in Economics." *Journal of Law and Economics* 17(2): 357–76.

Coelo, Philip. 1985. "Status as Utility: An Examination into the Causesof Economic Growth."*Research in Law and Economics* 7: 89–121.

Costain, Thomas. 1958. *The Three Edwards.* Buccaneer Books.

Czeck, Brian. (http://www.huffingtonpost.com/brian-czech/paul- krugman-on-limits to_b_5988532.html?utm_hp_ref=green.)

Daley, Alex and Doug Hornig. 2012. "Why Your Healthcare Is So Damn Expensive." *Casey Research*. July. http://www.caseyresearch.com/ articles/why-your-health-care-so-darn-expensive.

Darwin, Charles. 1871. *The Descent of Man*. London: J. Murray.

Darwin, Charles. 1859. *The Originof Speciesby Natural Selection.*

London: J. Murray.

Davidson, Richard J., PhD, and Sharon Begley. 2012. *The Emotional Life of Your Brain: How Its Unique Patterns Affect the Way You Think, Feel, and Live—and How You Can Change Them*. New York: Hudson Street.

Dawkins, Richard. 1986. *The Blind Watchmaker.* New York: Norton.

de Heinzelin, J. E. et al. 1999. "Environment and Behavior of 2.5-Million-Year-Old Bouri Hominids."*Science* 284: 625–629.

Decker, Ed. 2013. "The Future of Intelligence: Is the Human Brain Still Evolving?" *Rewire Me*, blog post, November 9. http://www. rewireme.com/journeys/the-future-of-intelligence-is-the-human-brain- still-evolving/.

Deiner and Scollon. 2014. "The What, Why, When, and How of Teaching the Science of Subjective Well-Being." *The Teaching of Psychology.*

de Menocal, Peter B. 2013. "Climate Shocks." *Scientific American* 311(3): 48f.

De Neve, Jan-Emmanuel, Ed Diener, Louis Tay, and Cody Xuereb. 2013. *The Objective Benefits of Subjective Well-Being.* CEP Discussion Papers, CEPDP1236. Centre for Economic Performance, London School of Economics and Political Science, London.

Deutsch, David. 2011. *The Beginning of Infinity: Explanations That Transform the World.* New York: Viking.

DeWaal, Frans. 1989. *Peacemaking among Primates.* Cambridge, MA: Harvard University Press.

DeWaal, Frans. 1997. *Bonobo: The Forgotten Ape.* Berkeley: University of California Press.

De Wahl, Frans. "One for all" Scientific American. 311: 68-71. (2014).

Diener, Edward, and M. Chan. 2011. "Happy People Live Longer: Subjective Well-Being Contributes to Health and Longevity." *Applied Psychology: Health and Wellbeing* 3: 1–43.

Diener, Edward, and Christie Napa Scollon. 2014. "The What, Why, When, and How of Teaching the Science of Subjective Well-Being." *Teaching of Psychology* 41(2): 175–183.

Dobel and Anderson. 2002. "Progress and the Promise of Public Policy." *In Making Progress.* Lexington Press.

Domínguez-Rodrigo, M. 1997. "Meat-Eating by Early Hominids at the FLK 22 Zinjanthropus Site, Olduvai Gorge (Tanzania): An Experimental Approach Using Cut-Mark Data." *Journal of Human Evolution* 33: 669–690.

Domínguez-Rodrigo, M. 1999. "Flesh Availability and Bone Modifications in Carcasses Consumed by Lions: Palaeoecological Relevance in Hominid Foraging Patterns." *Palaeogeography, Palaeoclimatology, and Palaeoecology* 149: 373–388.

Domínguez-Rodrigo, M. 2002. "Hunting and Scavenging by Early Humans: The State of the Debate." *Journal of World Prehistory* 16: 1–54.

Domínguez-Rodrigo, M., and T. R. Pickering2003. "Early Hominid Hunting and Scavenging: A Zooarchaeological Review." *Evolutionary Anthropology* 12: 275–292.

Domínguez-Rodrigo, M. et al. 2010. "Configurational Approach to Identifying the Earliest Hominin Butchers." *Proceedings of the National Academyof Sciences USA* 107: 20,929–20,934.

Domínguez-Rodrigo, M. et al. 2005. "Cutmarked Bones from Pliocene Archaeological Sites at Gona, Afar, Ethiopia: Implications for the Functions of the World's Oldest Stone Tools." *Journal of Human Evolution* 48:109–121.

Domínguez-Rodrigo, M. et al., eds. 2007. *Deconstructing Olduvai: A Taphonomic Study of the Bed I Sites.* Dordrecht, The Netherlands: Springer.

Downs, Anthony. 1957. *An Economic Theory of Democracy.* Boston: Addison-Wesley.

Egeland, C. P. et al. 2004. "Disentangling Early Stone Age Palimpsests: Determining the Functional Independence of Hominid- and Carnivore-Derived Portions of Archaeofaunas." *Journal of Human Evolution* 47: 343–357.

Ellenberg, Jordan. 2014. *How Not to Be Wrong: The Power of Mathematical Thinking.*NewYork:Penguin.

Elickson, Robert. 1986. Of Coase and Cattle: Dispute Resolution among Neighbors in Shasta County, 38 STAN. L. REV. 623–87.

Ellickson, Robert. 1994.*Orderwithout Law: How Neighbors Settle Disputes.* Cambridge, MA: Harvard University Press.

Ellickson, Robert, Carol Rose, and Henry Smith. 2014. *Property Law.* WolterKluver.

Erikson, Erik H. 1963. *Childhood and Society.* New York: Norton.

Erikson, Erik H. 1964. *Insightand Responsibility: Lectureson the Ethical Implications of Psychoanalytic Insight.* NewYork:W.W.Norton.

Fearon, James, and David Laitin. 1996. "Explaining Ethnic Cooperation." *American Political Science Review* 90:715–735.

Fernández-Jalvo, Y., and P.Andrews. 2011. "When Humans Chew Bones." *Journal of Human Evolution* 60: 117–123.

Ferraro et al. 2013. "Earliest Archaeological Evidence of Persistent Hominin Carnivory." *PLOS ONE* 9, e62174.

Fogel, Robert William. 2000. *The Fourth Great Awakening and the Future of Egalitarianism.* Chicago: University of Chicago Press.

Frank, Robert H., and Philip J. Cook. 1995. *The Winner-Take- All Society: How More and More Americans Compete for Ever Fewer and Bigger Prizes, Encouraging Economic Waste, Income Inequality, and an Impoverished Cultural Life.* New York: Free.

Galiana, Isabel and Chris Green. 2010. "An Analysis of a Technology-Led Climate Policy as a Response to Climate Change." *The Breakthrough.* http://thebreakthrough.org/blog/AP_Technology_Galiana_ Green_v.6.0.pdf.

Gaventa, John. 1982. *Power and Powerlessness: Quiescence and Rebellion in an Appalachian Valley.* Champaign: University of Illinois Press.

Gebauer et al. 2013. "The Psychological Benefits of Income Are Contingent on Individual-Level and Culture-Level Religiosity." *Social Psychological and Personality Science* 4(5): 569–578.

"Ghana—GDP per Capita." *Ghana.* Index Mundi, n.d. Web. 14 Aug. (2015).

"Ghana." *Economy: Population, GDP, Inflation, Business, Trade, FDI, Corruption.* The Heritage Foundation, n.d. Web. 14 Aug. (2015).

Gilbert, Martin. 1997. *A History of the Twentieth Century.* New York: W. Morrow.

Goren-Inbar, N., et al. 2004. "Evidence of Hominin Control of Fire at Gesher Benot Ya'aqov, Israel." *Science* 304: 725–727.

Greene, B. 2004. *The Fabric of the Cosmos: Space, Time, and the Texture of Reality.* New York: A.A. Knop.

Greitemeyer, Tobias, and Dirk O. Mugge. 2014. "Video Games Do Affect Social Outcomes: A Meta-Analysic Review of the Effects of Violent and Prosocial Video Game Play." *Personality and Social Psychology Bulletin* 40: 578–89. January 23.

Gwyne, S. C. Empire of the Summer Moon: Quanah Parker and the Rise and Fall of the Comanches, the Most Powerful Indian Tribe in American History.

Hacker, Jacob S., and Paul Pierson. 2010. *Winner-Take-All Politics: How Washington Madethe Rich Richer And Turned Its Back on the Middle Class.* New York: Simon & Schuster.

Hall, Peterand Michele Lamont, eds. 2000. *Successful Societies: How Institutions and Culture Affect Health.* New York: Cambridge University Press.

Hall, Peter, and David Soskice, eds. 2001. *Varieties of Capitalism: The Institutional Foundations of Comparative Advantage.* Oxford: Oxford University Press.

Harris, Marvin, , Cannibals and Kings, Landmark, 1991

Harrison, Mark. 1998. "The Economics of World War II: An Overview." In *The Economics of World War II: Six Great Powers in International Comparison*, edited by Mark Harrison, New York: Cambridge University Press.

Hess, Elizabeth. 2008. *Nim Chimpsky: The Chimp Who Would Be Human.* New York: Bantam.

"Hierarchyof Needs."*Abraham Maslow—Father of Modern Management Psychology.* N.p., n.d. Web.16 Oct.(2015).

Higgs, Robert. 1987. *Crisis and Leviathan: Critical Episodes in the Growth of American Government.* NewYork: Oxford University Press.

Hobbes, Thomas. 1651. *Leviathan.* N.p.: Oxford at the Clarendon. http://www.egs.edu/library/thomas-hobbes/quotes/.

Huntington, Samuel P., and Lawrence E. Harrison. 2000. *Culture Matters: How Values Shape Human Progress.* New York: Basic Books.

Iverson and Soskice. 2006. "Electoral Institutions and the Politics of Coalitions: Why Some Democracies Redistribute More Than Others." *American Political Science Review* 100(2).

Joyce, Richard. 2007. *The Evolution of Mortality.* Cambridge, MA: The MIT Press.

Kahneman, Daniel, and Angus Deaton. 2010. "High Income Improves Evaluation of Life but Not Emotional Well-Being." *Proceedings of the National Academy of the United States of America* 107(38).

Kenneally, Christine. 2014. *The Invisible Story of the Human Race.* NewYork: Viking Press.

Kohli, Atul. "Nationalist versus Dependent Capitalist Development: Alternate Pathways of Asia and Latin America in a Globalized World." *Studies in Comparative International Development* 44(4): 386–410.

"KAL's Cartoon." January 2015. *Economist* 17.

Konner, Melvin. 2015. *Women after All: Sex, Evolution, and the End of Male Supremacy.* New York: W.W. Norton & Company.

Larson, Shannon. "Comments." *Quora.* N.p., n.d. Web. 16 (2015).

Lister, Greg. "Is Happiness a Zero-Sum Game?" http://coffee theory. com/2012/07/06/

Luhrman, T. M. "Wheat People vs. Rice People: Why Are Some Cultures More Individualistic than Others?" Editorial, *New York Times,* 2014.

Maddison, Angus. 1991. *Dynamic Forces in Capitalist Development: A Long-Run Comparative View.* New York: Oxford Press.

Maddison, Angus. 2005. *Growth and Interaction in the World Economy: The Roots of Modernity.* Washington, DC: The AEI Press.

Marean, Curtis W. 2015. "The Most Invasive Species of All." *Scientific American* 14: 32–39.

Maslow, Abraham. 1943. "A Theory of Human Motivation." *Psychological Review* 50(4): 370–96.

Maslow, Abraham. 1954. *Motivation and Personality.* New York: Harper.

Mason, Wyatt. 2014. "The Revelations of Marilynne Robinson." *New York Times Magazine,* October 1.

Massey, Robert. 1992. *Dreadnaught.* New York: Ballantine Books.

Mayr, Ernst. 1997. *This Is Biology: The Science of the Living World.* Cambridge, MA: Harvard University Press.

McHenry, Henry M. 1994. "Behavioral Ecological Implications of Early Hominid Body Size." *Journal of Human Evolution* 27(1): 77–87.

Milanović, Branko. 2011. *The Haves and the Have-Nots: A Brief and Idiosyncratic History of Global Inequality.* New York: Basic Books.

Mitani, John C., and David P. Watts. 2001. "Why Do Chimpanzees Hunt and Share Meat?" *Animal Behaviour* 61(5): 915–24.

Mukherjee, Siddarth. 2016. "Same but Different." *New Yorker*, May 2.

Nisbett, Richard E., and Yuri Miyamoto. 2005. "The Influence of Culture: Holistic versus Analytic Perception." *Trends in Cognitive Sciences* 9(9).

Nordhaus, William. 2012. "Why Climate Change Skeptics Are Wrong." *The New York Review*, March 22, 2012.

North, Douglas. 1990. *Institutions, Institutional Change and Economic Performance*. New York: Cambridge University Press.

North, Douglas. "Institutions." *The Journal of Economic Perspectives* 5(1): 97–112.

Novick A. 1955. "Growth of Bacteria." *Annual Review of Microbiology* 9: 97–110. DOI: 9.1146/annurev.mi.09.100155.000525. PMID.

Nutter, Warren. 1962. *The Growth of Industrial Production in the Soviet Union. Princeton*, NJ: Princeton University Press.

O'Connell, Andrew. 2013. S*tats & Curiosities from Harvard Business Review.* Boston: Harvard Business Review.

Olson, Mancur. 1971. *The Logic of Collective Action*. Cambridge, MA: Harvard University Press.

Oppenheimer, Franz. 1914. *The State*. New York: Vanguard Press.

Oishi, S., S. Kesebir, and E. Diener. 2011. "Income Inequality and Happiness." *Psychological Science* 22: 1095–1100.

Ostrom, Elinor. 1990. *Governing the Commons*. New York: Cambridge University Press.

Palacios-Huerta, Ignacio, ed. 2013. *In 100 Years: Leading Economists Predict the Future.* Cambridge, MA: The MIT Press.

Pappas, Stephanie. http://www.livescience.com/14638-income- inequality-costing-americans-happiness.html.

Persson, Torsten, and G. Tabellini. 2004. "Constitutions and Economic Policy." *Journal of Economic Perspectives* 18, 75–98.

Piketty, Thomas. 2014. *Capital in the Twenty-First Century.*
Translated by Arthur Goldhammer. Cambridge, MA: Harvard University Press.

Picketty, Thomas, and Emmanuel Saez. 2003. "Income Inequality in the
United States, 1913–1998." *The Quarterly Journal of Economics* 118(1).

Pinker, Steven. 2011. *The Better Angels of Our Nature: Why Violence Has
Declined.* New York: Viking.

Pinker, Steven. 2002. *The Blank Slate: The Modern Denial of Human Nature.*
New York: Viking.

Pobiner, B. 2013. "Evidence for Meat-Eating by Early Humans."
Nature Education Knowledge 4(6):1.

Posner, Daniel. 2004. "The Political Salience of Cultural Difference: Why
Chewas and Tumbakas Are Allies in Zambia and AdversariesinMalawi."
American Political Science Review 98:529–46.

Rawls, John. 1971. *A Theory of Justice.* Cambridge, MA:
Harvard University Press.

Ridley, Matt. 2004. *The Agile Gene: How Nature Turnson Nurture.*
New York: Perennial.

Ridley, Mark. 2001. *The Cooperative Gene: How Mendel's Demon Explainsthe
Evolutionof Complex Beings.* New York: Free.

Ridley, Matt. 2010. *The Rational Optimist: How Prosperity Evolves.*
New York: Harper.

Rosin, Hanna. 2010. "The End of Men." *The Atlantic.* http://
- men/308135/?single_page=true.

Rothstein, Edward. 2000. "ASojourner in the Past Retraces His Steps."
New York Times.

"Social Progress Index." *The Social Progress Imperative.* N.p., n.d.
Web. 14 Aug. (2015).

Shermer, Michael. 2015. The Moral Arc: How Science and Reason Lead
Humanity toward Truth, Justice, andFreedom.

Smith, Robin Anne. 2013. "How Did Human Brains Get to Be So Big?"
Scientific American, blog post, February 21. http://blogs.scientificamerican.com/
guest-blog/2012/02/21/how-did-human-brains- get-to-be-so-big/.

Stark, Rodney. 1996. *The Rise of Christianity: A Sociologist Reconsiders History*. Princeton, NJ: Princeton University Press.

Steirin and Bram Lancee. 2011. "Does Income Inequality Negatively Affect General Trust?" Gini Discussion Paper, November 20.

Stringer, Christopher. 2014. SA Mind, Nov/Dec, 74.

William J. Talbott: *Which Rights Should Be Universal?* (New York: Oxford University Press, 2005).

William J. Talbott, Human Rights and Human Well-Being (New York: Oxford University Press, 2010).

Talhelm, Thomas, X. Zhang, C. Oishi, D. Duan, X. Lan, and

S. Kitihama. 2014 "Large Scale Psychological Differences within China Explained by Rice versus Wheat Agriculture." *Science* 344: 603–8.

Tattersall, Ian. 2014. *Scientific American* Sept p. 56.

Taylor et al. 1978. *Journal of Conflict Resolution* 578.

Thaler, Richard H. 1991. *Quasi Rational Economics*. New York: Russell Sage Foundation.

"The Sun Shines Bright." 2011. *The Economist,* December 3. Web.

"The Tragedy of the Arabs: Civilization That Used to Lead the World Is in Ruins—And Only the Locals Can Rebuild It." 2014. *The Economist.* July 5. Accessed May 17, 2015.

Todar, Kenneth. *Textbook of Bacteriology*. http://www. textbookofbacteriology. net/.

Toffler, Alvin. 1970. *Future Shock*. New York: Random House.

Tylor, Edward B. 1871. *Primitive Culture: Researches into the Development of Mythology, Philosophy, Religion, Art, and Custom.* London: John Murray

Venter, J. Craig. 2013. *Life at the Speed of Light: From the Double Helix to the Dawn of Digital Life*. New York: Penguin.

Wade, Nicholas. 2014. *A Troublesome Inheritance: Genes, Race, and Human History.* New York: Penguin.

Wade, Nicholas. 2007. *New York Times*, Science Section, August 7.

Waldfogel, Jane. 1997. "The Effect of Children on Women's Wages." *American Sociological Review* 62: 209-17

Weber, Max. 1946. *Essays in Sociology.* New York: Oxford University Press.

Wilkinson, Richard G., and Kate Pickett. 2010. *The Spirit Level: Why Greater Equality Makes Societies Stronger.* New York: Bloomsbury.

Wilson, Edward O. 2012. *The Social Conquest of Earth.* New York: Liveright Publishing.

Wilson, Edward O. 2005. "One Giant Leap: How Insects Achieved Altruism and Colonial Life." *Bioscience* 58: 17–25.

Wilson, James Q. 2000. *Bureaucracy.* New York: Basic Books.

Winkelmann, Liliana, and Rainer Winkelmann. 1998. "Why Are the Unemployed So Unhappy? Evidence from Panel Data." *Economica*, New Series 65(257): 1–15.

Wittfogel, Karl. 1957. *Oriental Despotism: A Comparative Study of Total Power.* New Haven, CT: Yale University Press.

Wolff, Edward N. 2009. *Poverty and Income Distribution, 2nd ed.* Chichester, UK: Wiley-Blackwell.

Young, Michael, and Peter Willmott. 1957. *Family and Kinship in East London.* London: Routledge and Kegan Paul.

Zerbe, Richard O. 1985. "Is the Attempt to Gain Status a Zero- Sum Game? A Comment on Coelho." *Research in Law and Economics* 7: 117–21.

Zerbe, Richard O. 2001. *Economic Efficiency in Law and Economics.* Northampton, MA: Edward Elgar.

Zerbe, Richard O., and C. Leigh Anderson. 2001. "Culture and Fairness in the Development of Institutions in the California Gold Fields." *The Journal of Economic History* 61(01): 114–43.

Zuljan, Ralph. On War.com. Wars, Military History, International Relations. http://www.onwar.com/articles/f0302.

Zuljan, Ralph. 2003. "Allied and Axis GDP, Articles on War" n.p. Web 9

Proof

74718194R10157

Made in the USA
Columbia, SC
05 August 2017